Academic ambassadors, Pacific allies

Manchester University Press

Key Studies in Diplomacy

Series Editors: J. Simon Rofe and Giles Scott-Smith

Emeritus Editor: Lorna Lloyd

This innovative series of books examines the procedures and processes of diplomacy, focusing on the interaction between states through their accredited representatives, that is, diplomats. Volumes in the series focus on factors affecting foreign policy and the ways in which it is implemented through the diplomatic system in both bilateral and multilateral contexts. They examine how diplomats can shape not just the presentation, but the substance of their state's foreign policy. Since the diplomatic system is global, each book aims to contribute to an understanding of the nature of diplomacy. Authors comprise both scholarly experts and former diplomats, able to emphasise the actual practice of diplomacy and to analyse it in a clear and accessible manner. The series offers essential primary reading for beginning practitioners and advanced level university students.

Previously published by Bloomsbury:

21st Century Diplomacy: A Practitioner's Guide by Kishan S. Rana
A Cornerstone of Modern Diplomacy: Britain and the Negotiation of the 1961 Vienna Convention on Diplomatic Relations by Kai Bruns
David Bruce and Diplomatic Practice: An American Ambassador in London, 1961–9 by John W. Young
Embassies in Armed Conflict by G.R. Berridge

Published by Manchester University Press:

Reasserting America in the 1970s edited by Hallvard Notaker, Giles Scott-Smith and David J. Snyder
Human rights and humanitarian diplomacy: Negotiating for human rights protection and humanitarian access by Kelly-Kate Pease
The diplomacy of decolonisation: America, Britain and the United Nations during the Congo crisis 1960–64 by Alanna O'Malley
Sport and diplomacy: Games within games edited by J. Simon Rofe
The TransAtlantic reconsidered edited by Charlotte A. Lerg, Susanne Lachenicht and Michael Kimmage

Academic ambassadors, Pacific allies
Australia, America and the
Fulbright Program

Alice Garner and Diane Kirkby

Manchester University Press

Published by Manchester University Press
Altrincham Street, Manchester M1 7JA
www.manchesteruniversitypress.co.uk

British Library Cataloguing-in-Publication Data
A catalogue record for this book is available from the British Library

ISBN 978 1 5261 2897 3 hardback

First published 2019

Typeset by Out of House Publishing
Printed in Great Britain
by CPI Group (UK) Ltd, Croydon, CR0 4YY

Contents

Figures

Every effort has been made to obtain permission to reproduce copyright
material, and the publisher will be pleased to be informed of any errors and
omissions for correction in future editions.

Acknowledgements

This research has been supported by an Australian Research Council Linkage Project grant with partners the Australian-American Fulbright Commission and the National Library of Australia Oral History Unit. We are grateful for the support of Mark Darby, who was executive director of the Fulbright Commission when the project was first conceived. Subsequently, Executive Director Tangerine Holt saw the importance and exciting potential of this material during her tenure at the helm of the Fulbright Commission. We owe thanks for their unstinting and always very practical support. Staff at the Commission also supported the research process in many ways, for which we are grateful. We thank the many Fulbright scholars and alumni who shared stories and reflections with us, in surveys, interviews and informal conversations and emails. Margy Burn of the National Library of Australia, as well as Kevin Bradley, Shelly Grant and David Blanken from the Oral History Unit, were generous with their time and expertise. Dennis Altman has been a special friend to us, offering helpful advice and his considerable expertise. Others we wish to thank include David Walker, Patricia Grimshaw and Chips Sowerwine; Kate Laing who helped out with some occasional research; and Caroline Jordan who is both a one-person cheer squad and a critic with an unerring eye for fine and relevant detail. Her assistance at key moments was invaluable. Thanks also to Giles Scott-Smith for his encouragement of this work and its publication, and the anonymous readers for their helpful comments. A special mention is saved for John Salmond who was professor of history at La Trobe for many years and chaired the Victorian Fulbright Selection Committee which gave Diane a post-doctoral award in 1984. He subsequently invited her to serve on that Committee in the 1990s. That direct experience of the Fulbright Program has been invaluable. The project was at times interrupted by personal health, family and employment difficulties causing unfortunate delays. We are grateful to the Commission and the National Library of Australia for their patience; and to our families for sharing the ups and downs of the journey.

Abbreviations

AAA	Australian-American Association
AAEF	Australian-American Educational Foundation
AAFC	Australian-American Fulbright Commission
ABC	Australian Broadcasting Commission
ACER	Australian Council for Educational Research
ACLS	American Council of Learned Societies
AFUW	Australian Federation of University Women
AIATSIS	Australian Institute of Aboriginal and Torres Strait Islander Studies
ALP	Australian Labor Party
ANU	Australian National University
ANZUS	Australia-New Zealand-United States
ASIO	Australian Security and Intelligence Organisation
ATSIC	Aboriginal and Torres Strait Islander Commission
BFS	Board of Foreign Scholarships
CCNY	Carnegie Corporation of New York
CPA	Communist Party of Australia
CSIRO	Commonwealth Scientific and Industrial Research Organisation
CU	Bureau of Educational and Cultural Affairs (now known as ECA)
DOS	Department of State
HECS	Higher Education Contribution Scheme
IIE	Institute of International Education
NAA	National Archives of Australia
NARA	National Archives and Records Administration
NLA	National Library of Australia
SEATO	South-East Asian Treaty Organization
USEF	United States Educational Foundation
USIA	United States Information Agency
USIS	United States Information Service
UWA	University of Western Australia

Introduction

Since 1946 the Fulbright Program has been a significant force in shaping a global scholarly community. A US government venture with an unprecedented reach across the world, it has been held responsible for 'the largest migration of students and scholars in modern history'.[1] Although the idea of international educational exchange did not originate with Senator Fulbright, the program has played a distinctive role in the history of international exchange to become 'the world's pre-eminent exchange program for scholars and students'.[2] The Fulbright Program placed academics in the forefront of foreign policy, not as purposeful instruments of government but as the educators and carriers of culture.[3] The intricate relationship of academic exchange with government is a critical, central feature of the program's history. At the outset it was held up as 'the greatest step taken ... towards an American cultural diplomacy'.[4]

The Fulbright Program's origins in the aftermath of the Second World War are well-established.[5] The usual narrative locates it as a unique proposal, emerging in a brief moment of liberal international optimism, when many believed that the free exchange of knowledge and ideas between individuals of different nations would, in the long term, improve international understanding and lead to more peaceful relations worldwide.[6] In this account, Rhodes Scholar and US Democratic Party Senator for Arkansas, J. William Fulbright, devised the program in the immediate wake of the United States' 1945 atomic bombing of Hiroshima and Nagasaki and was inspired by his own mind-broadening experience at Oxford University in the 1920s. He had, as examples, several smaller-scale US exchange schemes such as the Belgian Relief Fund and Chinese Boxer Indemnity.[7]

Built on the cooperation between the United States and partner nations' governments and their educational and research institutions, it was a novel initiative in foreign policy, not to be confused with private, philanthropic schemes of exchange. The Fulbright Program of working with academics, 'the educated ... the intellectual elites', as the 'significant molders of opinion and shapers of policy', was preceded by earlier initiatives designed to place 'truth' and 'the independence of intellect' in support of the nation's foreign policy.[8] In 1938 this 'liberal internationalist' approach had led to the creation of the Division of Cultural Relations in the Department of State.[9] Senator

Fulbright then saw a way to fund a scheme that he claimed would nurture 'mutual understanding' between the United States and other countries through people-to-people exchanges, at a time when US power was burgeoning and resentment from many sides building.[10]

An alternative account takes a more critical approach, arguing against the establishment of the Fulbright Program as 'an idealist creation of benevolent internationalism' and seeing it rather as born out of an ideology of liberal universalism and the emergence of US hegemony with the end of war. It was, Lebovic argues, in that moment of triumphalism, when national self-interest and altruistic globalism collapsed into one, that the Fulbright Program originated, 'simultaneously structured by nationalist priorities and asymmetries of power'.[11]

Reflecting twenty years later on his vision at the time of its inception, Fulbright explained that the program's aim was 'to bring a little more knowledge, a little more reason, and a little more compassion into world affairs'.[12] He saw the scheme as being for 'the better understanding of education in international relations' and argued that the 'search for understanding among all peoples … can only be effective when learning is pursued on a world-wide basis'. Rather than see this as a one-way track in which the United States might bring its expertise to the world through 'unidirectional' 'information', he considered that 'the greater our intellectual involvement with the world beyond our frontiers, the greater the gain for both America and the world'.[13]

These were noble, high-sounding ideals that demand scrutiny. A sincere belief in the value of educational exchange was not incompatible with the pursuit of national self-interest, but emphasising the idealistic and overlooking the cultural assumptions and power imbalance of the exchange could lead to a distortion of the history. The ideals were to be implemented as a concrete program, administered through the mechanisms of the State Department and conveniently, ingeniously avoiding the expenditure of US funds. Fulbright's biographer Randall Woods claims Fulbright designed the program to bring an educated, enlightened, intellectual elite into existence to improve (or internationalise) US foreign policy.[14] Being dedicated to 'scholarship and intellectual creativity', its results could not be immediate, and nor could they be measured easily, for any achievements would be long-term, 'a cultivation of ideas and values' that was continuing, and not for short-term political benefit.[15] Yet this could also obscure the unequal power dynamics of cultural diplomacy, the belief that the United States could transform the world in its own image.

It is now over seventy years since the first countries signed up to the Fulbright Program and the international exchange of scholars began. The long-term benefit, or otherwise, of the program can surely now be seen, if that is the goal. Examining raw numbers alone tells one, impressive, story. There have been thousands of scholars who have travelled on exchange as academic ambassadors between the United States and other host countries. In the first twenty years alone, 25,000 US scholars and students, and close to 38,000 from other countries, participated in the scheme. By 2018 there were over 30,000 Fulbright alumni around the world.[16] Assessing the scheme's impact is challenging precisely because of this wide global reach. But there are other questions that can and should be asked if the goal is to shine a light on the Fulbright Program's significance and meaning in the late twentieth century.

The program's 'unique historical achievement', in the words of Richard T. Arndt, was 'making binationalism into a cogent and bountiful reality'.[17] Binationalism has meant relative autonomy for the administration and implementation of Fulbright commissions and foundations throughout the world. A volume of essays by former Fulbright scholars called for close analysis of the differences the Fulbright Program had made to individual countries.[18] Yet critical, academic studies of the program and its history in individual countries are surprisingly rare and book-length studies are virtually non-existent. The one substantial account of a single country (India) covered only the first decade.[19] There are official histories by Fulbright commissions, and wider studies which focus on exchanges between the United States and other countries but are not specifically on Fulbright.[20] Other studies have considered educational exchange and cultural diplomacy more broadly, in an international relations framework.[21] This book takes a step towards filling this lacuna in the literature by exploring the history of the Fulbright Program in Australia. Our aim is to expose the mechanics of the program in a single country, demonstrating the role of national priorities and power relations in structuring the exchange of scholars. We hold that Fulbright history is not an 'inevitably American' narrative.[22] We ask how the Fulbright Program evolved in practice, during the political and foreign policy context of the Cold War, and the challenges posed by involvement in the Vietnam War; what impact did the neo-liberal reforms of the last decades of the century have on the Fulbright vision?; what does Australia's program reveal about the complex issues of racial and gender diversity?; in short, what did it mean to place academic exchange in this particular relationship with government?; and how did the funding support and its decline impact on the direction of academic enquiry?

Pacific allies

Focusing on Australia shifts attention to a region of the world that is often overlooked, yet is crucial to understanding the cultural diplomacy origins of the program and revealing historic shifts in post-war alliances. The seeds of the Australian-American Fulbright educational exchange story were sown during the war in the Pacific 1941–45, which culminated in the atomic bombing of Japan and suddenly left surplus war materials in Australia and around the Pacific. The Pacific war had also brought the United States and Australia together as allies against a common enemy, underscoring the reality of Australia's location in the Asia-Pacific. To Australia it brought new vulnerability with the removal of Britain from the region. This turned the nation's defence priorities to cultivating a close relationship with its more powerful neighbour across the Pacific. To the United States, Australia's location in the Pacific had strategic military and intelligence importance, not only during the war but subsequently. New treaties for their mutual defence – the Australia-New Zealand-United States (ANZUS) alliance and the South-East Asian Treaty Organization (SEATO) – meant Australia joined the United States in its war in Korea and became (with New Zealand) the only western ally of the United States in its war in Vietnam.[23] That strategic dependence only increased in the era of satellite communication as the United States built ground bases in Australia to control and monitor US strategic surveillance and communication satellites, and also radio facilities to send commands to its submarines in the Indian Ocean, 'the most important and controversial issue posed by the American Alliance or Australian foreign policy generally'.[24]

The Fulbright Program belongs in the context of the unique relationship between these Pacific allies who were working towards securing their mutual interests in the region. In the Fulbright division of the world, Australia and New Zealand are firmly located by their geography in the east Asia-Pacific sphere of the globe (see Figure I.1).[25] Furthermore, Australia was an ex-colony of Britain, located close to other former

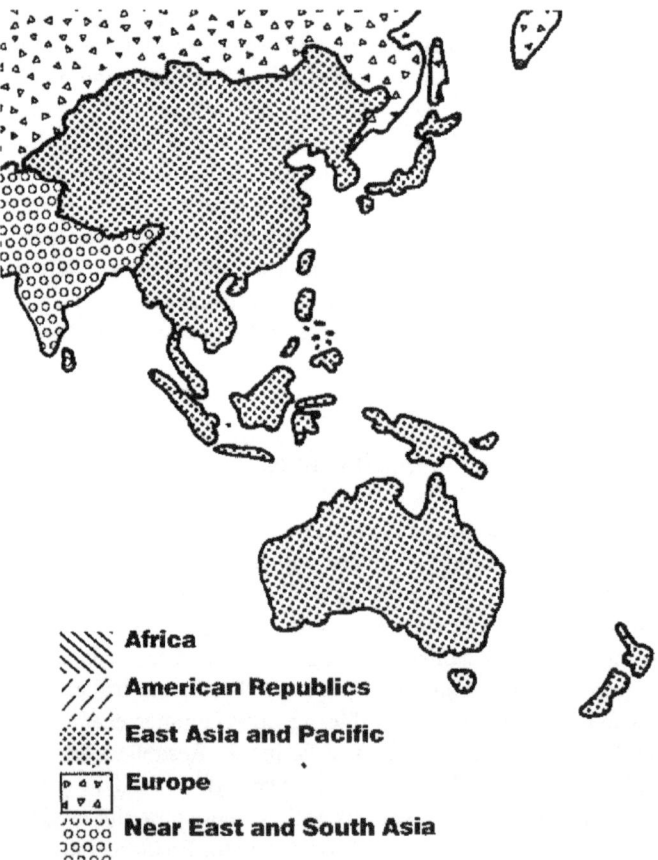

Figure I.1 Detail of Fulbright world map from *Forty Years: The Fulbright Program 1946–1986*

colonies, at a time when the decolonising momentum was growing. Coupled with its geographic and geopolitical features are shared characteristics with the United States, in both being settler colonial nations with dispossessed Indigenous peoples and diverse, multicultural immigrant populations. This has given a particular cultural and social inflection to national and transnational issues and policies that we can see reflected in the development of the program, as well as in research projects by scholars and universities seeking Fulbright awards.

The Australian-American Fulbright Program, signed into existence in November 1949 and launched early in 1950, correlated with the unfolding wartime relationship between the two nations and its continued evolution over the next six decades. The pursuit of peace and education occurred against the backdrop of a military diplomatic alliance of strategic value to both nations. The scheme sat at an awkward crossroads of foreign policy, education and research. In the post-war expansion of higher education, which also played out in the national agenda, these were not always distinct. The reality of Cold War polarisation soon eclipsed the post-war moment of liberal internationalism that had given the program substance, and in turn gave way to globalisation and neo-liberalisation, with their massive impacts on the public sector.[26] The story of the Fulbright Program also belongs in this literature on higher education, the unfolding of academic disciplines and the transformation of the public university over the past sixty years.[27] It has been a journey from liberal internationalism to neo-liberalism that is well documented by scholars.

The story starts with a long drawn-out negotiation (1946–49) between US State Department and Australian External Affairs officials of what was, in fact, the first formal treaty between the two countries. The Fulbright Agreement pre-dated the ANZUS Treaty. The narrative then moves through early Cold War challenges, a mid-1960s renegotiation on the cusp of the Vietnam War, and up to the early twenty-first century, when new security threats and technologies brought the allies closer, and transformed the ease of communication and mobility of scholarly travellers across the Pacific. Drawing on Fulbright Commission and government archives, newspapers, interviews with key players and scholars, letters, memoirs and surveys, this history both analyses the administration of the scheme and weaves in experiences of individual Fulbright scholars from a broad range of fields and institutions across six decades. It pays particular attention to the array of political and cultural challenges that have accompanied bi-national dealings. This rich web of stories touches on matters of historical and current interest, including the development of new academic disciplines and transnational networks, social upheavals, cultures of protest, Senator Fulbright's and many scholars' opposition to the Vietnam War, changing campus cultures, civil and Indigenous rights movements, soft-power approaches to peace-building, as well as struggles with funding cuts and increasing reliance on corporate funding with its accompanying ethical dilemmas in the 1980s and 1990s.

Threaded throughout the narrative is an examination of the ways 'mutual understanding' has driven decision-making, been understood and pursued by those involved in the program, and how this has changed over time. Social scientists and public servants might attempt to measure the 'impact' of the program and its 'success' in achieving the stated goal of mutual understanding between people of different nations (and, much more ambitiously, achieving world peace). For historians, however, it is ultimately more fruitful to look into 'the richness and complexity of reality, and the contingent and changeable nature of events'.[28] Observing closely and critically the experience of people engaged in the program enables us to understand their efforts to make the program, and William Fulbright's vision, work.

There were always unexpected dimensions to 'mutual understanding' that could never have been spelt out because they could not be predicted, and the learning experience could not be wholly controlled by program or government administrators. The personal impacts of exchange are, despite their diversity, also the easiest to identify. Scholars frequently express their belief that the time they spent on their award 'was the most transformative experience in my life' with some elaborating further on how much they learned, 'about life, and scholarship, politics and commitments'.[29] For others the impact came through the shock of experience. The history of the Fulbright Program in Australia is a shimmering spiderweb of stories. They reveal much about the cultural impact of the exchange experience and suggest more that can be said about the effects of travel on the transfer and reshaping of knowledge.

It is valuable to trace broader trends in the impacts on fields or institutions, and on occasion on policy. These include the establishment of networks across national boundaries which had the effect of Fulbright alumni encouraging other colleagues in their field, or from their institution, to apply. And the administration of the program also had sometimes unexpected influences on particular areas of research and the development of new fields of study. Isolating the *Fulbright* element, as opposed to other interlinked factors, poses some difficulties. Ideally we would know more about the impact of scholars' research projects in effecting change in their fields, perhaps their disciplines, and from there, the impact of their cohort and the program overall, in transforming organisations, social systems and political culture. Much research of this kind remains to be done if we are to understand the full implications of this trans-pacific exchange of scholars.

We have been able only to hint at the possibilities and richness of scholar experience in this study. Some stories beg to be told simply because they bring a moment of intercultural experience to life. One such moment was recounted to us by early Australian scholar and micropalaeontologist William Riedel. In 1951, Riedel was studying deep sea sediments at the Oceanografiska Institut in Sweden, when he learnt he had won a Fulbright award along with a John Murray Travelling Studentship in Oceanography, to study radiolarians at the Scripps Institute in California. When his plane landed in New York, en route from Sweden, Riedel realised too late that it was a weekend, the banks were closed, and he had no cash – only a scholarship cheque. Not knowing how he would get out of the airport, let alone pay for accommodation or food on his first night, the tall young man from the rural town of Tanunda, South Australia, burst into tears in the international terminal. A kind American approached and offered to take him to a hotel in a cab. Riedel watched in wonder as the man paid for the taxi fare and booked a room with something he didn't know existed: credit.[30]

Stories we have unearthed concern not only individual scholars and their exchange experience, but also the intricacies involved in the administration of the program through some tumultuous periods. This history is not a 'report' in the style of the many commissioned analyses that have peppered the Fulbright Program's history.[31] It does not seek to make recommendations for the future of the program – though some might find it useful in their own formulation of policy.[32] It is neither an official nor a celebratory history, though it has benefited throughout from the support and encouragement of the Australian-American Fulbright Commission. Nor can it do justice to the full spectrum of experience that scholars have shared in their interviews, memoirs, survey responses and conversation – no book could do that.[33] Rather, this history traces the story of the Australian–US exchange program from its origins, exploring how scholars in many different fields, as well as program administrators and diplomats, have perceived, talked to and about each other. One thing is clear: 'mutual understanding', the program's stated goal, can be interpreted in many ways. Though this flexibility in meaning has always posed a challenge for those seeking to justify ongoing funding for the program to members of Congress or Federal Parliament – and particularly to those crunching the numbers – the fact that mutual understanding can never be pinned down to a limited view has also, in the end, been a great strength of the scheme.

This book explores in depth some key moments (high and low) in the administration of the program and the cross-currents shaping them; we have taken both a synchronic and diachronic approach. At certain key moments in the development of the scheme, we drill down into government and Fulbright organisation archives in an attempt to understand the important questions administrators and policy-makers were grappling with. At other times we draw back to consider a bigger picture, exposing the landscape in which the program sits. Synchronic scrutiny, if applied across the life of the program, would have resulted in a very heavy tome. That was not one we wanted to write, and would have left no room for the stories of the scholars themselves. The first four chapters of this book delve quite deeply into the complicated binational machinery of administration for the exchange program – a behind-the-scenes view without which we cannot fully understand the nature and significance of the scheme.

Some aspects of the program demanded a diachronic treatment – a consideration of changes over time. Tracking the evolution of selection and programming policies and procedures over sixty years of the program, for example, has helped us discern the shifting shape and focus of the program and where it has been positioned in relation to, say, changing national research priorities, or changing political agendas of presidential administrations and federal governments. Evolving scholar demographics have also been considered, especially regarding the participation of women. The Australian Fulbright Program has exchanged over 5,000 scholars – researchers, lecturers, postgraduate students, schoolteachers and other professionals – in nearly every field of academic and artistic endeavour. Only a small minority of them were women, particularly in the first forty years, and even fewer were Aboriginal, or reflected the multicultural and ethnically diverse nation Australia had become over the years of the program. In later years the program has tried to address this shortcoming with more diversity becoming apparent among award recipients. These issues and how the program administrators managed them are also investigated in this book.

With the hardening of the Cold War, and campus unrest and anti-war protests during the Vietnam War, political interference was a constant threat to the program's integrity. No doubt national security organisations in both countries instituted surveillance of Fulbright scholars along with other political dissidents. Political turmoil surrounded the scholars who went on exchange – going both ways – and posed personal, political and social dilemmas for many. As one early scholar remarked, his experience in the United States had been a very positive one, 'though we in Australia cannot always agree with American foreign policy'.[34] Anti-Americanism has been a phenomenon in Australia as well as many other parts of the world.[35] Academics on both sides of the Pacific who understood the program's educational promise and were heavily involved in policy and selection, also worked to ensure the program's autonomy – as did Senator Fulbright himself. Australian alumni interviewed in the 1970s were unanimous in thinking the program should be expanded to allow more Australian academics to travel to the United States to 'learn that many of the things they had come to believe about the United States was terribly distorted [sic]'.[36]

Last, but not least, there is the immense variety of learning experiences reported by scholars. This is at once the heart of the story, and the hardest part to capture. There are certain themes that come through in the sources, for example regarding scholars' negotiation of academic and cultural differences, which the book seeks to tease out without flattening the great diversity of experience with bland generalisations. What is apparent is that the Fulbright Program has generated a stimulating, ever-expanding, transnational conversation – not only transnational but global, when we take into account the connections many scholars have made with colleagues from all around the world during their Fulbright award. Nevertheless, this conversation – or these conversations – cannot easily be constrained or *owned* by the program, and thus writing them up as history poses all sorts of challenges. While many scholars talk about their Fulbright grant as a moment of transformation, personal and/or professional, and link much of what came after to that moment, others are less clear on the direct impact of their exchange, making a simple cause-and-effect narrative impossible to construct. Many brilliant careers – such as that of Sir Zelman Cowen who subsequently became Australia's governor-general – would still have been brilliant without receipt of a Fulbright travel award. Some experiences which were miserable at the time seared themselves in the memory and led to later positive outcomes.[37] Less starry successes also occurred, for the stark characteristic of the Fulbright Program is the breadth of institutions it has involved, and the ordinariness rather than the celebrity status of the scholars it has sent on exchange.

Exploring this variety of experience leads to the rejection of any simplistic framework for discussing the impact of the program. Efforts to quantify effects in the domain of 'mutual understanding' tend to result in statements empty of meaning. It is in the specifics of individual experience, and the scholars' telling of these in their own, idiosyncratic voices, along with the complicated backdrop of administrative-political work that enables their exchange to take place, that we find out how a program like this works on the ground, and how (if not why) it has stayed the course for so long. In asking how this program evolved and endured as a cultural diplomacy initiative, and what the driving factors of change and endurance were, we also explore the consequences in a broader frame. We argue for seeing the scheme's role in enhancing the Australia–US diplomatic relationship and reorienting Australia's traditional ties away from Britain. We show how academics who took up opportunities offered by the Fulbright Program to conduct their research, also promoted women's careers, expanded the tertiary curriculum, diversified the profile of academic staff, pressed in many cases for social and political change, and generally found their own, unique ways of interpreting what it meant to be ambassadors working for 'mutual understanding'.

Notes

1 Randall Bennett Woods, 'Fulbright Internationalism', *Annals of the American Academy of Political and Social Sciences*, vol. 491 (May 1987), pp. 22–35.
2 Sam Lebovic, 'From War Junk to Educational Exchange: The World War II Origins of the Fulbright Program and the Foundations of American Cultural Globalism, 1945–50', *Diplomatic History*, vol. 37:2 (April 2013), pp. 280–312.
3 See Akira Iriye, *Cultural Internationalism and World Order* (Baltimore, 1997) for a conceptual discussion of the relations between culture and power.
4 Richard T. Arndt, *The First Resort of Kings: American Cultural Diplomacy in the Twentieth Century* (Dulles, 2005), p. 66; Kenneth A. Osgood and Brian C. Etheridge, *United States and Public Diplomacy: New Directions in Cultural and International History*, edited by Brian Craig Etheridge (Leiden and Boston, 2010).
5 Randall Bennett Woods, *Fulbright: A Biography* (Cambridge, 1995).
6 Beate Jahn, *Liberal Internationalism: Theory, History, Practice* (Basingstoke, UK, 2013).
7 Arndt, *First Resort of Kings*, pp. 172–9, 226, 230; Woods, 'Fulbright Internationalism'; Woods, *Fulbright: A Biography*.
8 Walter Johnson and Francis J. Colligan, *The Fulbright Program: A History* (Chicago, 1965), pp. 10, 9; Arndt, *First Resort of Kings*, p. 60.
9 Arndt, *First Resort of Kings*, pp. 61, 66, speaks of 'the political soil out of which an American cultural diplomacy had sprung'.
10 See Johnson and Colligan, *Fulbright Program*, pp. 6–9.
11 Lebovic, 'From War Junk to Educational Exchange', p. 283.
12 William Fulbright, 'Foreword', in Johnson and Colligan, *Fulbright Program*, p. vii.
13 Arndt, *First Resort of Kings*, p. 232; Johnson and Colligan, *Fulbright Program*, pp. ix, vii.
14 Woods, 'Fulbright Internationalism', p. 3.
15 Johnson and Colligan, *Fulbright Program*, p. 9.
16 ECA website, https://eca.state.gov/impact/facts-and-figures (accessed 1 July 2018).
17 Arndt, *First Resort of Kings*, p. 232.
18 Richard T. Arndt and David L. Rubin, eds, *The Fulbright Difference, 1948–1992* (New Brunswick, 1993).
19 N. Dawes, *A Two-Way Street: the Indo-American Fulbright Program 1950–1960* (Bombay, 1962). Johnson and Colligan's history is an early work which analyses

the foundation and development of the program for the first twenty years from an American perspective; Xu Guangqiu, 'The Ideological and Political Impact of US Fulbrighters on Chinese Students 1979–89', *Asian Affairs: an American Review*, vol. 26:3 (Fall 1999), pp. 139–57; Leonard Sussman, *The Culture of Freedom: The Small World of Fulbright Scholars* (Lanham, 1992); Sven Groennings, 'The Fulbright Program in the Global Knowledge Economy: The Nation's Neglected Comparative Advantage', *Journal of Studies in International Education*, vol. 1:1 (Spring 1997), pp. 95–105; Jan Rupp, 'The Fulbright Program or the Surplus Value of Officially Organized Academic Exchange', *Journal of Studies in International Education*, vol. 3:1 (Spring 1999), pp. 57–81; Giles Scott-Smith, 'The Fulbright Program in the Netherlands: An Example of Science Diplomacy', in Jeroen van Dongen, ed., *Cold War Science and the Transatlantic Circulation of Knowledge* (Leiden, 2015), pp. 128–54.

20 Notably Whitney Walton on French–US exchanges in *Internationalism, National Identities and Study Abroad* (Stanford, 2010); Liping Bu, *Making the World Like Us: Education, Cultural Expansion, and the American Century* (New York, 2003); and Philip Ziegler, *Legacy: Cecil Rhodes, the Rhodes Trust and Rhodes Scholarships* (New Haven, 2008).

21 Giles Scott-Smith, *Networks of Empire: The US State Department's Foreign Leader Program in the Netherlands, France, and Britain 1950–1970* (Brussels, 2008); Jessica Gienow-Hecht, 'Shame on US? Academics, Cultural Transfer and the Cold War: A Critical Review', *Diplomatic History*, vol. 24:3 (Summer 2000), pp. 465–94.

22 Johnson and Colligan, *Fulbright Program*, p xii.

23 Joseph Camilleri, *Australian-American Relations: The Web of Dependence* (Melbourne, 1980); Coral Bell, *Dependent Ally: A Study in Australian Foreign Policy* (Sydney, 1988).

24 Peter King, 'Whither Whitlam?' *International Journal, Pacific Affairs*, vol. 29:3 (Summer 1974), pp. 422–40; Andrew Mack, 'US Bases in Australia: The Debate Continues', *Australian Outlook*, vol. 42:2 (1988), pp. 77–85.

25 See also Peter I. Rose, *Academic Sojourners: A Report on the Senior Fulbright Programs in East Asia and the Pacific* (United States Bureau of Educational and Cultural Affairs, Office of Policy and Plans, 1976) Background Paper for Review Meeting AAEF, December 1976.

26 David Harvey, *A Brief History of Neoliberalism* (Oxford, 2005).

27 Simon Marginson, *Educating Australia: Government, Economy, and Citizen Since 1960* (Cambridge, 1997), esp. pp. 20–45; Stuart Macintyre, *The Poor Relation: A History of Social Sciences in Australia* (Melbourne, 2010), pp. 22–9, 87–121, 203–4, 233–53, 298–311; Philip G. Altbach and Ulrich Teichler, 'Internationalization and Exchanges in a Globalized University', *Journal of Studies in International Education*, vol. 5:1 (Spring 2001), pp. 5–25.

28 Marginson, *Educating Australia*, p. xii.

29 Sondra Farganis, response to Survey, La Trobe University, 2011; see also examples of scholars' reports in United States Educational Foundation, *The Fulbright Programme: The First Eight Years and the Future* (Canberra, 1958).

30 William R. Riedel, and Alice Garner, William Riedel interviewed by Alice Garner in Fulbright scholars oral history project [sound recording], 2010. A short biography of Riedel can be found on the University of California San Diego library website at: scilib.ucsd.edu/sio/biogr/Riedel_Biogr.pdf (accessed 17 August 2012).

31 See, for example, Joan Druett, *Fulbright in New Zealand* (Wellington, 1988); Anon., 'The Fiftieth Anniversary of the Fulbright Program', *International Educator*, vol. 5:4 (1996), pp. 13–24.

32 As for example Sussman, *The Culture of Freedom.*

33 Sally Ninham, *A Cohort of Pioneers: Australian Postgraduate Students and American Postgraduate Degrees 1949–1964* (Melbourne, 2011) is a study of scholars' experiences that has some areas of crossover in dealing with Australian postgraduates in the United States during the 1950s and 1960s but does not explore organisational aspects specific to program of scholarly exchange such as the Fulbright; Arthur Dudden and R. Dynes, *The Fulbright Experience 1946–86* (New Brunswick, 1987) is an example of the reminiscences of scholars.

34 Douglas J. Cole (electrical engineer, 1954) in USEF, *The First Eight Years and the Future*, p. 19.

35 Brendon O'Connor, 'Anti-Americanism in Australia', in Vol. 3: *Comparative Perspectives of B. O'Connor, Anti-Americanism: History, Causes and Themes*, 4 vols. (Westport, CT, 2007); Ann Capling, ' "Allies But Not Friends": Anti-Americanism in Australia', in Richard A. Higgott and Ivona Malbasic, eds, *The Political Consequences of Anti-Americanism* (New York, 2008); Paul Hollander, ed., *Understanding Anti-Americanism: Its Origins and Impact at Home and Abroad* (Chicago, 2004); Ian Tyrrell, 'Anti-Americanism Historicized' [review of above], *Reviews in American History*, vol. 41:3 (September 2013), pp. 445–50; Alan Bloomfield and Kim Nossal, 'End of an Era? Anti-Americanism in the Australian Labor Party', *Australian Journal of Politics and History*, vol. 56:4 (December 2010), pp. 592–611.

36 Peter I. Rose, *Academic Sojourners: A Report on the Senior Fulbright Programs in East Asia and the Pacific* (United States Bureau of Educational and Cultural Affairs, Office of Policy and Plans, 1976) Background Paper for Review Meeting AAEF, December 1976.

37 See scholars' memoirs, Zelman Cowen, *A Public Life: The Memoirs of Zelman Cowen* (Melbourne, 2006); Dennis Altman, *Defying Gravity: A Political Life* (Sydney, 1997).

1

'Free gift' or 'infiltration'?: Negotiating the Fulbright Agreement

The Australian Fulbright Program was born of a simple idea. That was Senator J. William Fulbright's proposal that people–people exchange between nations was a better disposal of Allied countries' funds than repaying the debt they had incurred purchasing US war materials. In September 1945, only weeks after the atomic bombing of Japanese cities brought an end to the war, Fulbright framed a bill as an Amendment to the Surplus Property Act of 1944, to 'utilize foreign credits in many countries in lieu of American dollars for American surplus property'.[1] He had designed a program which did not, in its initial form, require any congressional dollar appropriations. That was its genius politically and it slipped through Congress with almost no publicity. In a nutshell, he conceived of a scheme whereby the United States would renegotiate the debt and governments would instead sponsor the travel for educational exchange of people identified as leaders of the future.

There were two principal elements. The first related to matters of currency and the expenditure of US government funds. The second was the bi-national nature of the agreement between governments, each of them negotiated separately with the partner country. What became known as 'the Fulbright Act' (Public Law 79–584) enabled the US State Department to negotiate executive agreements with wartime allies who owed the US government money for military material supplied under wartime Lend-Lease arrangements. These had been abruptly terminated in September 1945. Now, instead of repaying the United States in the scarce currency of US dollars, debtor countries could set up a fund in their own currency, to be spent on travel to the United States by their own citizens – academics, graduate students and schoolteachers. Equally, the United States gained the prerogative of access, indeed the right, of sending US academics and students on exchange to the partner countries to study or teach in their institutions. The amounts available for the exchange depended on the terms of separate agreements negotiated with each partner country.

The scheme of sponsoring future international leadership depended heavily on these bi-national, government–government, agreements. Negotiation of the terms was therefore a critical foundation for the scheme's future success. It is in negotiating terms that were better for Australia than the United States initially proposed (and other countries had achieved) that the Australian Fulbright experience first becomes noticeably important.

The genesis of Senator Fulbright's exchange scheme has been recounted many times by others, but, until now, the Australian negotiation story has never been told.[2] Indeed even Australian studies of the period, or of key personnel involved in the negotiations, have not included the Fulbright story. Yet Australia's scheme was negotiated in conjunction with the post-war reconstruction program rolled out by the Chifley Labor government (1945–49) and rightly belongs in consideration of the period.[3] From the first announcement of the scheme in the United States in 1946, Australian officials began planning to bring the scheme to Australia. The path of negotiation was, however, rocky and fraught with disagreements and delays. Negotiations were conducted in an atmosphere of tension at a time of delicate relations between the United States and Australia.

The biggest obstacle the Australian Fulbright Program faced was just getting started. The Australian government had, only two months before the Fulbright Act was signed into law by President Truman on 1 August 1946, concluded a Lend-Lease Settlement with the United States, which meant it was eligible for the scheme.[4] In his autobiography, veteran Australian public servant H.C. 'Nugget' Coombs recalled his role. In his capacity as director-general of the Australian Department of Post-War Reconstruction Coombs accompanied Prime Minister Ben Chifley to Washington in May 1946, to discuss post-war Pacific policy with US officials.[5] They experienced a 'terrifying' trip in a converted bomber over a foggy Atlantic Ocean from London. There Coombs had been in discussion about the establishment of the new Australian National University (ANU) with expatriate scientist, Mark Oliphant, whom he was recruiting to head up the ANU school of nuclear physics.[6] In Washington, Coombs and Australian External Affairs Department Secretary John Burton set to work on obtaining an agreement with the US government concerning the amount Australia would pay the United States for unconsumed post-VJ (Victory in Japan) supplies, and how and when this would be repaid.

The Americans were inclined to be generous, wiping millions of dollars from their initial estimate of the Australian Lend-Lease debt in one phone call with Chifley, to settle on a figure of $27 million. The Australians were required to repay $20 million (in US dollars) within ninety days, but the remaining $7 million were to be held as unconverted Australian pounds, and deposited in a fund which would be spent thus: $2 million on US Embassy buildings on Australian soil, and the rest on the development of educational and cultural relations between the two countries. In return, however, the US government sought some key concessions in civil aviation rights and trade policy – exactly as Chifley and others had anticipated in the lead-up to these discussions. Coombs remembered that, despite enthusiasm for the proposal amongst Treasury Department and Commonwealth Bank officials in Australia, discussions around the educational and cultural use of the Australian currency portion 'ran into an unexpectedly hostile reaction' from Chifley. The prime minister saw this as 'the beginnings of a new imperial domination' and a restriction on 'future freedom', just when Australians were 'escaping from the tutelage of Whitehall and the City of London'. Chifley told Coombs and Burton, 'They can have their cultural fund', and, before picking up the phone to Secretary of State Dean Acheson to conclude the

Lend-Lease Settlement, added, 'but that is the end of it'.[7] Australian politicians in the throes of exploring just what cultural and political independence from the 'mother country' Britain might look like, were reluctant to bow to the new global powerhouse.

The Lend-Lease Settlement of June 1946 was widely reported in Australian newspapers, even described as a 'triumph' for Australian negotiators by a *Sydney Morning Herald* correspondent.[8] Two months later, on 1 August, Senator Fulbright's Amendment to the Surplus Property Act was signed into law and took effect, placing in State Department hands the responsibility for negotiating exchange agreements with Lend-Lease debtor countries, including Australia. It wasn't long before sharp-eyed Australian and US citizens with an interest in the proposed exchange program began to write to their respective governments seeking information about how to apply, but they would have a long wait before the first Fulbright scholars would cross the Pacific. First, the Australian and US governments had to conclude their own Fulbright treaty, and then bed down complex bi-national administration, programming and selection processes. This would take more than four years, a period marked by a rapid build-up of international Cold War tensions. This, among other things, complicated Australian–US diplomatic relations and raised troubling questions about the relationship of educational exchange to national foreign policy.

'In the nature of an arrangement between equals'

Coombs took the first steps towards the negotiation of an Australian Fulbright Agreement straight after the August 1946 enactment of the Fulbright Bill. He wrote to US Chargé d'Affaires John Minter, eleven days after the Act was signed, to outline his thoughts on the possible use of the $5 million available for educational and cultural purposes. Discussion followed with 'interested persons' including Professor Mills of the Commonwealth Office of Education, the barrister, former solicitor-general and ANU champion Sir Robert Garran, physicist Sir Victor Bailey and officials from the Departments of Treasury and the Interior. Coombs envisaged that, if the funds were stretched over several years at AU £45,500 per year, they might pay for:

- Two professorial chairs at the new National University in Canberra, in American History and Sociology, to be occupied by Americans (£9,000/year each).
- Visits by 'eminent Americans in the academic, scientific, literary or artistic fields' (£7,500/year).
- Postgraduate scholarships for Australians and Americans in the partner country (£8,000/year total).
- Staff for an American library in Australia (£2,000).
- £10,000 worth of 'general cultural activities', including the purchase of prints, books, films, and the presentation of American plays and other cultural works.[9]

Speculation along similar lines continued in Australia well into the next year. Formal negotiations were delayed at the US end by disagreements between State

Department divisions over the apportionment of the $7 million in foreign currency. The Buildings Division felt its share ($2 million), which was to finance the construction of US Embassy buildings in Australia, should be greater, and Educational and Cultural Affairs had to fight to hang on to its $5 million.[10] The State Department may also have been waiting on the passage of the Smith-Mundt Bill in January 1948, which allowed for the negotiation of educational exchange agreements with countries that did not have Lend-Lease arrangements with the United States.

The Smith-Mundt Act, officially known as the U.S. Information and Educational Exchange Act of 1948 (Public Law 80–402), supported American 'information' campaigns abroad, as well as cultural and educational exchanges with other nations.[11] It had made slow progress through Congress, beginning back in 1945 (when it was known as the Bloom Bill), partly due to suspicions amongst anti-Communist Congressmen that the State Department, which initiated the Bill, was riddled with Communists and fellow travellers who could not be trusted with promoting the 'right' image of the United States abroad. By the time it passed into law, however, the Smith-Mundt Act was being touted as an essential component of the United States' Cold War armoury. For those partner countries negotiating Fulbright agreements, it proved to be something of a poisoned chalice. It promised full scholarships to study in the United States for some of their citizens (as opposed to travel grants only). But the Act's support for educational exchange programs alongside US government propaganda ('information') abroad was guaranteed to cause discomfort amongst some negotiators, including the Australian public servants working for Chifley's Labor government.

State Department officials finalised their draft Australian–US agreement in January 1948, by which time they had already concluded two Fulbright agreements with other countries, both of them in the Asia-Pacific region, notably China and Burma.[12] When the draft reached the Australian government two months later, negotiations began in earnest. Well before the Department of External Affairs received this draft Fulbright Agreement from the State Department, Australian negotiators had already learnt the broad outlines of US terms. They were discussed in some detail in inter-departmental meetings throughout 1947. Records of these discussions foreshadow some sources of contention that would periodically dog the program in the years to come. These included the balance of power in the bi-national administration; the rate of currency exchange; taxation of grants; whether the program would be broadly cultural as well as educational; and what benefits the program might offer Australians.

Australian officials evidently saw potential value in the exchange program for educational development in this intense period of post-war reconstruction. Nevertheless they insisted on taking a good look at the gift horse. They challenged clauses relating to the setting of an exchange rate, legal immunity for the bi-national commission, and a waiver of taxation on scholars which the Australians argued (and Americans denied) should be reciprocal. The Australians also thought the program secretariat should be headed up by an Australian, who would be 'fully acquainted with Australian conditions and those aspects of Australian education, sciences, arts and culture related to the programme', while the Americans favoured one of their own.[13] Despite these early differences of opinion, the Australians recorded their 'desire for early action', in April and again in September.[14]

Above all, though, Australian negotiators were concerned about the proposed make-up of the bi-national Fulbright Foundation's board of directors, to be based in Canberra. In April 1947, L.F. [Fin] Crisp of Post-War Reconstruction noted a difference of opinion over the make-up of the proposed bi-national governing board of the Australian program. The Americans proposed a majority would be Americans while the Australians aimed for even numbers of each nationality with the US ambassador in the chair holding the veto. According to an April 1947 External Affairs memo, the State Department visualised the board as 'consisting of three United States officials, two non-Government American residents in Australia and two Australians'. Perhaps it was not only the 5:2 ratio but also the positions the Americans would hold (chair, secretary and treasurer) that posed a stumbling block for the Australians.[15] As an alternative, Australia proposed equal numbers from both countries, and that the American directors not be attached to the embassy, namely: three Americans resident in Australia and three Australians appointed by the Australian government, with the honorary chairman being an American, notably the US ambassador to Australia.[16] The Australians did not even like the terminology of 'board of directors' for what was a government-funded educational scheme. This corporate speak may have suited the highly privatised education system of the United States, but was foreign to the centralised public Australian system.[17]

External Affairs' memos recognised that 'The United States naturally expects to hold a dominant position in implementing the programme', given it was funded out of money owed to the United States. They complained that the American proposal would make the purportedly bi-national program 'a façade concealing complete control by the U.S. Department of State'.[18] One External Affairs officer expressed the fear that the program would bring 'more of an American infiltration into Australian life than an Australian infiltration into American life'.[19]

They probably raised their eyebrows when, late in 1947, the Chinese (Nationalist) government signed the very first Fulbright executive agreement, with a 100 per cent US board of directors.[20] The New Zealand agreement of 1948 was also 'wholly financed and controlled by the United States'.[21] Australia continued to press its case for an agreement that was 'much more in the nature of an arrangement between equals'.[22] Exasperated US officials, who argued that 'the money is American' and that the board should not be bound by 'regulations and controls', rejected the 'Australian idea', namely, the expectation that 'the program should be conducted by an inter-Governmental authority acting with explicitly defined functions and limitations', and, particularly, 'that Australia should share more equally in this authority as a matter of right rather than of courtesy on our [US] part'.[23] In later despatches, US officers explicitly interpreted this Australian intransigence in the light of broader events, painting the federal Labor government as 'suspicious and hostile toward what it regards [as] American economic imperialism', while its attitude 'toward international problems and especially toward the United States-Soviet conflict is too well-known to need elaboration here'.[24]

In early 1949, one key Australian negotiator even proposed abandoning the Fulbright Agreement entirely. A Treasury official, noting that the UK–US agreement of September 1948 was more favourable to the British than that proposed for Australia, argued that Australia would be better off paying her debts immediately to the US government rather than 'accept what the American Government described as a friendly gesture on terms which the Australian Government thought were unwise'.[25] This was not a decision to be taken lightly, for five million US dollars were at stake.

'In defence of national interests'

It is important to appreciate the diplomatic context in which these discussions were being conducted. Coombs' Post-War Reconstruction Department, as well as Department of Treasury and the Office of Education (then part of the Prime Minister's Department) were all privy to discussions. It was, however, officials in the Department of External Affairs who dealt most directly and regularly with the State Department about the educational exchange program. So while the scheme was educational in focus, it lay from its very beginnings firmly within the foreign policy domain. The minister for External Affairs at that time was Herbert Vere ('Doc') Evatt, Australian Labor Party (ALP) member for Barton and a former justice of the High Court.[26] He had made his international reputation in the immediate post-war period championing the role of small and middling powers in the new United Nations. He was the first president of the UN Atomic Energy Commission in 1946, and presided over the UN General Assembly's third session from September 1948 to May 1949.[27]

Evatt's relations with his US counterparts were famously tense during that time at the UN. His efforts to seek a mediating role for Australia between the Great Powers, refusal on key occasions to endorse US positions in UN debates, his stress on Pacific over European security, differences over policies on Japanese reconstruction, and the future of Manus Island as a military base, were some especially sore points over this period.[28] Evatt took a liberal internationalist stance to the UN, but this was mingled with a realism towards the dominance of the Great Powers, which meant that the national interests of smaller powers could only be protected within a stable international order.[29] His biographer, John Murphy, argues that 'When he asserted the claim of smaller powers to take their part in designing the United Nations system, he was motivated by nationalism, even as he helped to shape an international constitution', and 'we should equally note his impassioned, legalistic defence of national interests'.[30]

His awkwardness with the United States actually dated from his term as foreign minister during the Second World War. Murphy reminds us that Evatt was the first Australian foreign minister 'to articulate an independent foreign policy, and that ... his enthusiasm grew out of his advocacy of Australian national interests in negotiating with Britain and America about prosecuting the war'. Compared to his predecessor in the role, Richard Casey, Evatt was single-minded in his nationalism, seen to be 'brash and often offensive', and Americans considered him 'rude and ill-mannered'.

Murphy says American journalist Hartley Grattan, who had been a Carnegie Fellow to Australia in 1939, had seen 'one of Evatt's contributions' in being 'to establish in the American mind the idea that there was an Australian nation. In Evatt they had before them an Australian nationalist of forceful, authoritarian personality'.[31]

Grattan emphasised Evatt's sheer physical presence and stubborn demanding advocacy. The Americans were facing someone who was patently not a diplomat, and who did not sound like an Englishman. Instead, Grattan wrote, in Evatt they were confronted with 'a kind of brute fact of nature': 'The Americans had on their hands an Ayers Rock Australian nationalist, standing brutally there and meaning ... [that] in the present context that the British curtain around Australia had been rent – permanently ... suddenly it was understood that Australia would have to be dealt with direct and qua Australia as an autonomous nation.' Grattan frequently commented that Evatt's approach was that of 'an advocate, a lawyer'. 'He had a "case" to make and he set about to make it in the only way he knew – the way of an advocate defending a client before a court. In this case the court was the government of the United States.' Murphy concludes that 'Evatt's relative success in having his voice heard reflects Grattan's comment about his forceful advocacy, often belligerent but impossible to ignore'.[32]

Consistent with this perception, in a secret policy statement on Australasia of August 1948, State Department officials described some of Evatt's actions in the UN context as 'embarrassing to us', and observed too that Australian 'suspicion of American financial and military power has deep roots'.[33] Wartime cooperation had in many ways strengthened Australian–US links, symbolised by the raising of the Australian legation in Washington to embassy status in 1946 and vice versa soon after. Yet this was a complex relationship whose vagaries inevitably affected Fulbright negotiations. Indeed, the broader Fulbright story offers a new window on to that relationship, a window of special interest because of its framing in an internationalist language that assumed both parties were seeking a higher good, an exchange of knowledge and experience that would, ideally, contribute to world peace. Negotiators interpreted this higher good – and the means of achieving it – in the light of their own government's broader interests and also of their particular understanding of the role of education in society. Australian concerns about the nature and extent of US power, about the value (or threat) of US educational models, about the dilution of an Australian (and to many, 'British') culture, played out in the Fulbright negotiations.

We have seen some of the grounds for dispute in the ratio of Americans to Australians on the proposed board of directors. J.W.C. Cumes of External Affairs, in his notes on the US draft agreement in March 1948, expressed concern that the board was in danger of being controlled by the State Department; nevertheless he understood that the program offered Australia an alternative to payment in scarce US dollars. He acknowledged the US expectation of holding a position of dominance and also expressed his desire that it would be 'an agreement between equals'. This was hard for the American negotiators to swallow.[34] Though they were very keen to conclude an agreement, the Americans were troubled by the divergence between their view that the money was theirs, and by the Australian government's unapologetic desire for an equal share of control of the board.[35] Orsen Neilsen, reporting at length on a meeting he had held with External Affairs Secretary John Burton, complained about the Australians' 'sensitiveness to being outnumbered and out-weighed' on the board, and revealed that Burton *et al.* proposed that the body be called an Advisory Committee 'or some other title from which the sting of *directing* has been removed'.[36]

We cannot overlook the cultural dimension to this conversation. For this was as much about the two nations' different approaches to education as it was about an uneven power balance in the administration of the program. As a State Department officer reported in August, 'The scope of "free enterprise" is more narrowly defined and does not enjoy the same veneration in Australia as in the U.S.'.[37] The Fulbright Program at the US end was designed to rely on the cooperation of non-governmental organisations. These were mostly student and academic support associations, such as the Institute of International Education (IIE), established with funding from the Carnegie Corporation of New York (CCNY) in 1919, and the Conference Board of Associated Research Councils. This arrangement was presented to the world as a positive example of US reliance on private (that is, non-government) initiative. For example, in May 1948, George V. Allen, US assistant secretary of state for public affairs, told a conference on international exchange in Michigan, 'it is a privilege to be associated with a field of endeavour in which our Government's participation is welcomed, and not feared, by private citizens'. He spoke of 'a world in which certain Governments manage all the affairs of their citizens, with the result that the initiative of the latter is either stifled or ruthlessly manipulated from above'.[38]

In contrast to the US educational landscape, the Australian state-funded education system was highly centralised, and its language was that of the public service, virtually untouched by commercial considerations. Australian public servants' resistance to the 'board of directors' terminology reflected this difference, but also indicated a deeper and broader resistance within the educational world to US models of teaching, learning, devolved administration and private funding.

State Department officers commented quite often in their despatches on Australia's powerful historical connection to British educational models, which was particularly evident in Australian universities. This could manifest as a certain sense of superiority vis-à-vis American educationalists, tied in with an anxiety about existing practices and principles being diluted or supplanted by American approaches. External Affairs officer John E. Oldham's response to the US draft agreement in April 1948 is a perfect example of this combination of anxiety and superiority. Oldham expressed concern that the Fulbright Program would involve 'American infiltration' rather than the reverse, or Australia affecting the United States. He then went on to wonder whether 'the American students with their lower standards will be able to make the grade at certain Australian universities, such as Sydney, Melbourne and Adelaide, where standards are very high in comparison with the rest of the world'.[39] Although Oldham's comments were meant for the ears of other Australian departmental officers and certainly did not appear in official communications with the State Department, the archival record of the next few years shows that US foreign service officers were very aware of Australian public servants' and educators' fears and assumptions. These concerns were later to affect the operation of the program at particular moments. For now, it was a preoccupation apparent in the earliest stages of the program's development.

An 'approach ... generally negative and uncooperative'

Australia might have been one of, or even the first, country to sign a Fulbright Agreement had things proceeded smoothly from the outset. The process of negotiation was, however, slow, and then it stalled. The records reveal that there was a break in communications in mid-1948, after the Australians sent their response to the US draft. It is possible that the Australian suggestions simply took time to make their way through the various bodies involved in the program at the US end – including the Bureau of Educational and Cultural Affairs (CU) in the State Department, the Board of Foreign Scholarships (BFS), and the non-governmental organisations that supported the program. But when we look at the larger picture of Australian–US diplomatic relations at this time, a different set of possibilities emerges.

In June 1948, the US government placed an embargo on the transmission of certain classified information to the Australian government, due to suspicions, based on British and American intelligence officers' analysis of VENONA decrypts, that a security leak to the Soviet Embassy had originated with the Department of External Affairs.[40] John Burton, secretary of External Affairs, who was personally involved in Fulbright discussions over this period, was already believed by some in the State Department to be, if not a Communist, then at the very least a 'fellow traveller'.[41] The Fulbright records for that month, while they make no specific mention of the decision to stop intelligence sharing, suggest that the silence extended beyond matters of security and defence. On 1 June, David Cuthell of the US Embassy, noting in a meeting with Australian officials 'a considerable divergence of opinion over the fundamental principles of the Foundation', thought that the Australians' proposed amendments would 'bring a speedy reply' from his government. The response was anything but speedy. In September, a secret telegram from External Affairs to the Australian Embassy in Washington noted that though they had sent their formal response to the US draft three months earlier, they were 'still awaiting advice as to any comments from the Department of State'.[42]

In November, Coombs wrote to an unnamed Australian minister, possibly Evatt, about two treaties under discussion at the time: the American proposal for a 'Treaty of Friendship, Commerce and Navigation', which troubled the Australian government on a number of fronts, and the Lend-Lease (aka Fulbright) Agreement. Officers from several Commonwealth departments had met and agreed that that the Treaty of Friendship was 'still full of economic and social difficulties from Australia's point of view and in any case would yield few and small advantages to Australia, while being of great potential value to America'. Meanwhile, they revealed they were still waiting on a reply from State Department about the Australian response to the draft Fulbright Agreement.[43] Indeed, they had 'pressed for a reply, both through the United States Embassy in Canberra and our Embassy in Washington, but [had] received no indication of the reactions of the United States Government'.[44]

The long silence from Washington may have stemmed from growing frustration on the American side with the Australian determination to act like 'equals' in the negotiations process, exacerbated by the broader resentment of Evatt and Burton's approach to international, economic and security issues. In March 1949, State Department despatches declared that 'the approach of the Australian Government toward the Fulbright Agreement since negotiations were begun a year ago has been generally negative and uncooperative … the Australian Government has tended to consider the Agreement wholly bilateral while ignoring the fact that the fund of $5,000,000 belongs to the United States and is in payment of value received'.[45] Yet the United States was also untrusting of the Australians.

A month later, Andrew B. Foster, chargé d'affaires at the American Embassy in Canberra, went further, reporting that 'the Australian Government has taken from the beginning of the negotiations … a peculiarly obstructionist and unyielding attitude'. He went on to speculate about the reasons for this. 'As reported by the Embassy in other despatches', he said, 'the Australian Labor Government has made clear that it is not interested in either a Treaty of Friendship, Commerce, and Navigation with the United States or an agreement for the avoidance of double taxation'.[46] Here Foster was referring to Evatt's interventions on the international stage and his – and Burton's – unwillingness to fully embrace the anti-Soviet language that was now *de rigueur* in US foreign policy circles and was also impinging increasingly on the world of higher education.

Thus, the Fulbright negotiations were caught up in a complex web of bi-national (and international) preoccupations and arguments. The exchange program was, inevitably, weighed up alongside other, related measures with economic and social impacts that stretched beyond the limited focus of academic exchange. In both countries at that time education was primarily a state government concern and was only minimally represented at federal level. The fact that the negotiations were being carried out by foreign policy – State and External Affairs – rather than Education departments guaranteed a certain overflow from larger foreign policy concerns into the educational questions the proposed program raised.

Despite these disagreements and delays, there is plenty of evidence in the government archives that Australians more generally were very interested in the proposed exchange program, which had been mentioned regularly in the mainstream press since the Lend-Lease Settlement of June 1946 and the passage of the Fulbright Bill in August. Hundreds wrote to inquire about opportunities to study in the United States throughout the negotiation period.[47] By 1949, public critique of the delay was building in the Australian press, and Evatt was blamed for what was considered a pointless intransigence and a failure to appreciate the value of the proposed scheme.[48] The matter was being politicised as the federal election drew near.

In the final year of negotiation, 1949, Australian newspapers began to paint the long delay in concluding a Fulbright deal as damning evidence of the Chifley Labor government's poor relations with the United States. Journalists, and opposition politicians writing opinion pieces, stressed the significance of the scheme. In April 1949, one *Canberra Times* journalist claimed that 'These negotiations are regarded in Washington as the greatest of importance of all outstanding matters between the two countries'.[49] Such mounting public criticism may have spurred Evatt to move things along, for US archives suggest that he made special efforts to conclude the agreement in early 1949.

According to US Ambassador Myron Cowen, writing in February 1949, Evatt was 'largely instrumental [in] bringing Australian Treasury in [to] line especially on tax exemption' and wanted 'very much to sign the agreement himself' before going overseas. An indication of the Treasury position appears in an account of a meeting between Office of Education officials and Bert Goodes, the assistant secretary of Treasury. It was Goodes who had managed to get hold of a copy of the UK binational agreement and found that 'the English agreement included almost all the provisions for which the Australian government had been standing out'. Indeed, some provisions were even more favourable to the Government of the United Kingdom. Goodes was concerned that if 'each side was engaged in a game of bluff' then the Australians would be better off pulling out of the negotiations, even at this late stage.[50] Australia, committed to the Sterling area, was trying to minimise drawing on scarce dollar reserves. US Embassy negotiators were also digging in their heels. Andrew B. Foster reported in his April 1949 despatch that Ambassador Cowen was convinced that 'if Australia refused to grant unconditional tax exemption for Fulbright grantees[,] the United States should drop further efforts to get an agreement and should ask the Australian Government to pay the fund of five million dollars to the United States in dollars as provided in the Agreement of June 7, 1946'.[51]

So, despite Evatt's intervention, the taxation issue was not resolved at all, and was thrashed out again and again through the year. Misunderstandings between Australian federal departments over this article of the agreement were at the heart of the delay, one External Affairs officer claimed. But compounding this was another clause that the Australians refused to accept. The Americans, responding to the devaluation of the Australian pound, sought an exchange rate (applying to the program funds) more favourable to the United States than the one agreed to in the June 1946 Lend-Lease Settlement Act that laid out the basic terms making possible a Fulbright Agreement. The Australians pointed out that if current exchange rates were used, they would in effect be repaying the US government 'over half a million pounds' more than originally agreed.[52] There was a distinct lack of bi-national mutual understanding at this stage of the negotiations.

In October, Liberal Member of the House of Representatives Richard Casey – who had been Australian minister to Washington nine years earlier – published an opinion piece criticising the Chifley government's 'chilly reception' to the Americans' 'free gift to Australia' (namely the Fulbright Program). Their attitude, along with the refusal to consider an agreement to eliminate double taxation, was he considered 'quite fantastic when the plain fact is that we need the friendship and support of America far more than she needs ours'.[53] This echoed the substance of Andrew B. Foster's April despatch, in which he declared that 'Australia needs the United States far more than the United States needs Australia, although this does not prevent the Australian Government from adopting the complacent attitude that the United States is bound to bail Australia out in the next war just as we did last time'.[54]

Here we get to the crux of the matter. The question is: was the mutual understanding allegedly being sought here simply to be an understanding that the United States was more powerful and that therefore other countries must bend to its will? While Casey and Foster's comments seemed to suggest this, Australian External Affairs negotiators took a different view. If the program were to have any chance of generating positive and productive relations between the people (and governments) of two countries, it must surely proceed from a basis of equality (or something resembling it) in its fundamental arrangements.

Growing public interest in the program and frustration at delays in its implementation were now used to pressure the Australian government into capitulation. From the US Embassy Andrew B. Foster claimed that 'For at least a year there has been deep and wide interest throughout Australia in the proposed agreement. Countless inquiries have been received by the Embassy and the consulates from students, scholars, professors, research workers, and educators desiring to apply for grants under the program or hoping to arrange for visiting American grantees to become associated with their institutions'. He also noted that the Australian press 'has repeatedly published news and background stories about the program and I am called every few days by various newspaper men wanting to know whether any progress has been made'. He took this as evidence that '[t]he Australian people as a whole appear to be aware of the generosity and high purpose of the Fulbright program and to be impatient with the Australian Government for its failure to reach agreement with the United States'.[55]

The Americans continued to blame the Australian government but despite the obstacles to reaching agreement, things were moving along. In the same month as Casey's article, US Ambassador Pete Jarman described the attitude of the Australian negotiators as 'capricious, uncooperative and obstructionist' in his despatch to Washington, but now he also acknowledged some fault on the American side. On the troublesome exchange rate question, he said 'our position is so weak, at least in terms of the evidence thus far submitted, that we cannot conceive of an impartial arbiter deciding in our favor'.[56]

In the end, both sides made compromises, or capitulations. The Australians agreed finally to a taxation waiver on Fulbright grants, and to the narrowing of the program's focus to 'educational' concerns (rather than 'educational and cultural' as they had sought[57] – perhaps perversely, given the prevailing fear of American cultural imperialism). The Americans agreed to honour the June 1946 Lend-Lease Settlement exchange rate for Fulbright funds, and also that the Australian minister for External Affairs and the US chief of mission would *together* select the Australian directors on the bi-national board (Article 5).

Despite several years' worth of disagreements and delays, this was a major achievement. Finally, on 26 November 1949, Evatt and US Ambassador Pete Jarman (see Figure 1.1) signed the executive agreement enabling the Fulbright exchange scheme – the first ever formal treaty between the two countries. The ANZUS Treaty was still two years away. This was only a fortnight before the Australian federal election. If Evatt hoped to gain some political mileage from the conclusion of the deal, or to demonstrate that he was on better terms with the Americans than critics claimed, he was to be disappointed. Two days later, a *Sydney Morning Herald* editorial titled 'Missing Our Chances With The U.S.A' declared that Evatt's 'praise of the Fulbright agreement signed

Figure 1.1 The US ambassador to Australia, Pete Jarman, signing the Fulbright Agreement for the United States, watched by the Australian minister for External Affairs, Dr H.V. Evatt, Canberra, November 1949

in Canberra during the week-end, invites the comment that the Government might well have shown a year or two sooner appreciation of such ties with the United States'.[58] Less than a fortnight after that, Robert Menzies' Liberal-Country Party (L-CP) coalition won the federal election with a 5 per cent swing. When Percy Spender replaced Evatt as minister for External Affairs, he took a very different approach to Australian–US relations, pulling away from Evatt's beloved UN, and embracing the language of the Cold War in a way that Evatt and Chifley had tried to avoid.

Historian David Lowe argues that, in the late 1940s, one of the problems facing the Australians and Americans in their diplomatic dealings with each other, aside from many substantive policy differences, was that they 'did not speak the same language' – that is, that Chifley and Evatt refused to subscribe to the rhetoric of 'clashing civilisations' that dominated public discourse in the United States.[59] Over this period, however, it became increasingly difficult for the Labor government to hold to an independent line and remain aloof from the hardening Cold War divide. In contrast, the L-CP Coalition was rhetorically much more in tune with American Cold Warriors. Spender, for example, was strongly influenced by American thinkers on the Cold War. Indeed, Lowe claims that while in opposition Spender 'did his best to bring the origins of US containment policy into Australian awareness'.[60] In April 1948 he declared that 'A vote for Labor in Australia is a vote which will bring closer all the dangers of this foul philosophy which Christian and freedom-loving people abhor'.[61]

Finally, the Australian Fulbright Agreement was a reality. Australia was still among the first ten countries to sign, even with the difficulties of negotiation and the mutual distrust on both sides. The ALP government and the official bureaucrats in the several government departments had fought for and gained a better deal for Australia, a fact that would become clear in the longer term.

Soon after the signing, External Affairs staff asked Evatt to consider candidates for the three Australian seats on the board. By then, he had other things on his mind. Evatt, who was also Chifley's Attorney-General, was coming into the final week of a federal election campaign being fought tooth and nail over bank nationalisation, post-war rationing and Communism in the unions. His campaign hit a bump when the University of Tasmania's Vice-Chancellor Torleiv Hytten, an economist who opposed Labor's bank nationalisation policy, announced his intention to sue Evatt for claiming that Hytten had advocated 'a pool of unemployment of between 6 and 11 per cent' in a conference paper, at a time when both sides of politics aimed for full employment. Then, adding fuel to the fire, a man declared that Evatt had had him interned during the war for chairing an anti-Communist meeting – a story lapped up by the press.[62] Spender condemned Evatt's 'splurge of socialistic legislation' at a public meeting, declaring: 'it is well said that the Devil himself knows not the mind of man, and it would take a multitude of devils to penetrate the dark recesses of Dr. Evatt's mind'.[63] It is little wonder Evatt was slow to reply to the External Affairs request. Nine days later, the Labor government was voted out, and nine days after that, Spender was named the new minister for External Affairs. One of Spender's first ministerial tasks, then, was to implement the freshly signed Fulbright Agreement, and oversee the setting up of the program. The new L-CP coalition government had inherited the agreement, and with it, the responsibility of establishing the administrative machinery and appointing bi-national board members so the program could be implemented immediately.

Delay in getting the agreement signed was indicative of some of the tensions implicit within a scheme that was both a US government initiative but was not, and could never survive as, an unmediated extension of US foreign policy. While the proposal for the Fulbright scheme came out of the Second World War, and negotiations for these agreements began as early as 1946, they were being conducted over three years of deepening Cold War tensions, and the scheme was only implemented during the height of Cold War polarisation. What is apparent is a shift in the Chifley government's attitude towards the negotiations. From an initial eagerness to get a quick agreement, a later hard line on the negotiation emerged in 1948, which was only mollified by the end of 1949 in time to sign the agreement before losing the election. The archives reveal the relief felt by the American foreign service establishment in Australia when the L-CP coalition won government in the December 1949 election.[64]

Notes

1 Statement by Assistant Secretary William Benton on the Fulbright Bill, Department of State Press release, 1 August 1946, No. 532. In A9790 8132, National Archives of Australia (hereafter NAA); see Lebovic, 'From War Junk to Educational Exchange: The World War II Origins of the Fulbright Program and the Foundations of American Cultural Globalism, 1945–50', *Diplomatic History*, vol. 37:2 (April 2013), pp. 280–312.
2 On the US back story, see Randall Bennett Woods, *Fulbright: A Biography* (Cambridge, 1995); Walter Johnson and Francis James Colligan, *The Fulbright Program: A History* (Chicago, 1965); Richard T. Arndt, *The First Resort of Kings: American Cultural Diplomacy in the Twentieth Century* (Dulles, 2005).
3 Stuart Macintyre, *Australia's Boldest Experiment: War and Reconstruction in the 1940s* (Sydney, 2015).
4 Agreement between the Government of the United States of America and the Government of the Commonwealth of Australia on Settlement for Lend-Lease, Reciprocal Aid, Surplus War Property, and Claims, signed at Washington and New York on 7 June 1946, by James F. Byrnes, Secretary of State of the USA, and H. Evatt, Minister of External Affairs of the Commonwealth of Australia. 60 Stat. 1707; Treaties and Other International Act Series 1528, NAA.
5 H.C. Coombs, *Trial Balance* (Melbourne, 1981).
6 Macintyre, *Boldest Experiment*, p. 305; see also S.G. Foster and M. Varghese, *The Making of the Australian National University, 1946–1996* (Sydney, 1996), p. 18.
7 Coombs, *Trial Balance*, pp. 85–6.
8 'Australia Settles Lend-Lease Account', *Sydney Morning Herald*, 10 June 1946, p. 3.
9 12 August 1946, Letter (and notes) from H.C. Coombs, Director, Ministry of Post-War Reconstruction, to John Minter, U.S. Embassy. In 'Lend Lease Educational and Cultural (Fulbright) Agreement', NAA: A9790 8132.
10 1 April 1947, Cablegram SECRET I.7027 XM0031. From Department of External Affairs to Australian Embassy Washington, concerning delays to agreement. And 11 Sept 1947 Cablegram SECRET from Aust Emb Wash to Dept Ext Aff I. 18289 XMO.30. Both documents in NAA: A9790 8132.
11 Arndt, *First Resort of Kings*, pp. 161–86.
12 3 March 1948, Telegram Australian Embassy Washington to Department of External Affairs, noting receipt of draft agreement on 2 March. In '[1948 file – pink tab] [Foreign policy] – (U.S.) – lend lease – Cultural fund – (under Fulbright Act) (general policy)' in NAA: A3300 874.
13 Department of State preference for an American Executive Officer was mentioned in a Confidential Despatch No. 65 from DOS to the U.S. Embassy in Australia, 29 November 1948, in NARA RG 59 811.42747 SE/6–1848. Also 23 November 1949, DOS incoming telegram no. 257, U.S. Embassy Canberra to Secretary of State, in NARA RG 59 811.42747 Box 4805.
14 30 April 1947, Dept of Post-War Reconstruction Minute. To the Minister (from L. F. Crisp). Cover letter for submission by Inter-Departmental Committee on Education, for PM, Coombs and Evatt. 1 April 1947, Cablegram SECRET I.7027 XM0031 [see n. 13].
15 1 April 1947, Cablegram SECRET I.7027 XM0031. A9790 8132, NAA.
16 30 April 1947, Dept of Post-War Reconstruction Minute. To the Minister (from L. F. Crisp) Cover letter for submission by Inter-Departmental Committee on Education, for PM, Coombs and Evatt. A9790 8132, NAA.

17 9 June 1948, Confidential Despatch from American Embassy, Canberra, to Secretary of State. 'Subj: Proposed Agreement with Australia for the Use of Funds Available under U.S. Public Law 584', RG 59, CDF 1945 Box 4805, NARA.

18 16 March 1948, 'Lend-Lease Cultural Agreement' (Notes on articles of draft agreement by J.W.C. Cumes). A1067 A46/2/4/10, NAA.

19 19 April 1948, 'External Affairs – For the Secretary – Additional Detailed Comment on U.S. Draft Agreement' [signed J[ohn]. E. Oldham]. In A1067 A46/2/4/10, NAA. This was in response to US comments of 1 April 1948.

20 10 November 1947, 'Central News Agency – English Service – Agreement for Estab'g US Educ'l Foundation in China Signed'. A1361 4/7/5 part 1, NAA.

21 Geraldine McDonald, Pam Kennedy and Barb Bishop, *Coming and Going:Forty Years of the Fulbright Program in New Zealand* (Wellington, 1989), p. ix.

22 16 March 1948, Document titled 'Lend-Lease Cultural Agreement'. Notes on U.S. draft agreement by J.W.C. Cumes (External Affairs). In 'Social and Cultural Matters. Land-lease [*sic*] Cultural fund. "Fulbright Agreement"', NAA A1067 A46/2/4/10.

23 2 June 1948, Memo of Conversation [CONFIDENTIAL] To Orsen N Neilsen. From David C. Cuthell [Foreign Service officer] 'Subj: Draft Agreement of Fulbright Act'. RG 59 DOS CDF 1945 Box 4805, NARA.

24 14 April 1949, AmEmbassy (Foster) to Sec of State. 'Re-establishment and rehabilitation in overseas countries – Lend-lease settlement funds – Available for culture (Fulbright bill)', RG 59 811.42747 Box 4805, NARA.

25 No date, but estimated as January 1949 going by its position in the files, and reference to dates in a later State Department despatch. A1361 4/7/5 PART 1, NAA.

26 Peter Bayne, 'Evatt, Herbert Vere', in Michael Coper, Tony Blackshield and George Williams, eds, *Oxford Companion to the High Court of Australia*, 1st edn (Melbourne, 2001).

27 John Murphy, *Evatt: A Life* (Sydney, 2016), pp. 214–22, 250–6.

28 3 February 1950, Sydney to DOS: USIE Country Paper – Aims and Objectives of the USIE Program in Australia. In NARA RG 59 R59 511.43 – 811.43, Box 2359; see also Murphy, *Evatt*, pp. 214–58.

29 Murphy, *Evatt*, pp. 218, 222–3.

30 Murphy, *Evatt*, p. 239.

31 Murphy, quoting Grattan, *Evatt*, pp. 186–7.

32 Murphy, *Evatt*, pp. 187, 192.

33 'United States Relations with Australia: Policy Statement of the Department of State', classified Secret, Washington, 18 August 1948. In United States Department of State, *Foreign Relations of the United States, 1948*, vol. 6: The Far East and Australasia, pp. 2 and 7. At http://digicoll.library.wisc.edu/cgi-bin/FRUS/FRUS-idx?type=div&did=FRUS.FRUS1948v06.i0006&isize=M (accessed 23 August 2012).

34 16 March 1948, 'Lend-Lease Cultural Agreement'. (Cumes).

35 2 June 1948, Memo of Conversation [CONFIDENTIAL] to Orsen N Neilsen from David C. Cuthell. Subject: Draft Agreement of Fulbright Act. In NARA: RG 59 DOS CDF 1945 Box 4805.

36 9 June 1948, Despatch no. 111 – CONFIDENTIAL. American Embassy, Canberra, to Secretary of State. Subject: Proposed Agreement with Australia for the Use of Funds Available under U.S. Public Law 584. In NARA: RG 59 DOS CDF 1945 Box 4805.

37 'United States Relations with Australia: Policy Statement of the Department of State', classified Secret, Washington, 18 August 1948. In United States Department of State, *Foreign Relations of the United States, 1948*, vol. 6: The Far East and Australasia, p. 7.

38　'Extract from United States State Department Wireless Bulletin dated 10th May, 1948: Allen Cites Cooperation in U.S. Educational Exchange' in 'Social and Cultural Matters. Land-lease [*sic*] Cultural fund. "Fulbright Agreement"', A1067 A46/2/4/10, NAA.

39　19 April 1948, External Affairs – For the Secretary – 'Additional Detailed Comment on U.S. Draft Agreement' [signed J[ohn]. E. Oldham]. NAA: A1067 A46/2/4/10.

40　Phillip Deery, 'Decoding the Cold War: Venona, Espionage and "The Communist Threat"', in Peter Love and Paul Strangio, eds, *Arguing the Cold War* (Melbourne, 2001), pp. 113–14. Deery was a Fulbright scholar in 1989.

41　David Lowe, *Menzies and the 'Great World Struggle': Australia's Cold War 1948–1954* (Sydney, 1999), p. 35.

42　6 September 1948 [received 7 September], Telegram from DEA to Australian Embassy Washington. '[1948 file – pink tab] [Foreign policy] – (U.S.) – lend lease – Culturalfund – (under Fulbright Act) (general policy)' in NAA: A3300 874.

43　15 November 1948, Cover letter to item 22, from Coombs to the Minister [Evatt? Department not named] on 'Treaty of Friendship, Commerce and Navigation. Lend-Lease Settlement – Educational and Cultural Agreement'. 'Lend Lease Educational and Cultural (Fulbright) Agreement', NAA: A9790 8132.

44　[n.d. – mid-to-late November 1948?], Lend Lease Educational Cultural Agreement: overview of events/discussions to date – includes a table of US proposals and Australian counter proposals. In 'Lend Lease Educational and Cultural (Fulbright) Agreement', NAA: A9790 8132.

45　21 March 1949, AmEmbassy to Sec of State, No. 6. Subject: Misunderstanding within the Australian Government concerning Taxation Provisions of the Pending United States-Australian Fulbright Agreement. NARA: General Records of Dept of State Central Decimal File 1945–49, RG 59, 811.42747 Box 4805.

46　14 April 1949, AmEmbassy to Secretary of State. Re: Pending United States-Australian Fulbright Agreement. Signed Andrew B. Foster, Chargé d'Affaires. In 'Exchange of scholars/professors', in 811.42747 Box 4805 RG 59 General Records of Dept of State Central Decimal File 1945–49, NARA.

47　A1067 A46/2/4/10, NAA; and A1838 250/9/8/3 PART 1, NAA.

48　'Slow Negotiations Disappoint U.S.: Strong Views on Taxation and Student Plan', *The Advertiser*, 14 April 1949, p. 2; 'Delay in Fulbright Act Negotiations', *The West Australian*, 2 May 1949, p. 14.

49　'Australia May End Drawn-Out Negotiations', *Canberra Times*, 30 April 1949, p. 1.

50　7 February 1949, Commonwealth Office of Education document (no title) addressed to Prof. Mills and others reporting on a meeting held with Bert Goodes of Treasury. In 'Re-establishment and rehabilitation in overseas countries – Lend-Lease settlement funds – available for culture (Fulbright bill)', A1361 4/7/5 PART 1, NAA. The UK Fulbright Agreement had been concluded in September 1948.

51　14 April 1949, AmEmbassy to Secretary of State. In 'Exchange of scholars/professors', 811.42747 Box 4805 RG 59 CDF 1945–49, NARA.

52　22 September 1949, External Affairs Memorandum 'For the Minister: Lend Lease Educational Fund: Fulbright Agreement' in A1838 250/9/8/2, NAA.

53　R.G. Casey, 'Our Relations with America', *Morning Bulletin* (Rockhampton, Qld.), 13 October 1949, p. 3.

54　14 April 1949, AmEmbassy to Secretary of State. In 'Exchange of scholars/professors', 811.42747 Box 4805 RG 59 CDF 1945–49, NARA.

55 14 April 1949, AmEmbassy to Secretary of State. In 'Exchange of scholars/professors', 811.42747 Box 4805 RG 59 CDF 1945–49, NARA.

56 4 October 1949, Telegram Canberra to Department of State: Despatch 103. In 'Exchange of scholars/professors', in 811.42747 Box 4805 RG 59 General Records of Dept of State Central Decimal File 1945–49, NARA. Andrew B. Foster had said something similar in April 1949 in a despatch: 'Our case is so weak, and the advocacy of it would put us in such an embarrassing position, that I believe we should accept the risk of possible depreciation of the Australian pound in terms of the dollar.' AmEmbassy to Secretary of State. Re: Pending United States-Australian Fulbright Agreement. Signed Andrew B. Foster, Chargé d'Affaires. In 'Exchange of scholars/ professors', in 811.42747 Box 4805 RG 59 CDF 1945–49, NARA.

57 In this post-war period, Coombs was developing an interest in creating opportunities for cultural development in Australia, to be boosted/inspired by the example of tours by performance groups from overseas. He flagged the possibility of a Commonwealth cultural council. Tim Rowse, *Nugget Coombs: A Reforming Life* (Cambridge, 2002), pp. 192–7. If cultural relations had been included in the Australian–US Fulbright Agreement, this might have facilitated tours by US performing groups to Australia.

58 *Sydney Morning Herald* editorial, 28 November 1949, p. 2.

59 Lowe, *Menzies*, p. 41.

60 David Lowe, *Australian Between Empires: The Life of Percy Spender* (London, 2010), p. 118.

61 Speech given by Spender at Masonic Hall, Randwick, 28 April 1948, Spender Papers Box 2, fol. 11, MS4875, National Library of Australia (henceforth NLA), quoted by Lowe, *Australian Between Empires*, p. 117.

62 'Action Against Evatt', *Central Queensland Herald* (Rockhampton, Qld.), 1 December 1949, p. 13 and 'Attack on Evatt', *Sydney Morning Herald*, 3 December 1949, p. 3.

63 'Mr. Spender Dr. Evatt Attacked', *Sydney Morning Herald*, 2 December 1949, p. 4.

64 Lowe, in *Menzies*, p. 42, notes he found in the Truman papers Jarman's admission that he had prepared congratulatory letters to Menzies and Fadden over a week before the election results were known.

2

'A steady stream of new problems':
Politics and teething issues

Negotiating the terms of the Fulbright Agreement had been concluded but, now, setting up the scheme brought a new suite of problems. Charles Odegaard, executive director of the American Council of Learned Societies (ACLS), offered some advice to those charged with establishing a working exchange program. Odegaard was a history lecturer who would become president of the University of Washington, and was also a member of the Committee on International Exchange of Persons established by the Conference Board of Associated Research Councils.[1] Odegaard reflected on the difficulty to be encountered in administering the Fulbright Program in this initial period. He emphasised the challenge for American administrators who had to take into account 'the wishes of innumerable institutions in a variety of lands with very diverse traditions', and foresaw 'a steady stream of new problems calling for rational analysis and policy determination'. He called, finally, for 'the indulgent sympathy of the entire educational world in America and abroad' while these problems were sorted out.[2] Many obstacles, however, were more likely to be local and administrative, with no road map yet in place. In Australia, the tensions which had inflected the negotiations did not disappear immediately, even with the change of government.

As soon as word got out that the long-awaited Fulbright Agreement had been signed, External Affairs began to receive notes of congratulation. Among these were carefully worded letters from people hoping to be named to the bi-national board of seven directors who would oversee finances, selections and programming for the exchange program. One of the first was a telegram from Conrad F. Horley, a prominent Sydney accountant and president of the Australian-American Association (AAA). This was an organisation of private citizens, many American-born, dedicated to fostering social, intellectual and business ties between the two countries.[3] Horley wrote on 26 November to express the Association's 'gratification that this most generous gesture of the American government has been brought into realization'.[4] Back in May, the AAA's secretary, P.M. Hamilton, had sent an anticipatory letter to External Affairs proposing a role for Association members in the planned administrative machinery of the program, so their interest in the program was on the record.[5] But Conrad Horley's November missive clearly annoyed External Affairs Minister Evatt, who scribbled on its margins the following barbed reply: 'Many thanks ... The conclusion of this agreement was marred only by unfortunate statements calculated to spoil Aust-USA relations which have been & are ~~completely~~ [crossed out by hand] the closest. I hope your association can use its influence to prevent these ill-informed utterances.'[6]

The public criticism of the delay in signing the Fulbright Agreement over the previous months had clearly rattled the minister, and he rightly saw the AAA as instrumental in fomenting trouble. In October, the Adelaide *Advertiser* and Brisbane *Courier Mail* had reported the accusation by the AAA's Victorian delegate to the federal council that the federal government had dealt Australian–US relations a 'great blow' by (allegedly) refusing to 'surrender these millions for such worthy objects such as the Fulbright scholarship scheme'.[7] The Victorian delegate was none other than Sir Keith Murdoch, father of today's media mogul Rupert, owner of both newspapers and an important member of the AAA. His wife Dame Elizabeth was the patron of the Victorian chapter for many years (until her death in 2012).[8] Now, as the Australian-American Fulbright Program or United States Educational Foundation (USEF) was getting underway, the AAA was angling for a seat on the board. A disgruntled Evatt, however, was unlikely to grant that wish.

Getting started

Before the election result was known, External Affairs officials had already drawn up a list of potential Australian board members. It included several senior public servants who had been involved in the negotiations – 'Nugget' Coombs of (the soon-to-be dismantled) Post-War Reconstruction, R.C. Mills of the Office of Education and Bert Goodes of the Treasury (Goodes was the official who had at one point in the Fulbright negotiations suggested ditching the agreement if the Americans would not budge on certain conditions). Also suggested were three judges, including Sir Charles Lowe, who was both chancellor of Melbourne University and a justice of the Victorian Supreme Court; two vice-chancellors – the ANU's Douglas Copland and Melbourne University's John Medley; the headmaster of Melbourne private school, Wesley College; and a Rhodes Trust representative. The list did not include anyone from the AAA. Officers from External Affairs had also begun to prepare briefs for the three, as yet unnamed, Australian board members, 'trying to anticipate, for their benefit, the decisions which will have to be made and what experience in other countries has been'.[9]

By this time nine other countries had signed Fulbright agreements and exchange programs were underway. Although not all were actually in operation, agreements had been signed in China (1947), Burma (1947), England/UK (1948), Belgium (1948), Greece (1948), France (1948), Italy (1948), New Zealand (1948) and the Philippines (1948). As well as Australia, in 1949, Norway, Iran, Turkey and United Arab Republic signed on. So Australia had several models to draw on for its planning. In a 1948 External Affairs file a number of early agreements can be found, including the Burmese and Chinese agreements, as well as press releases on other completed negotiations. In June 1948, for example, Ralph Harry in External Affairs wrote to the secretary concerning the new Philippines agreement, noting that, with respect to articles on board membership and payment procedures, these 'appear to be more favourable to the Philippines than the corresponding articles of the proposed Australian agreement to Australia. The State Department explain that special conditions applied in this case due to the close association between the United States and Philippines Governments'. Other memos in the file concerned the make-up of the New Zealand, Belgium and Chinese boards.[10] So, the Australians were not working entirely in isolation; they were grappling with these new schemes alongside others and knowledge was, to some extent, being shared amongst the different partner nations.

It was clear that the USEF board's main responsibilities would be to 'maintain the funds of the Foundation', to 'plan, adopt and carry out programmes' and to recommend to the US Board of Foreign Scholarships those Australian 'students, professors etc. qualified to participate'. The board would also oversee institutional placement and hosting of US scholars. Each of these aspects required a host of local and transnational policy and procedural decisions to be made, before any scholars could embark on their intellectual journey.

The US administrators were keen that preparations now pick up speed. On Minister Spender's first day with his new portfolio, 19 December, he learnt that the US ambassador was ready to nominate the American members and hoped to establish the full board as soon as possible.[11] Six weeks later, the American Section of External Affairs recorded Spender's final selection. The Australian board members would be the minister himself (as stipulated by the agreement), the judge Sir Charles Lowe, and Professor Currie, vice-chancellor of the University of Western Australia.[12] All, notably, had public sector careers. Currie had not been on the original list of potential directors, but Douglas Copland, who was, had recommended Currie, who had recently been elected chair of the Vice-Chancellors' Committee.[13] The announcement came just as Spender was heading off to the Commonwealth Foreign Ministers' Conference in Colombo. There he would play a key role in the establishment of the Colombo Plan for technical aid in Southeast Asia (initially named the 'Spender Plan').[14] This was a regional program of educational exchange that in subsequent years would be better known in Australia than the Fulbright Program. Their relationship as policy initiatives of the incoming Menzies L-CP coalition government deserves further investigation.

Soon after, in early February 1950, US Ambassador Jarman named the American board members: two US Embassy officers, Paul J. Sturm and Doyle V. Martin, and an American businessman who had been resident in Australia since the 1930s, W.R. Hauslaib. An External Affairs memo recorded their credentials: Sturm, second secretary in the embassy, had taught French at Yale in the late 1930s before joining the foreign service, Martin was the US Embassy's disbursing officer, and Hauslaib, managing director of Ira L.& A. C. Berk Ltd, which imported Packard cars to Australia, owned 'one of the best collections of ties I've ever seen!'[15] That Hauslaib was a former president of the AAA (1946–47) and the AAA had thus succeeded in getting itself represented on the USEF was a piece of information (discreetly) omitted.[16]

Further efforts were made by the AAA to promote the new program by linking it to the long-standing Rhodes scholarship. In mid-1950, a member of the AAA in a long article in the Association's magazine, *Pacific Neighbors*, traced the connections between the Rhodes scholarships and the Fulbright Program. He noted that Senator Fulbright had been a Rhodes Scholar, and the newly appointed USEF executive officer (Geoffrey Rossiter) had been too. The political goal of linking the two in the minds of the educated Australian public showed in the final paragraph when Hamilton declared that '[t]he torch of international co-operation through educational exchanges, first lit by Cecil Rhodes fifty years ago, is now being handed on by the Fulbright scholarships'. With an overblown rhetorical flourish, he continued: 'Its light will continue to shine in an ever-widening sphere, and the spirit of Rhodes may well say "well done" to one who has followed its gleam in the realms of firmer friendship and finer understanding through personal contacts and enduring endeavour in a world-wide field.'[17]

While the AAA, as a supporter of the Fulbright Program, evidently hoped the reflected glow and powerful cultural capital of the Rhodes scholarships might help nurture interest in the new program, its perspective was misleading. These were in fact very different schemes. One was philanthropic, centred on a single institution (Oxford University), still confined at that time to single men with demonstrated sporting prowess, and designed to bolster British imperial ties. The other was government-funded, open to academically gifted men *and* women in almost any field, who hailed from and were hosted by a wide range of public and private educational institutions. Arguably the AAA missed the point of the true genius of the Fulbright Program. Its efforts to make it equivalent to the Rhodes scholarship also failed. Sixty years later, in responses to the survey conducted for this book, many Australian scholars noted that while they had discovered upon arriving in the United States the power of the Fulbright 'brand' (in the marketing speak of the late twentieth century), in Australia the program still did not have the recognition factor of its imperial predecessor.

A government-sponsored exchange program was indeed a new sort of challenge for Australia's public servants. Now that membership of the board was settled, other matters demanded attention. Well before the board swung into action, officers of the US Embassy and the Department of External Affairs had taken the first administrative steps required to establish the new program. These public servants' primary responsibilities, however, lay elsewhere, and it soon became apparent to them, 'judging from the amount of work already received', that the program urgently required a full-time executive officer with a small staff.[18] Running a bi-national academic exchange program would be no walk in the park. It involved daily liaison between a medley of Australian and US federal and state government departments, non-government organisations, selection committees, higher educational institutions and schools, not to mention individual applicants for awards. Furthermore, the machinery already established in the United States was complicated, and the USEF in Australia would soon add several more layers of administrative procedure.

The USEF board's first meeting was held at the American Embassy on 21 February 1950. First tasks were to appoint an executive committee, arrange for the investment of the £1.5 million program funds held by the Treasury, advertise for an executive officer, and seek advice from Australian vice-chancellors on the creation of state-based advisory committees. These were to help appoint the executive officer and assist with initial screening of applicants. The board agreed that a house would need to be bought for the executive officer out of Fulbright funds, given the 'acute housing shortage' in Canberra at the time,[19] and £10,000 was set aside for this purpose (eventually a house was bought for £7,000).[20]

Three weeks later, the board met with Frederick Bundy, from the State Department's Exchange of Persons Division. He explained to them the existing arrangements for administering the program at the US end, and gave an overview of key US Board of Foreign Scholarships (BFS) policies governing selection and programming. This made it clear that ultimate control remained with the United States. The Washington-based BFS was responsible for final approval of candidates, from both countries, with initial selection of US scholars supported by three non-government organisations: the Institute of International Education (IIE) for graduate students, the United States Office of Education for exchange teachers, and the Governing Board of the Associated Research Councils (or Conference Board) for advanced research scholars and lecturers. The USEF in Australia would be expected to oversee the initial selection of Australian candidates in all categories, but final approval rested with the BFS. The USEF would also determine institutional affiliations for US scholars proposed by the BFS. If no suitable institution could be found for any individual scholar approved by the BFS, the award would not be offered to the candidate.

An additional control came with the stipulations on currency. Under the terms of the Fulbright Act, grants could only be awarded in the partner (non-US) country's currency – in this case, Australian pounds. This meant that Australian scholars would only have their travel costs covered. Consequently all applicants had to prove they had (or expected to gain) access to US dollars from other quarters. This was usually from US university or philanthropic scholarships, fellowships and assistantships, but was sometimes from the State Department's Smith-Mundt scheme. Young scientist Patricia Lee, for example, had a Fulbright award covering fares from Australia to the United States, an Australian Federation of University Women International Grant covering living expenses and textbooks, and a Rockefeller Foundation Fellowship to give her extra time to finish her course.[21] Again the border with government foreign policy goals was blurred by the administrative requirements imposed by the United States. On the other hand, this restriction did not apply to US candidates. Awards made to US scholars would cover travel, living and (where needed) dependants' allowances, for the duration of their Australian exchange.

The USEF board members must have begun to realise at this point that this binational administration was a very complicated beast. From the State Department, Fred Bundy expressed the hope that the Foundation would make use of the existing Committee on Study and Training in the United States (CoSaT). This had been established in Sydney by the US Embassy in 1949, partly in anticipation of the Fulbright Agreement, but mainly to administer other US government scholarships enabled by the Smith-Mundt Act (or 'United States Informational Exchange and Educational Exchange Act of 1948', Public Law 402). Awards under this Act included stipends for selected foreign graduate students and research scholars visiting the United States, as well as more overtly political Foreign Leader and Specialist Awards. The Department hoped that those Australian postgraduates granted a Smith-Mundt award would then be offered a Fulbright award to cover their travel. The Sydney CoSaT did prove useful to the Foundation in carrying out initial screening of Australian graduate students for Fulbright awards. On occasion, however, it also caused consternation among board members and USEF staff who were anxious to ensure that the character of the Fulbright Program was apolitical. From the outset, the shaping influence of State Department loomed large over the program's administration and would return to bedevil it at key intervals.

In this first year, Fred Bundy and the USEF board agreed that given the time of year and the work that remained to be done to establish the Australian program, the Foundation would offer only a small number of awards. This would be a pilot year, during which the Foundation staff could test their procedures and prepare more fully for later years according to BFS programming guidelines. In 1950 USEF would offer travel grants only for Australians, and the first scholars would be selected 'almost entirely from among those persons who can demonstrate immediate dollar support in the United States'.[22] There was some urgency, as most of these scholars would need to be in the United States by September, in time for the start of the academic year. This led to an extraordinary situation of confusion over the identity of the first scholar.

The first Australian scholar?

In January 1950, a month before the bi-national board was even named, there was a flurry of correspondence between External Affairs in Canberra and its Melbourne office, concerning an Australian travelling to the United States on an alleged Fulbright scholarship. According to the Melbourne office, Maxwell Kennedy, a mining engineer from Ballarat, was on his way to study Petroleum Production at the Colorado School of Mines, on a 'Fullbright [*sic*] scholarship valid for four years', supposedly granted through the Victorian Department of Education. This scholarship did not cover his fare, and Kennedy was now seeking financial assistance for this from External Affairs.

There were clearly some problems with this story. First, according to the Fulbright Act, grants to Australians, being in Australian currency, would cover travel only, not tuition or living expenses which Kennedy had been granted. Second, there were no selection procedures in place, as the board had not yet met. What was going on here?

Kennedy was very fortunate in his timing. External Affairs knew that the USEF board, once established, would need immediately to find Australians with confirmed US dollar support and institutional affiliation, to whom they could offer the first awards. It looked as though Kennedy might fit the bill – if they could only find out what scholarship he was really on (for it clearly couldn't be a Fulbright). External Affairs may also have been encouraged into immediate action in this case by a little sting in the tail of the Melbourne branch's message of 11 January. This was to the effect that the US Embassy had already granted Kennedy a visa, and the US Consulate 'wishes to make a test case of him as they are of the opinion that the Australian government has been very unco-operative over the Fullbright [*sic*] scheme'.[23] As before, during the negotiation stage, pressure from American interests was putting heat on the Australians who seemed to be dawdling. Kennedy gave them an opportunity to precipitate action. For his part, Spender, who was determined to demonstrate that his L-CP government was on more harmonious terms with the United States than its ALP predecessors, was unlikely to let his department fail this 'test case'. This might explain why the Liberal Party Premier of Victoria, Thomas Hollway – like Kennedy also a Ballarat man – was also drawn briefly into the matter when he forwarded the documents to Canberra.[24]

External Affairs' American Section thus sought to speed up the Victorian Education Department's response to their enquiry about the true nature of Kennedy's scholarship. It turned out that Kennedy had in fact won a four-year scholarship from the Colorado School of Mines, which covered tuition, and he had then been advised (by whom is not made clear) to apply for a Fulbright award to pay his passage across the Pacific. With no Fulbright selection body or process in place at this time, his application letter had ended up in the Melbourne office of External Affairs' in-tray. Somewhere in the paper trail, the message had become confused, and his Colorado scholarship was wrongly described as a Fulbright. So it seems Kennedy himself was not claiming to be a Fulbright scholar but he conveniently provided a means to push things along.[25]

This 'test case' resulted in Kennedy being granted one of the first Australian Fulbright awards, albeit without going through the normal process. His application was approved by the Foundation at its June 1950 meeting. Such an ad-hoc selection process was possible only in this teething period. Once the board appointed an executive officer, and formally established its selection procedures, there would be no room for pre-emptive decisions succumbing to externally applied pressures, or side-stepping of approval processes, by administrators or board members. This would not, however, spell the end of political meddling at the edges of the program – or, at least, anxiety about the *possibility* of political meddling – particularly as the Cold War sharpened. Navigating the fine line of political imperatives and competing government interests would continue as the abiding character of the Australian-American Fulbright Program.

The genius of Rossiter

That the Fulbright Program did succeed in getting off the ground and laying the foundation for a successful future owes much to the brilliance of the USEF board's first appointment. This was the executive officer, Geoffrey Rossiter (see Figure 2.1), appointed by the board in April 1950, to face the Antipodean end of what ACLS's Odegaard anticipated as a 'steady stream of new problems'. Rossiter was chosen from a large field and a shortlist of eighteen applicants for the position, which had been advertised nationally after the first board meeting.

Rossiter had impeccable credentials. He was a history lecturer with a BA from the University of Western Australia and a Master's degree in Modern History from Oxford University. During the war Rossiter had been a RAAF Wing Commander and was awarded a Distinguished Flying Cross.[26] Even in 1950 he certainly looked the part of a wing commander, sporting a fine Errol Flynn-style moustache. In 1946,

Figure 2.1 Geoffrey Rossiter, wife Margaret and children at home in the Fulbright House, Canberra, 1954

he had been named a Western Australian Rhodes Scholar, following in the footsteps of his older brother Roger who had won a Rhodes in 1935.[27] Hailed as a 'brilliant member of one of Western Australia's most brilliant families', who had represented his university and his state in both athletics and rugby, media profiles welcomed this appointment of the new executive officer.[28] It turns out that he was also a smart choice to lead the program – which he went on to do for the next fourteen years. One 1960 US Fulbright scholar – an historian of the American West – reflected recently: 'I have always thought the Fulbright Program was well administered. Does anyone remember Geoffrey Rossiter? I do.'[29]

Here was another illustration of the wisdom of Australian negotiators in standing firm for their principles. During the pre-1949 Fulbright negotiations, the State Department had expressed a preference for an American in this key administrative role.[30] Australian negotiators, however, argued successfully for someone with local knowledge. The program needed a person who could talk convincingly to the Oxbridge-oriented academic community about US educational possibilities, in a time when anti-Americanism was still a powerful force on campuses, despite (and in some cases exacerbated by) the recent experience of wartime collaboration. Though many Australian academics responded positively to the establishment of the exchange program, there were plenty of others who would and did actively discourage their students from seeking US postgraduate opportunities. This attitude was slow to recede. Even forty years later anecdotal evidence about university selection procedures highlighted discrimination against US degrees and US academic references. This worked in reverse too, with Australian degrees not being appealing to US students. An important part of Rossiter's job was to sell the potential benefits of an American educational experience to a community known for its suspicion of US cultural influence and inclined to look askance at US approaches to school and university education. A preference for Oxbridge-educated academics was deeply institutionalised.

Without the backing of the academic community, the program would never get off the ground. Academics were needed not just as candidates to apply for and take up awards. Their voluntary contributions of expertise were crucial, to advise the Foundation on local institutional requirements, sit on regional selection committees, act as academic hosts, and mentor students and colleagues to apply for awards, write references for applicants, and supervise and submit reports on visiting scholars.

Rossiter had not only to come to grips with the complex administrative requirements of his position, but also to build support and interest amongst Australian academics for the exchange program. The scheme's first years coincided with the intensification of Cold War ideological battles, and this would present a range of challenges for Rossiter, the binational board, as well as for scholars and academic hosts. Rossiter's first annual report provides a useful overview of essential dilemmas and attempted solutions. The core elements of the program – selection, programming and orientation – are examined in later chapters.

In March 1952, Geoffrey Rossiter submitted a long draft annual report covering the Australian program's first two years (January 1950 to December 1951) for consideration by the USEF board. He explained in detail the challenges facing the Foundation in this teething period, when many procedures were being tried and tested. He applauded the Foundation board's decision to take a 'cautious approach', starting with small-scale programs in the first few years, thus allowing the inexperienced administrators time to find their feet. He acknowledged (without elaborating) that the Foundation had 'made many errors' and was grateful that scholars and other interested parties had been 'ready to point to mistakes of administration but also quick to offer suggestions for improvement'.[31]

Some of the Foundation's early administrative difficulties would prove to be perennial frustrations, as later chapters will show. Others were short-term and would be resolved with improvements in the speed of communication and transport in ensuing decades. The first of these was the issue of location and the isolation of Canberra. It is perhaps hard to appreciate how small and isolated Canberra must have seemed in 1950 – even to a West Australian. As Rossiter put it, the capital was 'not a city in the usual sense of the word'. When we consider that the lake was not yet filled, that most of the ANU buildings were either half-built or still only architectural plans, that the National Library was still housed in the Commonwealth Parliamentary Library, and that there was a very limited social life on offer (outside of people's homes), Rossiter's complaint becomes more understandable. For a sense of the still embryonic, post-war Canberra of this period, one has only to read 1994 Fulbright Senior Scholar Frank Moorhouse's carefully researched novel *Cold Light*. Rossiter and his wife Margaret had moved to Canberra to take up the position, when the national capital was experiencing a shortage of accommodation. The board agreed that a house would need to be bought for them out of Fulbright funds[32] and Margaret Rossiter played an important role alongside her husband in regularly entertaining scholars in the family home. Their daughter Fran Rossiter Ballard recalls how hard her mother worked, how the children's bedrooms became the Fulbright office, but also how much her father had enjoyed and valued his work with the Fulbright Program. The close involvement with their home 'gave the whole family a wonderful opportunity to meet with Fulbright scholars regularly', which she now says 'provided us with a deep connection to America which I still retain today and which has been passed on to Dad's grandchildren as well'.[33]

The Foundation office, with an initial staff of two, increased to four in 1951, was based in two rooms in the US Embassy building in Canberra. Although this ensured good access to embassy staff, the Department of External Affairs, and the ANU, as well as members of the Canberra press gallery, it meant that relations with the main state universities, which hosted the majority of scholars, were somewhat hampered. The Foundation faced some difficulties when making travel and accommodation arrangements for scholars, in particular for Americans, most of whom disembarked in Sydney. Rossiter and his staff had to place many long-distance phone calls, which were prohibitively expensive at that time, and write volumes of letters to finalise details of individual scholars' housing, transportation and institutional placement.

Distances also meant that the Foundation often could not 'discharge its proper duties of counselling grantees' when problems arose. In some cases US Fulbright scholars had returned home after completing their exchange period, having had no contact at all with the Foundation office. From 1952, Rossiter began making regular tours of the states so that he could meet Fulbright scholars, engage with participating institutions, and deal in person with complaints and difficulties. This was a big undertaking when air travel was expensive, less available and much slower than it is today.

With key Foundation board members residing in other states, and with little time to spare from their professional lives, it was usually impossible for Rossiter to bring them together for special meetings to address urgent problems that entailed policy interpretation or procedural changes. An executive sub-committee of Canberra-based directors did its best to deal with such matters, but Rossiter expressed some uncertainty about the status of their decisions. This may have been because the sub-committee members comprised mostly foreign service officers, meaning that the representatives of the academic and business worlds were missing from some important decisions. Although the executive sub-committee's resolutions had to be confirmed by the full board, sometimes it was too late for objections or reversals.

'A land far away'

Rossiter's frustrations with geographic (and perhaps social) isolation and its impact on administrative processes were, of course, compounded by the great distance between the Foundation in Australia and the various agencies in the United States with whom he had to deal on a regular basis. This was to be expected when running a bi-national scheme whose partner countries were separated by a vast ocean, in a time of slow travel and communications. More troubling than the miles of land and sea that stretched between Canberra and Washington, however, was the chronological mismatch between the two countries.

From an administrative point of view, the incompatibility of Australian and US academic calendars was probably (and continues to be) one of the greatest frustrations in the Australian–US Fulbright exchange. The Australian school and university teaching years started in February and March, while the American academic year began in September. Fulbright administrators working across two hemispheres, powerless to alter this geographically determined phenomenon, tried to ameliorate it at various times by tinkering with the timing of calls for applications and of approval processes. Once initial selections were made, the calendar mismatch complicated the process of institutional placement. For example, Australian academics took their long summer break in the very period when they were supposed to approve (or reject) proposed institutional placements of US scholars for the following year. Moreover, some departmental heads and school principals (on both sides of the Pacific) were unhappy about having to release their staff, or receive and integrate visiting scholars, part-way through the teaching year.

Lecturers in particular had trouble with this chronological incompatibility, because their teaching programs were inevitably affected. This proved an obstacle to the enthusiastic take-up of Australian awards by senior US scholars, particularly in the early years, when Australia also suffered from an image as an intellectual backwater. Except in certain fields Australia could hardly compete with an Ivy League PhD or an Oxbridge institution. For Americans considering an overseas research period, Australia, 'a land far away', was not particularly attractive. Australia thus struggled to compete with some other Fulbright partner countries to attract Senior Scholars (to be discussed in subsequent chapters). For now, Rossiter had another, immediate challenge on his hands: that of building interest in the exchange program at home, in Australian universities.

Rossiter reported in early 1952 that universities and other educational institutions in Australia, 'traditionally conservative in their approach to new and untried ventures', were now 'coming to accept' the program. Here we glimpse the cultural challenge for the Foundation in convincing educated Australians of the program's worth, for many were doubtful of the benefits of an American academic exchange experience. Rossiter claimed in early 1952 that the word 'Fulbright' was already 'beginning to acquire significance in informed circles'. But eighteen months later, a Foundation memo to the State Department declared that 'In some academic circles here, it is a fact that the standard of American education, particularly at the college and university level, is regarded as open to question, even though this attitude may be without justifiable foundation'.[34]

The USEF and the US Embassy knew that accounts by returning Australian scholars of their exchange experiences would be an important tool for convincing their university colleagues of the benefits of exposure to US universities and schools, but it took time for these to filter through. In 1958, an Australian Fulbright alumnus reflected that one of his 'more foolish preconceptions' before his exchange had been that 'American universities were, on the whole, second rate, particularly in the humanities'. As noted earlier in relation to the preference for Oxbridge degrees, he, too, found that this 'prejudice ... dies hard in Australian academic circles'.[35]

US foreign service officers working in the information and culture areas in Australia reflected quite often on the problem of convincing a suspicious Australian educated public of the worth of the US educational system(s). In a December 1952 report to the State Department, Melbourne-based Public Affairs Officer Joseph Thoman (who would later sit on the Fulbright board) noted 'a certain amount of anti-American sentiment' in government circles and at the University of Melbourne, which had 'some faculty members' who 'feel the same way and they exert some influence there in developing among the students the same prejudices'. On those intellectuals who had 'more of a condescending and sometimes antagonistic attitude towards American culture and our universities', he opined that this was 'largely because they suffer from inferiority complexes or because they have had little contact with people in their fields in the U.S. as they have done any of their overseas graduate work in England or on the Continent; most of them have a complete lack of knowledge of American cultural achievements'.[36] Putting aside inferiority complexes (a fairly common fallback for puzzled US foreign service officers), Fulbright scholars' reports and reflections suggest that Thoman was right about the lack of awareness of what the United States had to offer in the cultural and educational sphere. There was no lack of awareness in Australia of American popular culture, of course, and this was often bemoaned by both visiting American Fulbrighters in their reports, as well as by embassy staff. The problem was that Hollywood movies and their companions cast a deep shadow over other American kinds of cultural production.

The Foundation had hoped that in 1951, when American scholars first came to Australia under the program, they would prove an impressive enough bunch to convince their academic hosts and the broader Australian public that American educators and students had something to offer. The Senior Scholars were seen as particularly important in this establishing period, as they were likely to draw more press attention, and would be more experienced at presenting in public, than would recent graduates.

Rossiter wrote of the first group of twenty-six Americans who came in 1951, that though they were 'largely unknown and untried' to Australians and indeed to the Foundation, 'apart from one or two notable exceptions', they had proved 'excellent representatives of their country abroad' and 'reflected high credit' on the American committees which had selected them at such short notice. Rossiter believed their impact had been 'extremely valuable in establishing the programme upon a sure foundation'. And only by ensuring that visiting scholars were 'of the highest order possible', could the Foundation hope to achieve 'the effective correction of the view of American education' that prevailed in Australian universities.[37] So, although Rossiter felt progress was being made, the program was still vulnerable, and in 1953, the Foundation faced its biggest public relations challenge to date.

Promoting the program

By 1953, the exchange program was in its third year of operation, but only its first year of programming at full strength. This was also the first year that the Foundation introduced formal orientation for visiting scholars. The board, very aware of the importance of publicity for the program in this establishment phase, had, in February, discussed making better use of the United States Information Service (USIS), and trialling a 'system of coordinated press releases' about their scholars' activities and movements.

When a group of twenty American Fulbrighters – the largest contingent to travel together to Australia so far – set sail for Sydney two months later on the *Aorangi*, USEF and USIS publicity machines went into full swing. Newspapers across the country reported their impending April arrival, and the scholars even starred in a newsreel, produced by the Film Division of the Australian News and Information Bureau. In 'Fulbright Scholars Extend Knowledge In Australia', we see a group of mostly mature, bespectacled men and women wandering around Sydney's Royal Agricultural Show, patting cows. Cut to the group standing around rather awkwardly, chatting in scraggly bushland, while chunks of skewered meat sizzle over a campfire, and a voiceover points out enthusiastically how cheap meat is in Australia. The newsreel ends with a shot of the Americans looking out over the sweep of a Sydney beach, one scholar stripped down to a stylish one-piece bathing suit.[38]

This was something of a publicity coup. But only months later, the Foundation was faced with the undesirable flipside of press attention. On 21 June 1953, the University of Tasmania prepared to receive its second ever Fulbright scholar. Dr Walter Krause, an economist from Utah, arrived in Hobart just as a cold snap hit the island and snow started to fall. He was met by Professor Gerald Firth, of the Economics Department, who took him to the house where he was to live for the next nine months.[39] Less than 48 hours later, Krause had left town. The economist travelled directly to Canberra, and arrived, unexpectedly, at the Fulbright Foundation office, which was still housed in the US Embassy. There, Krause told Rossiter that he had left Tasmania because he could not bear the cold. According to the Foundation's subsequent report to State Department, Krause had 'tried living in a hotel in addition to the private house in which accommodations had originally been secured for him', but the heating was 'hopelessly inadequate' and he found it impossible to work. Rossiter arranged for Krause to stay in Canberra for the next few months, changing his affiliation to the ANU and organising access to the centrally heated National Library (then in Parliament House), in the hope that he might 'overcome his adjustment difficulties' and decide to remain for the full term of his award. But once three months were up, Krause returned his ticket to the Foundation, headed to Sydney, bought himself a Pan Am ticket and flew back to the United States the following day.

Rossiter acknowledged that unheated Australian houses were a shock to many American scholars accustomed to central heating – indeed such complaints have regularly been made by Fulbrighters throughout the decades[40] – but he also noted that Krause 'did not attempt to clothe himself suitably' in Hobart, indeed, 'he persisted in wearing light tropical clothing which was unsuitable in every way'. In fact, Rossiter had come to the conclusion that Krause had not really wanted his Fulbright award, even before he stepped onto Australian soil. He 'seemed to feel that he had made a mistake in accepting the award', and would probably not have remained for the full award period 'regardless of the conditions he encountered'.[41] It seems that Krause, who had planned to study (among other things) the effect on the Australian wool industry of the introduction of synthetics – a question of genuine interest to his host country – agreed to stay on for three months in Canberra mainly to avoid causing embarrassment to the Foundation, which had only recently faced the premature departure of another Senior Scholar, University of Oklahoma Mechanical Engineering Professor Merl Creech.

Professor Creech had left Australia about a fortnight before Krause arrived, after having spent only four days in Sydney. His sudden flight had been reported on the front page of the *Sydney Morning Herald* under the attention-grabbing headline 'Mysterious Departure of U.S. Professor'. Other newspapers around the nation, from Rockhampton to Adelaide, had then run with the story. The Adelaide *Advertiser* article began thus: 'American Professor Merl D. Creech flew 10,000 miles to Sydney to lecture to Australian students, stayed for four days, and then left without an explanation.' The *Morning Bulletin* of Rockhampton titled its article 'No Lecture, No Explanation'. The lengthy reports on events leading to his departure hint that Professor Creech's issues were personal, perhaps health-related. Krause's story was not so clear-cut. But together, along with the premature departure of a third, unnamed scholar that same year, these cases did the program some damage. Rossiter reported that 'the Australian press has shown a great interest in this incident and in inquiries to the Foundation reporters have continued to hint that there was some reason underlying Professor Creech's departure which the Foundation wished to hide'. Foundation staff's pleas of ignorance did not satisfy their questioners.

These difficulties raised several important policy issues in this teething period, concerning selection criteria relating to scholars' emotional stability and adaptability. This was a particularly sensitive area (and in the case of American scholars, as we will see, almost entirely out of the Foundation's control). Also concerning was how best to prepare scholars for living and working conditions in Australia. The Creech and Krause cases were anomalous, however, and most visiting scholars, even if shocked at times by under-resourced universities and unheated housing, or a little unsettled by different social practices, were keen to make the most of their experience.

Take Kenneth Brill, an American geologist who arrived in Hobart three months before Walter Krause's very brief stay. Brill warned future grantees in his scholar report that the University of Tasmania 'consists chiefly of a number of slab huts in a paddock'. Brill was, despite this unexpected simplicity, happy to live with the limitations of his host institution, perhaps in part because he spent much of his time out in the bush rather than sitting in an unheated office. He found, though, that he could not carry out his field research in the manner he had expected. He had intended to make 'lithofacies studies of the Permian strata' in Tasmania, but discovered, upon arriving, that Tasmania had not yet been mapped 'in sufficient detail to permit the stratigrapher to do detailed work'. This meant Brill had to spend much of his time 'beating the bush for outcrops that were rumoured to be present, mapping areas where no geological work had been done, and making structural studies in regions that had been incorrectly mapped'.[42] Brill might have predicted this state of affairs, considering that the map of Australia that he received from the Australian Government Tourist Bureau before he left the United States 'didn't even have Tasmania on it'. Instead of despairing, though, he plunged in and carried out this basic mapping work, thus contributing a resource of great value to his hosts and subsequent researchers.

Brill's pragmatism and adaptability caught none of the press attention afforded the other, more troublesome professors, but several other visiting lecturers more than made up for this. Rossiter and the Foundation must have heaved a sigh of relief when, only a fortnight after the media jumped on Creech's departure, a very different sort of senior scholar turned up. Some fifteen American women came to Australia under Fulbright auspices in 1953 (up from seven in 1952), including eight postgraduates, five schoolteachers, and one senior scholar, who made a big impression. This was Professor Mary E. Murphy, who held the Chair of Economics and Business Administration at the Los Angeles State College of Applied Arts and Science, the first woman in the United States to become a certified public accountant.

According to an article in the Women's Pages of the Adelaide *Advertiser*, the two Fulbrighters considered to have been the most successful 'ambassadors' so far were Professor Murphy and, before her, Harriet Creighton, a professor of botany and first woman to be appointed secretary of the Botanical Society of America, who had come to Australia in 1952. Professor Murphy travelled to every Australian university, giving talks that were guaranteed to pique interest, not only among accountants and commerce students, but amongst women and men in the broader community. The *Advertiser* reported that, during her tour, Murphy 'studied our economic and indus-trial set-up at first hand', spoke to 'businessmen, bankers and administrators' and, 'in short', spent most of her time in 'a man's world'. But she also talked to Australian businesswomen, and made some pronouncements which seem, from our twenty-first-century perspective, quite radical for Australia in the early 1950s.[43]

Murphy's criticisms and exhortations got surprisingly positive coverage. The report Murphy submitted to the Foundation at the end of her seven-month stay was a thor-ough and bracing account of her activities and impressions, providing an insightful overview of the state of the program in Australia from the perspective of a high-powered, publicity-conscious professional woman. Murphy was less than impressed by her accommodation in Queensland, her first port of call, and found the university unprepared to take on the responsibility for ensuring adequate and affordable housing for her for the two months she stayed in Brisbane. She thought the Foundation needed to do more groundwork to 'encourage host Universities to extend a welcome hand to the visitors'. In Sydney she felt the Economics Department did not give her a cordial welcome or use her services as fully as she had expected, whereas in Western Australia, the welcome was so warm that it more than made up for the department's 'non-existent' office facilities. Answering a question about 'additional information' that might have been useful before her arrival, she said she would have appreciated knowing more about the status of university education in each city, and being given 'names of people, for instance, favorable or unfavorable to the Fulbright Plan'.[44]

This last is an interesting observation, for it confirms a continuing level of resistance to or suspicion of the program amongst some Australian academics. Murphy elaborated on this in response to a question about the program's success in realising its goal of furthering 'mutual understanding'. She had found a 'variation of interest in the Fulbright Plan', and thought the Foundation needed to work harder 'to "convert" certain universities or Departments ... to the efficacy of using the Lecturers assigned to the greatest extent'. She also thought the Foundation needed to publicise the scheme more widely, to the general public, informing them of the 'background of the Plan, how it is used' and 'what the professional qualifications are of the people brought out'. She also hoped the Foundation might do something about the attitude 'prevalent' in Australian universities that an Australian bachelor's degree was superior to a Master's degree or a PhD 'granted by an English or an American university', which she considered 'antipathetic to the advancement of scholarship here'.[45]

Murphy's report concluded with some reflections on the future of the program. First, she noted the scarcity of information available to Americans about Australia. Scholars preparing for their journey across the Pacific depended 'almost entirely' on American literary critic Hartley Grattan's books on Australia. 'There is still the feeling that Australia is a land far away from America cut off from the rest of the world, and rather lagging behind England, America and Canada.' Murphy saw that this would change, but it required that more be written about Australia; she hoped to fill this gap by producing some 'popular articles and technical papers on developments here' upon her return to the United States. Murphy also explained that Americans were often reluctant to accept a Fulbright appointment in Australia, because they felt that 'little can be learned or contributed to University life here'. She had found this was to be quite untrue, and argued that Australia presented 'a great challenge to the serious teacher or student, and the best representatives of American education should be given the privilege of coming here in the years ahead'.[46]

This brings us, then, to the difficult matter of selecting scholars. This was and is, after all, the core of the scheme, for the program's success rested on the quality of its participants. The story of selections is a complicated one, and concerns the creation and re-interpretation of selection criteria, an administrative machinery whose parts were scattered across Australian and US states and institutions, reliance on the work of volunteer selection committees, and changing ideas about which kinds of research are nationally or internationally important. It deserves its own chapter.

Notes

1   'Charles C. Odegaard PhD., a Personal History by William H. Burnett', Living History Interview, Coastal Research Group, www.coastalresearch.org/1997/03/07/charles-e-odegaard-ph-d-living-history-interviewccfw553d/ (accessed 27 July 2017).
2   Charles Odegaard, 'The Fulbright Exchange Program in Operation', *ACLS Newsletter* (December 1949), pp. 13–14.

3 The Victorian Branch claims it was founded in the pre-Second World War period. See Australian-American Association website: https://australianamerican.org/ (accessed 14 September 2017). This is not to be confused with the Washington organisation founded in 1989.

4 Telegram from Conrad F. Horley, President of the Australian-American Association, to Hon H.V. Evatt, 26 or 28 November 1949. In A1838 250/9/8/2 PART 4, NAA.

5 19 May 1949, Letter from p. M. Hamilton, Secretary of the Australian-American Association to Evatt, in A1838 250/9/8/2 PART 4, NAA.

6 Telegram from Conrad F. Horley to Minister Evatt, 26 or 28 November 1949. A telegram with the same text (minus the crossed-out word) was sent to Horley on 28 November. In A1838 250/9/8/2 PART 4, NAA.

7 'Fulbright Play Delay Criticised', *Advertiser* (Adelaide), 4 October 1949, p. 3; and 'Blows to Ties with U.S.A.', *The Courier-Mail* (Brisbane), 4 October 1949, p. 5.

8 Geoffrey Serle, 'Murdoch, Sir Keith Arthur (1885–1952)', *Australian Dictionary of Biography*, National Centre of Biography, Australian National University, http:// adb.anu.edu.au/biography/murdoch-sir-keith-arthur-7693/text13467, published first in hardcopy 1986 (accessed 26 July 2017); see AAA Victorian Branch, https:// australianamerican.org/ (accessed 14 September 2017).

9 9 December 1949, Memo from JWB [John Wear Burton, Secretary, External Affairs] to Australian Embassy, Washington. A1838 250/9/8/2 PART 4, NAA.

10 4 June 1948, Ralph Harry to Sec, DEA. Re status of negotiations (on Philippines); 25 June 1948, Ralph Harry Memo to Mr G Temby (on Chinese board, all American); 13 September 1948 on New Zealand and 22 September 1948 on UK agreement; 8 October 1948, DOS Press release re Belgium and Luxembourg signing Fulbright (on board ratio). All in A3300 874, NAA.

11 Spender noted in the margins of a 19 December departmental memo: 'I am in discussion with Ambassador'. 19 December 1949, Department of External Affairs: For Minister: USEF. Re appointment of members. A1838 250/9/8/2 PART 4, NAA.

12 30 January 1950, American Section. For the Minister. Re Fulbright Agreement. In A1838 250/9/8/2 PART 4, NAA.

13 5 December 1949, 'For the Secretary: Appointment of Australian members of the Fulbright Agreement Board of Directors', from the same NAA file: A1838 250/9/ 8/2 PART 4, NAA. To see the digital copy click here and jump to page 206: https:// recordsearch.naa.gov.au/SearchNRetrieve/Interface/ViewImage.aspx?B=565257.

14 David Lowe, *Australian Between Empires: The Life of Percy Spender* (London, 2010); David Lowe and Daniel Oakman, *Australia and the Colombo Plan: 1949–1957* (Canberra, 2004); David Lowe, 'The Colombo Plan and Soft Regionalism in the Asia-Pacific: Australian and New Zealand Cultural Diplomacy in the 1950s and 1960s', Working Paper No.1, Alfred Deakin Research Institute, April 2010.

15 3 February 1950, For the Minister: Fullbright [*sic*] Board Appointees. A1838 250/9/8/2 PART 4, NAA.

16 James H. Coleman, 'Hauslaib, William Russell (1897–1970)', *Australian Dictionary of Biography*, National Centre of Biography, Australian National University, http://adb. anu.edu.au/biography/hauslaib-william-russell-10454/text18541, published first in hardcopy 1996 (accessed 26 July 2017).

17 'The Fulbright Story – Fulbright Scholarships implement the ideals of Cecil Rhodes'. By P. M. Hamilton, Executive Officer, Australian-American Association. Extract from *Pacific Neighbours*, vol. 5:3 (1950). Typescript in A1361 4/7/5 PART 2, NAA.

18 9 February 1950, 'United States Educational Foundation in Australia': Minutes of a meeting held in Department of External Affairs with US Embassy and External Affairs officers (Foster, Sturm and Martin; Harry, Cumpston, Birch). In A1838 250/9/8/2 PART 4, NAA.
19 First USEF Annual Report, p. 4.
20 USEF board minutes, 10 March 1950; USEF board minutes of 23 June 1950.
21 Interview with Patricia Lee Taylor by Diane Kirkby, Melbourne, January 2017.
22 USEF minutes, 10 March 1950.
23 10 January 1950, DEA Inward Teleprinter Message to Ext Aff Canberra for Mr Body. 'Confidential'. A1838 250/9/8/3 PART 1, NAA.
24 15 March 1950, Premier Hollway to Prime Minister, forwarding documents explaining Kennedy's situation – in A1838 250/9/8/3 part 1 NAA.
25 23 March 1950, External Affairs American Section, Telegram 're Maxwell Victor Kennedy' in NAA A1838 250/9/8/3 part 1.
26 'Perth Scholar in Sea Rescue', *Daily News* (Perth), 27 May 1943, http://trove.nla.gov.au/ndp/del/article/78314542?searchTerm=%22geoffrey%20rossiter%22&searchLimits='Six Days in Dingy', *West Australian* (Perth), 27 May 1943, p. 3, http://trove.nla.gov.au/ndp/del/article/46757553?searchTerm=%22geoffrey%20rossiter%22&searchLimits= (both accessed 1 August 2014).
27 'Geoff Rossiter Gains Rhodes Scholarship', *The Northern Miner* (Charters Towers, Qld.), 24 December 1945, p. 3.
28 'Interesting People', *Australian Women's Weekly*, 8 July 1950, p. 28; see also 'Geoffrey George Rossiter: A Big Educational Job', *Smith's Weekly*, 3 June 1950, p. 15; see also Alice Garner, 'Geoffrey Rossiter', in *Fulbrighter* Newsletter 2014.
29 Malcolm Rohrbough, response to survey, La Trobe University, 2011. In possession of the authors.
30 29 November 1948, No. 65 [despatch no?] [CONFIDENTIAL]. Response to Despatch no. 111 of June 9 1948, in NARA 811.42747 SE/6–1848; and on the Australian preference: 30 April 1947, Dept of Post-War Reconstruction Minute. To the Minister (from L. F. Crisp). Cover letter for submission by Inter-Departmental Committee on Education, for PM, Coombs and Evatt. 1 April 1947 Cablegram SECRET I.7027 XM0031. NAA.
31 First USEF Annual Report, p. 7.
32 First USEF Annual Report, p. 4.
33 Emails from Fran Ballard to Alice Garner, 22 October 2014, and to Diane Kirkby, January 2018, in possession of the authors.
34 USEF Memo No 169 to DOS (IES). 28 October 1953. On: Selection of American Grantees (Appendix 1 to USEF board meeting, 26 October 1953).
35 USEF, *The Fulbright Programme: The First Eight Years and the Future* (Canberra, 1958), p. 12.
36 I. 'The Situation' USIE Melbourne. I-A Local Factors Affecting USIE. In 31 December 1952, FSD, AMConsulate Sydney to DOS. Subj: IIA: Transmitting Combined Evaluation Report for the Period Dec 1 1951 to Nov 30 1952 [includes reports from 5 USIS posts in Australia]. DOS 59 Central Files 511.43 Box 2359, NARA.
37 First USEF Annual Report, pp. 2 and 19.
38 This two-minute newsreel was one of several stories appearing in Australian Diary no. 071, 1953, directed by Jack S. Allan. In the National Film and Sound Archive collection, title 67328.

39 'More rain and snow expected', *Advocate* (Burnie, Tas.), 23 June 1953, p. 9.
40 Leah Glasser in 'Students Here Like America', *The Mail*, 26 September 1953, p. 18. Another example was 1964 US scholar Norm Sanders, interviewed by Hamish Sewell in the Old Parliament House political and parliamentary oral history project (NLA, 2011) and 1968 US scholar Margaret Webster who wrote that it was 'impossible to overemphasise [...] the EXTREME COLD of Australian houses'. In Margaret Webster, Scholar report, 1968, in NAA: A463, 1965/2313.
41 21 September 1953, 'Report on Fulbright Research Scholar: Dr. Walter Krause', USEF Memorandum No. 143 to Department of State (IIA/IES), in A1838 250/9/8/4/2 Part 2, NAA.
42 Kenneth Gray Brill Jr, Report, 1953, p. 3, in 'United States of America – Relations with Australia – United States Educational Foundation – General', A1838 250/9/8/4/2 PART 2, NAA.
43 'Equality as "Quickest Way to Prosperity"', *Argus* (Melbourne), 15 July 1953, p. 6.
44 Mary E. Murphy, Scholar report, 1953, in 'United States Educational Foundation – General'. A1838 250/9/8/4/2 Part 2, NAA.
45 Murphy, Scholar report, 1953.
46 Murphy, Scholar report, 1953.

3

'Bright scientific moles' v. 'goodwill ambassador extroverts': Choosing a Fulbright scholar

A Fulbright scholar who came to Australia in the early 1960s now says 'who knew how important it would be for me, a young eager gal from nyc', to have this experience. 'I was open to learning and Australia was a perfect learning environment. Right time/right place to be tested, one might say.'[1] She embraced the social and cultural environment: drinking with labour movement leaders at the local pub, listening to folk music and jazz, hearing feminist Germaine Greer speak of 'ideas i had not ever thought about', watching 'a young Zoe Caldwell' act on stage, and talking civil rights with colleagues as the movement gained momentum in the United States. Did this mean she was a successful choice as a Fulbright scholar, acquiring and sharing cultural understanding, or was the purpose of the exchange a more narrowly academic one?

Differences over the selection criteria and process for choosing scholars for Fulbright awards had quickly emerged as a new area of tension between the Australian and US officials administering the program. Different interpretations of 'mutual understanding' were embedded in the evolving administrative machinery, and this shaped the interpretation of selection criteria over the coming decades. Selection was ultimately based on judgements and reactions to an endlessly variable set of personal and intellectual qualities of scholars working in a very broad range of fields. Without clear criteria and solid guidelines on how the selection process was to be administered, confusion crept in. Streamlining procedures took some time to achieve and it fell to Executive Officer Geoffrey Rossiter to make it happen at the Australian end.

A 'highly complex and … baffling'[2] administration

One of the very first challenges for Rossiter and the first USEF board was to set up the administrative machinery for Australian selections. This was not a simple matter, for there were several stages in the process, requiring approvals from different agencies on both sides of the Pacific. In Australia, as in all Fulbright partner countries, there was one central body dealing with all aspects of the exchange program – namely the USEF and its bi-national board. At the US end, however, there were numerous organisations and government departments involved in selections, including the Institute of International Education (for postgraduate students), the Conference Board of Associated Research Councils (for research scholars and lecturers), and the Federal Office of Education (for schoolteachers). The State Department's Bureau of Educational and Cultural Affairs also played an important role, as the conduit for information and decisions between the various US agencies, the policy-making BFS, and overseas foundations. Then there were the various universities and schools whose cooperation was necessary when organising placement and reception of scholars. This chapter concentrates on the selection of Australian scholars. The American selection process was, from the Australian perspective, more closely tied to questions of pro-gramming, explored in the next chapter.

According to the bi-national Fulbright Agreement, the US BFS had final approval of scholars of both nationalities, but preliminary selections, or recommendations, were carried out in the scholar's home country. It was the responsibility of the USEF in Canberra to oversee this screening process in Australia, before transmitting primary and reserve 'panels' (or lists) of candidates, via the State Department, for approval by the BFS in Washington DC.

The BFS, which first met in October 1947, worked over its first years to establish general selection guidelines for Fulbright exchanges, continuing to adjust and refine them as new partner countries signed executive agreements with the United States.[3] Once Australia signed on to the program in November 1949, the State Department communicated the most recent version of BFS guidelines to the USEF in Canberra.

As we have seen, Fulbright awards for Australians only covered travel costs at this time, because the terms of the Fulbright Act were that partner countries 'counterpart funds' could not be converted to US dollars. It was many years before this changed. The first Australian Fulbright awards to include more than travel and insurance were postdoctoral and junior lecturer/research scholar awards which came in 1979 with a one-off grant-in-aid, initially of $6,000. It wasn't until 1987 that the board decided to 'move gradually towards parity' in the Australian and US award benefits. So initially, for the first three decades of the program, Australians had to demonstrate they had suf-ficient US dollars from other sources to cover their living expenses in order even to be eligible for a Fulbright grant. This meant that most Australian applicants had already been through a prior stage of selection, a winnowing by other scholarship granting institutions or philanthropic bodies. So an applicant might, for example, have won a Frank Knox Scholarship to Harvard, or a teaching assistantship at a university where they hoped to study, or perhaps an Australian Federation of University Women Grant or a Carnegie Corporation of New York (CCNY) Commonwealth Travel Grant. Thus the USEF, though it had its own selection criteria, was to some degree piggybacking on these other schemes.[4]

In 1950, when the USEF, in order to get the program up and running, needed to select the first 'Travel Only' Australian Fulbright scholars very quickly, a call for applications was publicised in major newspapers in May. Some promising candidates – people known to have won other US grants – were even contacted directly and asked to apply. Essential eligibility criteria included a bachelor's degree, proof of admission (or of pending admission) to a US higher education institution, and sufficient US dollars to cover living expenses. There was no form to fill out, and letters of application were to be sent directly to the USEF office in Canberra. The board acted as the selection committee, and Rossiter listed the criteria: '1. Academic record; 2. Personality; 3. Length of stay in the United States; 4. Suitability of the project in terms of the wider objectives of the program; 5. Professional experience and standing where applicable.'[5]

In a document from this period outlining 'Selected Approved Policies and Principles of the Board of Foreign Scholarships', the section on 'Eligibility and Selection of Candidates' specified that 'Selection will be guided by excellence of scholastic achievement, academic requirements and facilities of the institution to be attended, academic or other experience which particularly qualifies the applicant to undertake the proposed project'.[6] The External Affairs officers involved in the initial setting up of the program understood this, for in February 1950, four of them met with representatives of the New Zealand High Commission and the secretary-general of the South Pacific Commission (SPC),[7] who wanted to know whether the Fulbright Program might enable research to be done for the SPC. According to the External Affairs record of the meeting, 'It was made clear that the USEF members are most anxious that the exchange should be kept primarily an educational one, and that it should operate not so much for the benefit of the two governments, but for the students and institutions concerned'. Furthermore, 'It was stressed that all the emphasis would have to be placed on the educational aspects of the work'.[8]

This coincided with the establishment of another technical and educational aid program, the Colombo Plan, which had an overtly Cold War political *raison d'être*, namely, shoring up Southeast Asia against Communism.[9] The Fulbright Program's first administrators were quite clear that the US–Australian exchange program would steer clear of such politicisation. Ensuring that Fulbright selection procedures were both efficient *and* fully in accordance with this educational focus would prove a challenge. Sometimes administrative convenience came at the expense of USEF control and oversight, and several experiences in the first decade brought this home to the bi-national board.

The Sydney Committee

Not long before the Australian–US Fulbright Agreement was signed, the US Embassy had established a Committee on Study and Training in the United States, in Sydney, which came to be known as the 'Sydney Committee'. The State Department established committees of this kind throughout the world after the Information and Educational Exchange ('Smith-Mundt') Act was passed in January 1948. The Smith-Mundt Act enabled the State Department to (among other things) grant a number of scholarships and fellowships to foreign students and scholars. These were different from Fulbright awards, in that they were funded by the US government in US dollars appropriated from the Treasury by Congress rather than by foreign currencies owed under Lend-Lease

Settlements; they covered tuition, and came with a stipend, but did not cover travel. The State Department encouraged Fulbright foundations in partner countries to consider granting Fulbright travel grants to those who were selected by the New York-based IIE for Smith-Mundt awards.[10]

Although the Sydney Committee's primary role was to recommend candidates to the IIE for Smith-Mundt grants, the timing of the Committee's creation in October 1949 meant that it became closely involved with Fulbright selection processes – something that State Department's Fred Bundy encouraged when he met with the new Australian–US Fulbright board in March 1950. The seven-member Sydney Committee comprised US embassy officers, American businessmen and prominent Australians including (initially) Sydney University's Challis Professor of Law, Kenneth Shatwell, Director of the Commonwealth Office of Education, Professor R.C. Mills, and Spender, then a member of the federal opposition but soon to become minister for External Affairs with the change of government. This was a committee with some heft.

Initially, procedures went something like this: Rossiter and the USEF staff in Canberra received and assessed paper applications for Fulbright postgraduate and junior research scholar awards from across Australia, compiling a shortlist of promising candidates which they then sent on to the Sydney Committee. The Sydney Committee then interviewed applicants and recommended a certain number for Smith-Mundt awards, before seeking approval from the USEF for these preferred Smith-Mundt candidates to be offered Fulbright travel grants as well. The remaining candidates on the primary panel were then forwarded to the BFS for approval for Travel Only Fulbright awards.

In 1951, it became apparent that there were some problems with this arrangement, namely, that lines of communication were becoming confused, with the USEF in Canberra and the Sydney Committee each receiving different information from the State Department, the IIE and the BFS. The Committee had apparently stepped over the line in making recommendations to the IIE without reference to USEF decisions. Feathers were ruffled and relations strained for a time.[11] This kind of confusion confirms an observation by the IIE's Student Program director back in 1949, in his introduction to a twenty-seven-page handbook for Committees on Study and Training, that 'the type of operation [they] conducted' was, 'to the uninitiated, highly complex and, at times, baffling'.[12]

Rossiter and American member of the USEF board, businessman W.R. Hauslaib, met with the chair of the Sydney Committee to improve the coordination of selection processes. In his 1952 draft annual report, Rossiter noted that a 'satisfactory relationship' between the two bodies had been established, with Rossiter now sitting in on the Sydney Committee meetings as a non-voting member. Although he wished the USEF would be 'afforded the opportunity of actively assisting in the selection of candidates' for joint Smith-Mundt/Fulbright awards, at least they had overcome the problem of 'divided authority', which had led to 'considerable confusion' and generated two slightly different lists of recommended candidates for the 1951–52 student program. In 1953, the board demonstrated its faith in the Sydney Committee when it resolved the body could 'pre-screen' Fulbright applicants.[13] That is, the Sydney Committee would be the first port of call for paper applications, and would consider Smith-Mundt grants and Fulbright travel awards together. They would then send a shortlist to the USEF selection committee, from which the board would make final recommendations to the BFS.

Keeping a degree of oversight over the Smith-Mundt side of things was clearly important to Rossiter and some Fulbright board members. In part this was because the Smith-Mundt Act embraced cultural and educational diplomacy as an explicit element of Cold War foreign policy, unlike the Fulbright Act and the bi-national agreement that flowed from it, which had a primarily educational focus. For example, in January 1951 the Advisory Commission on Educational Exchange, which was a body set up under the Smith-Mundt Act, launched a report called 'Two Way Street'. In it the Commission's chair, chancellor of Vanderbilt University, Dr Harvie Branscomb, said 'The free exchange of peoples and their ideas is one of the surest means of combatting communism'. This was because 'the Soviet masters are seeking to turn the world against the United States in hatred and suspicion through their shrewd, continuous and malicious untruths. Our counter-attack is to make the truth known … It is a vital part of our total effort, the Campaign of Truth'.[14]

Although the Commission was created under the Smith-Mundt (not the Fulbright) Act, Branscomb listed the Fulbright scheme as one of the programs serving this larger anti-Communist vision and goal. This despite Section 601 of the Smith-Mundt Act which spelt out that the Commissions created under that Act 'shall have no authority over the Board of Foreign Scholarships or the program created by Public Law 584' (that is, the Fulbright Program).[15] Perhaps Rossiter, conscious of many academics' sensitivity to any suggestions of government interference in their scholarly work, wanted to ensure that the embassy's Public Affairs Officer, who sat on both the Sydney Committee and USEF board, did not try to sway selections along particular lines, or blur the distinctions between the Fulbright and Smith-Mundt programs.

US Embassy despatches to the State Department at this time reveal some potentially worrying points of overlap. In December 1952, for example, US Cultural Affairs Assistant Violet J. Robinson wrote a report to the State Department under the heading 'Exchange of Persons'. Discussing the Smith-Mundt scheme, she noted that 'Target groups in educational exchange have followed closely those set forth in the Country Plan'.[16] The April 1952 Country Plan for Australia had outlined the following 'Psychological objectives'. First was 'To lend assistance wherever possible, particularly through labor channels, to efforts of anti-Communist forces in Australia in checking the growth of internal Communist influence'. Another was 'To counter a doubt prevalent in a considerable segment of opinion leaders and others that the United States lacks the wisdom and maturity for world leadership'.

Here we see how Cold War thinking framed the work of Information and Cultural Affairs staff in Australia as it did elsewhere. Senator Joe McCarthy's attacks on a State Department he believed to be riddled with Communist fellow travellers suggests that not all foreign service officers welcomed the ideological push shaping their jobs in this period. Nevertheless, regardless of their personal political convictions, embassy officers were required to write reports in terms of Cold War-generated 'objectives' and 'target groups'.[17]

The relevance of this to Fulbright selections becomes more apparent when we read what Violet Robinson had to say about how the Sydney Committee functioned. She reported that 'In selecting scholarship candidates, it has not been wholly possible to tailor the group to a target field, but selectors' "thinking" has been directed along these lines and in many instances final recommendations have embodied potential representatives in target groups'.[18] 1950 despatches identified priority target groups in Australia as 'middle class, white workers', 'Labor union members' and 'underpaid public school teachers'.[19] A 'secondary' target was 'the sophisticated, intellectual, international Australian' who, though 'he has opportunities to travel, is realistic, intelligent, and can and does understand rather accurately the motives of the United States to insure peace throughout the world', must nevertheless 'be kept informed'.[20] In 1951, the target group was revised slightly, with the secondary target being described more specifically as 'Universities and their instructors in political science and government ... because through their lectures they can inform the students about the fabric of the major political institutions'.[21]

Violet Robinson explained that USIS officers had 'attempted to weight the scales' of Smith-Mundt selections 'through choice of Committee on Study and Training membership'. She then clarified that 'No attempt is made in this report to assess the Fulbright program. All details in this regard are handled directly by the United States Educational USEF, American Embassy Canberra, and accurate and up-to-date information is not readily available here'.[22] Though she made an explicit distinction between the two exchange programs, her revelations help us understand why Rossiter and others on the USEF board might have held concerns about the role of the Sydney Committee's role in Fulbright pre-screening. Sitting as a non-voting member on the Sydney Committee, Rossiter would, we presume, have witnessed any efforts, subtle or otherwise, to shape selections. Even if such efforts were focused primarily on Smith-Mundt foreign leader and specialist grants, rather than educational exchange grants, the question was: how effectively could this particular body of selectors separate out the different goals and emphases of the two exchange programs, and would all members willingly or actively make this distinction?

In 1956, US Public Affairs Officer R.J. Boylan, who was at the time the treasurer on the Fulbright board, claimed in his 'Country Operating Plan' that there were 'deficiencies' at present in the cultural exchange program that they were working on. 'The Fulbright program tends to be somewhat handicapped by a tendency to exchange bright scientific "moles" instead of the goodwill ambassador kind of extrovert that may have been envisaged.' Despite this shortcoming, he concluded that 'on the whole it is a successful interchange that has been of benefit to about 350 Australians'.[23]

Unlike Robinson, who had been writing about Smith-Mundt awards, Boylan was explicitly discussing the Fulbright Program here. Boylan was a Cold War hard-hitter who ignored the distinction between Smith-Mundt and Fulbright goals and procedures. It seems, though, that he was frustrated by the Fulbright board's insistence on placing academic record before other personality factors – an indication that 'mutual understanding' went beyond the narrow world of scholars.

Boylan explained why political science and history lecturers in particular were worth targeting under the US Information Agency's number one 'Country objective' of encouraging 'Australia's maximum cooperation with United States' policies affecting the Far East, South Asia and the Pacific'. He wrote: 'Fulbright lecturers and professors before leaving for the United States are provided with background material to assist them in understanding our country. We feel that if we can make friends of these people before they leave, while they are in the United States and after they return we have potentially able defenders of United States domestic and perhaps foreign policy'.[24] This, however, was going somewhat further than the Fulbright's stated goal of encouraging 'mutual understanding'.

There was good reason, then, for anxiety among those who wished to preserve the apolitical character of Fulbright educational exchange in these Cold War years. Managing such political pressures on the program was a constant challenge (elaborated in chapter 5). The need for vigilance illustrates the way that the selection process needed to be carefully thought through, so as to avoid any undue influence.

'Reforms in the machinery of control are desirable'[25]

In early 1958, the State Department disbanded the Sydney Committee and created a new committee to be based in Canberra, following revisions to the department's (or USIA's) International Exchange Manual.[26] In March that year, Earl T. Crain, a US Foreign Service Inspector, reported that 'Some members of the old committee and some members of the board of the USEF in Australia felt that the new committee had too great a concentration of academicians on its membership and that other interests were not sufficiently represented'. And so, the new Canberra-based committee was enlarged with the addition of two businessmen, one of whom had sat on the old committee:[27] Walter Phillips, Australian manager of Atlantic Union Oil Company, and C.R. McKerihan, president of the Rural Bank of NSW.[28]

In the same year that the Sydney Committee was moved and renamed the 'Advisory Committee on Candidates', the USEF finally established regional selection committees, or 'advisory sub-committees', whose task it was to interview those shortlisted by the Advisory Committee. Two board members, the American businessman W.R. Hauslaib and Australian Arthur Denning (director of the NSW Department of Technical Education) had been particularly keen to see interviews introduced as part of the application process. Rossiter had considered this years earlier, but believed it was impossible on a national scale due to interstate distances and time considerations. Now that regional committees were finally in place, interviewing became feasible.[29]

In his 1952 draft annual report, Rossiter had acknowledged that while interviews would be desirable this was not yet logistically possible due to distance and time constraints. Selection committee members were busy professionals volunteering their time, and there was only so much that could be asked of them. In the meantime, he believed those selected on paper according to established criteria were 'usually adequately equipped to fulfil the objectives of the programme'.

The board, he noted, placed 'considerable reliance' on confidential reports, or letters of reference, that they received about candidates.

In fact, some students and scholars were already being interviewed at this time. These were the students and scholars applying for joint Smith-Mundt/Fulbright awards, through the Sydney Committee. Given that these applicants, if shortlisted by the Committee for a Smith-Mundt, were automatically considered for Fulbright travel grants, the interviewing process established by the Sydney Committee effectively formed a part of the Fulbright selection process. One of those interviewed in this early period was plant biologist Adele Millerd, who was amongst the very first Australian Fulbright scholars to leave Australia in 1950.

Over sixty years later, Millerd could recall vividly her interview experience, which took place in a boardroom on the top floor of the Shell building in Sydney. She described the meeting as 'fairly intimidating' – not so much because she felt unprepared, but because 'most of the people round the table had never done anything like it, and they didn't really know what to ask'. One panel member, on discovering that Millerd played golf, asked what her handicap was. 'The highest possible', she answered. The US ambassador (or perhaps it was the consul) reassured her that he shared a similar handicap. Though she doubted this was true, his friendly remark was comforting to her, particular as another 'gentleman' had taken a different tack to questioning her: he 'sat back in his chair', Millerd recounted, 'ran his eyes up and down' her, and asked how old she was, even though all her details were in the paperwork in front of him. Millerd found this very distressing, but decided to let it pass, thinking it was important to be 'well behaved', given she was 'hoping to get something from this interview'. Millerd was initially reluctant to share this particular story during her 2011 interview, until reminded how long ago it was. 'It still bears a scar', she acknowledged. This was one of the only negative memories Millerd had of her Fulbright experience, which took her to Caltech to work with inspiring scientists who (unlike the Sydney interviewer) had 'nothing to prove' and who treated her as an intellectual equal.[30]

When Rossiter acknowledged in his first annual report the 'shortcomings' and 'errors' of inexperienced USEF administrators in this teething period, he was not referring explicitly to the selection committees. Nevertheless, Millerd was keenly aware that the panel interviewing her was not adept at their task, especially when interviewing women, and did not know what questions to ask her, issues which go to the heart of the problem of selection. For it was all very well to conduct interviews, but what should selectors be looking for? And (we might ask) how could the USEF be sure that committee members were equipped to make sound decisions about the personal and academic qualifications of the applicants?

Eight years after Millerd's memorable interview, the board revisited the need for interviews specific to the Fulbright Program, as part of their broader discussions about selection procedures and committee structures. Proponents argued that conducting interviews was the best way to judge 'facts such as appearance, speech and general deportment' as well as for 'ascertaining the true purpose of a candidate's proposed programme', the 'likelihood of his [sic] return to Australia', and, not least, 'his emotional stability'.[31] There was still concern, however, about the 'serious obstacles in the way of

Figure 3.1 Bill Ford on board the *Himalaya*, known as the 'Scholar Ship', sailing from Sydney to the United States, 1958

establishing effective interviewing machinery'. In April 1958, there were ninety-four applications for postgraduate travel grants from across the nation.[32] The selection process by paper alone was already 'rushed',[33] and interviewing every applicant within the restricted timeframe allowable set by the BFS was not considered feasible. The board did, however, come up with a plan.

The new regional selection committees set up in 1958 were given the task of screening applications from their state or region, and interviewing selected candidates before forwarding their recommendations, in order of preference, to the Advisory Committee in Canberra, and thence to the board. In other words, the regional committees were now the first to screen applicants, relieving the Advisory Committee members of much preliminary work. In September that year, the USEF released a document for selection committees advising of the requirements and conditions to be applied to candidates for Fulbright travel grants. These were adapted from BFS and Department of State guidelines. Under 'Factors Applicable to Applicants in All Categories', the first item was 'General Responsibilities', which stated that

'Recipients of grants ... shall be representative and responsible citizens, selected not only on the basis of scholarly and professional standing but also in the expectation that they will contribute to a full and fair picture of Australia while in the US and [...] thereby contribute to understanding and friendship between the two countries'.[34]

This was a neat statement of the way in which the program brought together academic and ambassadorial aims. The 'full and fair picture' phrase is telling, in that it represents an Australian adaptation of US cultural diplomacy terminology most strongly identified with President Truman in the immediate post-war period. 'Full and fair' was what came before the more hard-hitting, anti-Communist 'Campaign of Truth' approach from 1950. That is, 'full and fair' was a cultural diplomacy based on the notion that the United States (or, in this case, Australia) did not have to invent stories about itself or pretend to be perfect in order to demonstrate its virtues and strengths; a cultural diplomacy which acknowledged that honesty about one's failings was a sign of strength. It is striking that the Australian Fulbright Program administrators should choose this terminology over the much more ideologically stark language that had come to infuse US foreign policy statements at this time.

In this list of General Requirements, 'Personality' came in at number 5, after items on the 'Scope and Nature of Projects' and 'Scholastic and/or Professional Achievement'. The document advised that 'Personality factors will be particularly important in the selection of candidates. Each applicant's personal suitability, adaptability and particularly emotional stability as they pertain to his selection as a representative of Australia overseas and as they relate to his proposed project shall be established prior to awarding him a grant'. Although this spelt things out more fully than the bald one-word criteria 'Personality' that appeared in Rossiter's 1952 list, there was still a good deal of room for disagreement amongst selection committee members in this area. For one selector's boor might be another selector's confident scholar. Was an extrovert necessarily more adaptable to a new and different living and working environment? Might not a quiet observer absorb more about the host culture than a big talker?

Assessing personality was a minefield. As Rossiter himself put it in a 1953 memo to the State Department, 'no system of selection is 100% reliable since personality is a factor which cannot be gauged accurately, nor is it possible to judge with any degree of certainty how an individual will react to the new and unaccustomed environment of his host country'.[35] And when a candidate's 'emotional stability' was listed among factors to be considered by selectors who may or may not be psychologically insightful (let alone trained), the difficulty becomes all the more apparent. By 1992, the board reached a decision to delete the references to emotional stability in its selection guidelines. It specified that 'Applicants should possess such personal qualities as will enable them to contribute to understanding between the two countries'. 'Personal qualities' (rather than 'Personality') were thus assessed, in this context, in relation to the informal ambassadorial expectations that attached to a Fulbright award, a matter to which we return in chapter 7.

For some reason, applicants for senior scholar awards were not interviewed (and so not assessed for their 'representational' or personal qualities) for the first six decades of the program. It was not until 2012 that shortlisted Australian senior and professional scholars were required to front up to a panel and answer questions. The reasons for this were never spelt out in discussions about interviews. There was perhaps an assumption that senior academics and professionals would have enough experience of high-pressure public presentations, travel and socialising with strangers, that their ability to cope with an exchange situation could be taken for granted. In fact the program's history reveals that age is no guarantee of adaptability to a new environment; in some ways the opposite might be true.

Academic track record was much less troubling territory, given there were nationally accepted indicators of achievement on which to rely. Selectors were more likely to disagree over the perceived value of a proposed research project or disciplinary focus, and this was where the make-up of selection committees was of particular importance. A collection in the archives of selection committee score sheets from 1960 to 1961, gives a rare indication of individual selectors' approaches, and reveals what may have been common sources of friction between these academic and business representatives. Handwritten notes (unattributed) accompanying these score sheets noted a wide divergence of views between academics and businessmen in this particular round over applications in the fields of Philosophy, Russian History and Poetry; according to the note-taker, 'clearly their subjects were too esoteric for "hard-headed" businessmen'.[36] Perhaps this is why, in 1960, the board decided to limit regional advisory sub-committees' responsibilities 'to the initial selection of candidates for interview and assessing them on factors of personality and maturity only'. While these committees would be 'free to rate candidates in order of preference if they wished', this was to be done 'on the basis of personality rather than academic attainment and field of study'. The personal interview of candidates was considered 'an opportunity to judge if a candidate was weaker or stronger than his application papers suggested'.[37] The board's selection committee would, in turn, focus more on academic qualities and experience.

In 1962, the board noted that regional advisory sub-committees currently consisted of three members 'appointed by the senior [US] Foreign Service representative in each area concerned'. The board sought to alter the constitution to increase the committee membership to four, 'to provide for better representation of the academic disciplines'. From now on, committees would include one American 'if possible', and 'representation should include, as far as possible, academic interests, sciences, the humanities, and business interests'.[38] Finding the right balance of interests and expertise on selection committees was an ongoing challenge.

Nine years in, the selection machinery had taken on a more definite shape, but the problems were not over: a new disagreement developed in early 1959, when the USEF board made some last-minute revisions to the new Advisory Committee's panels of recommended candidates, before sending them on to the relevant agencies in the United States. This was, it seems, a neat reversal of the 1951 dispute. The Advisory Committee felt its members' care and expertise had been disregarded, and argued that if a committee of prominent people were to be entrusted with this process, then the only grounds for the board to alter or overturn their decisions must be based on policy, and be transparent to all.[39] The board acknowledged that a committee of 'high standing' should have its recommendations 'treated with respect', but argued that 'any reasonable committee would understand that the Board could not delegate its final responsibility for travel grant selections and must retain the right of rejecting recommendations for reasons it considered valid'.[40]

At this point, the Fulbright board decided it was time to take greater control of the selection process, and took the 'opportunity of clearing up the present difficulties [and] of preventing similar occurrences in future'. The board was determined to have a greater say in the membership of the new Advisory Committee on Candidates, and decided to expand its membership to allow a 'broader geographical basis and a wider representation in academic disciplines' – seeking, it seems, a re-balancing after the recent infusion of business interests. The USEF also intended to establish its 'authority to alter the committee's recommendations for sufficient reasons'.[41] And so, for the sake of clarity, the board called for the articulation of clear terms of reference spelling out the roles and responsibilities of the 'various bodies involved in our travel grant selections'. The Australian–US exchange program was now approaching its tenth anniversary, which no doubt seemed like an appropriate time to re-evaluate selection procedures.

The unenviable task of articulating the terms of reference fell to Rossiter. He found that when he wrote the selection process down on paper, 'it look[ed] worse than it seemed to before'. He went further, joking that 'If ever anyone evolved a more Heath-Robinsonish device or a more complicated piece of nonsense to carry out a simple operation I would be very surprised'. Travel grant applications, for example, would now receive 'the full treatment', passing from an advisory sub-committee (regional), to the new Canberra-based Advisory Committee on Candidates (formerly the Committee on Study and Training), to the Committee on Selections (subset of the board), and finally, to the full board of directors.[42]

The joint Smith-Mundt/Fulbright selection process was a variation on this theme, with the added confusion that the Advisory Committee on Candidates functioned here under its original name, the Committee on Study and Training. It is hardly surprising that Rossiter, who had to keep the communications flowing between these many and various committees with changeable names, dreamed of 'some consistency and a slight note of simplicity'. He realised that the simplifications he hoped for – such as, for example, enabling the USEF to make selections for Smith-Mundt awards – probably weren't legally 'correct' under the relevant Acts.[43]

Two years later, in 1961, Les Moore, private secretary in the Prime Minister's Department, wrote to a colleague that 'from my experience as a member of the Selection Committee some years ago, I am sure that reforms in the machinery of control are desirable'.[44] Australian public servants were beginning to discuss the continuing future of the Fulbright Program, as a new funding model was needed to replace the original agreement. If, as was being suggested, 'Australian government money is to be used to finance the successor to the Fulbright scheme', Moor proposed that 'the Australian Government should have a more direct say in the control of the Scheme'. As a consequence of the eventual negotiation of a new Australian–US Fulbright Agreement, achieved in the early 1960s and signed off in August 1964, selection policies and procedures were indeed restructured.

1960s changes to selection policies and procedures

Selection procedures underwent significant changes in 1964, when the initial funding ran out and the partner countries signed a new Fulbright Agreement. The Menzies government agreed to co-fund the exchange program, and in return, insisted on having a greater say in the selection process, thus (eventually) sidelining the ex-'Sydney', now Advisory Selection Committee. The Office of Education within the Prime Minister's Department now took over responsibility for the constitution and management of a national selection committee for Australian travel grants, which became known as the Australian Selection Committee.

This did not really simplify things, however, as the administration of the Australian program was now effectively split between the Australian Office of Education and the USEF secretariat, and respective areas of responsibility were initially unclear. This was especially true in the first years after the change when public servants in the Prime Minister's Department had to familiarise themselves with the program. For a while, during the transitional period of 1963 to 1965, there was talk by the Office of Education of creating an Australian version of the BFS, with all Australian membership (just as the BFS had all American members), in an effort to make the program more truly bi-national. Six months before the new agreement was signed, External Affairs' Max Loveday reported that Les Moore from the Prime Minister's Department envisaged this Australian BFS as operating 'in conjunction with a joint USEF, the latter to have equal membership and functions somewhat more restricted than the present Educational USEF'. Loveday, who had more experience with the complexities of the program than Moore, pointed out that 'it was clear that Moore had not thought through the details of how the bodies would operate in relation to each other, nor of what was to happen to Rossiter's present office arrangements'.[45] Rossiter, apparently unhappy with developments, perhaps because he could foresee the diminution in the executive officer's responsibilities and freedom of action, flagged his intention to resign, but stayed on for six months to ease the transition until his replacement was appointed.

An Australian BFS never eventuated, probably because it could never, within the existing legislative framework, hold a completely equal place to the original BFS. Under the Fulbright Act, the BFS in Washington, DC was the prime policy-making body and had final approval of all awards from all partner countries. Individual Fulbright executive agreements could not override this. Thus, the Australian BFS would ultimately have played a subordinate role and would have added yet another (and possibly unnecessary) layer to an already overly complex administrative structure.

There were some changes of emphasis in selection criteria under the new system, with the new Australian Selection Committee giving greater weight to academic than to personal qualities. In a letter to Noel Flentje, South Australian Regional Selection Committee member and Fulbright alumnus, the Prime Minister's Department's Ken Jones acknowledged 'a tendency in the past for some Regional Committees to place a good deal of emphasis on the question of personality and representational capacity of applicants' – indeed, as we have seen, that had been the official board recommendation to these committees. However, the current board, 'while not discounting the merit of these qualities', did not want them to be given 'pride of place'. And so, it increased the proportion of academics in the reconstituted committees.[46]

It was swings and roundabouts, for in September the next year, during a board meeting discussion on selection procedures, the External Affairs representative 'queried the preponderance of academics' on the regional selection committees, and called for greater lay representation. LeVan Roberts, US public affairs officer, a board member for five years, pointed out that USEF experience 'showed that lay representation had been valuable' but that the US consuls who sat on each regional committee could play this lay role.[47]

Debates over the ideal constitution and functioning of selection committees would continue through the decades. Aside from the academic/lay balance, there was plenty of discussion about the disciplinary areas represented on selection committees by academic members. There was certainly a push from the BFS and State Department for a larger number of scholars in the humanities and social sciences to be selected, from the early 1950s right through the 1990s. The argument was that scholars whose work concerned the history and representations of their nations were best placed to further the goal of 'mutual understanding'. The US perception (shared by many Australian academics) was that more Australian scholars in the sciences were recommended for awards than their humanities/social science counterparts, that the Australian board was 'partial to science' as considered policy.[48] This bias was partly a reflection of the much larger proportion of applications coming in from the sciences (not surprising given the greater likelihood of success) and the weakness in Australia of social science disciplines. They could be strengthened by more international exchange, 'if some of those chaps could go to the United States', but the United States' lack of knowledge about Australian social scientists meant they were harder to place in US institutions and therefore missed out on awards.[49]

In March 1962, the board's selection committee, reflecting on the Australian travel grants for the coming year, noted the 'preponderance of scientists in the field' despite its efforts 'in arranging the panels of candidates' to seek 'balance among the disciplines represented'. Expressing concern at the lack of candidates in the social sciences and humanities, the board agreed that 'effort should be made to encourage a wider field of applicants in future competitions'.[50] A few months later, board member L.G. Huxley, vice-chancellor of the ANU, reported on a meeting at his university about this shortfall; it was suggested that the prerequisite of a PhD might be discouraging applicants in the humanities and social sciences. Huxley suggested that 'a more flexible wording of the information circular, while maintaining the high academic standard required, might well induce more scholars in these fields to apply for awards'.[51]

The post-1964 decision by the Office of Education and the board to recalibrate selection processes to place extra emphasis on academic record over personality, may well have reinforced the tendency for scientists to be selected before scholars in the humanities, because their university records were usually more straightforward. This tendency was still apparent twenty years later when the partiality to science was still evident. A political scientist (and 1966 Australian Fulbright alumnus) who joined the ACT selection committee in the mid-1980s recalled in an interview that there had been a preponderance of scientists on the committee until he came along. He found there was a problem in their decision-making, and it was not just the lack of applications from competitive candidates that was causing the disparity between science and humanities. Instead the committee's conception of merit was based quite narrowly on university results and tended to focus on science and mathematics achievements. It seems they struggled even harder when humanities applicants were not 'chaps'. The political scientist remembered the occasion when a candidate came in with a 'really interesting and fresh' feminist approach to the classics. He worked hard to bring the scientists on the panel around to selecting her.[52] It seems gender bias may have been more operative in non-science disciplines.

Intermittent board attempts to encourage more applications from practising professionals (or non-academics) met a similar stumbling block: selection committees felt unqualified to assess the merit of their project or their record of work. Occasionally they would seek advice from external experts in particular fields regarding an applicant. In 1982, following on a program review, the board decided to create a new senior professional award category, and this raised questions about whether the advice of professional associations, such as the Australian Medical Association, should be sought during the selection process. How, board members wondered, could the USEF 'control any pre-selection undertaken by a professional body and would professional bodies accept such control anyway?' Was it possible that 'the best applicants from the Fulbright point of view could be lost through preselection by a professional body applying criteria that were irrelevant (even inimical) to the Fulbright purpose'? Also, a fundamental question was: how should they define a 'professional'? If they were to try to name all possible eligible professions the list would be 'unmanageably long'.

Through the mid-1980s the board began to worry that there was not enough communication with state selection committees, and in 1987 there were 'some reported anomalies' in the various state committees' procedures and decisions. When the board tried to plan a conference of board and selection committee members, another question arose: who should organise this, the USEF or the Department of Education? So the lack of clarity about administrative responsibilities identified twenty years earlier had not been resolved. It would be another two years (May 1988) before such a meeting of board and state selection committee members would be held.

For a long time, the USEF, under some pressure from the BFS, had talked about encouraging practising arts professionals to apply for awards. Artists tended not to put themselves forward, and when they did, selection committees often felt unqualified to judge the merit of their work. Artists' CVs rarely fit the template of successful academic exchange applicants. Art gallery director Jacqueline Hochmann (later Taylor), who was appointed to the board in 1985, helped overcome this problem by providing new expertise on selection committees.[53] In order to ensure that such applicants would have a chance of surviving the selection process, the board, under Hochmann Taylor's guidance, invited a representative of the visual and performing arts to join each state selection committee. This action led the board to take a closer look at the balance of all disciplines on these committees, and they produced lists of those fields needing better representation. For example, in 1992, the board agreed that the Victorian and Tasmanian committees needed someone from the 'hard sciences', while South Australia required someone in humanities or social sciences, and New South Wales a management or business representative.[54]

The fact that the Fulbright Program was open to all academic fields posed some problems for selectors, but in many ways this has proved to be a great strength. It has enabled the program to accommodate new and evolving disciplines, and has encouraged its administrators and selectors to contemplate, and appreciate, the full gamut of intellectual activity across a range of institutions, in each country. There have, from the beginning, been efforts to emphasise particular fields or 'projects' at different times, which inevitably had impacts on selections – particularly with respect to American scholars. So now we turn to the story of programming and American selections.

Notes

1 Sondra Farganis, response to Survey, La Trobe University, 2011, in possession of authors.
2 Handbook for Committees on Study and Training in the United States, 2nd edition, July 1949, in 'Scholarships, Bursaries, Fellowships – Foreign – Institute of International Education (New York)', A1361 20/4/12 PART 1, NAA.
3 Walter Johnson and Francis Colligan, *The Fulbright Program: A History* (Chicago, 1965), pp. 25–6, 39.
4 Sally Ninham, *A Cohort of Pioneers: Australian Postgraduate Students and American Postgraduate Degrees, 1949–64* (Melbourne, 2011), pp. 280–2, for a list of some of these schemes in the 1950s and 1960s.
5 USEF Draft Annual Report [Jan 1950 – Dec 1951], p. 21. In A1838 250/9/8/3 Pt2, NAA.
6 Item 8 of 'Selected Approved Policies and Principles of the Board of Foreign Scholarships', n.d. [c. 1950], in 'United States of America – Educational USEF Programmes', A1838 250/9/8/7 PART 1, NAA.
7 The South Pacific Commission was founded in Australia in 1947 under the Canberra Agreement by six governments that then administered territories in the Pacific: Australia, France, New Zealand, the Netherlands, the United Kingdom and the United States. The Commission's goal was to restore stability to the region after the upheavals of the Second World War, to assist in administering the territories and to benefit the people of the Pacific. Website of the Secretariat of the Pacific Community (the Commission's successor), at www.spc.int/en/about-spc/history.html (accessed 16 October 2012).
8 Note of meeting in Dept of External Affairs, 21 February 1950. Present: Dept officers, Mr Gabites of NZ High Commissioner's Office and Mr Forsyth, Sec-Gen of the South Pacific Commission. In A1838 250/9/8/7 PART 1, NAA.
9 Daniel Oakman and David Lowe and Department of Foreign Affairs and Trade (Australia), Australia and the Colombo Plan: 1949–1957 (Canberra, 2004).
10 Johnson and Colligan, *Fulbright Program*, pp. 29–30.
11 USEF board minutes, 23 July 1951 and Draft annual report for year 1952, A1838 250/9/8/3 Pt2, NAA.
12 Handbook for Committees on Study and Training in the United States, 2nd edition, July 1949, in 'Scholarships, Bursaries, Fellowships – Foreign – Institute of International Education (New York)', A1361 20/4/12 PART 1, NAA.

13 USEF board minutes, 27 April 1953.
14 DOS press release, 3 January 1951 (no. 4): 'Two Way Street' Issued by US Advisory Commission on Educational Exchange. In 'United States of America – Relations with Australia – Cultural', A1838 250/9/8/1 PART 1, NAA.
15 'United States Information and Educational Exchange Act of 1948', Public Law 402, H.R. 3342, January 27, 1948.
16 31 December 1952, FSD AMConsulate Sydney to DOS. Subj: IIA: Transmitting Combined Evaluation Report for the Period Dec 1 1951 to Nov 30 1952. In Department of State Central Files 511. 43, R59 Box 2359.
17 Combined Evaluation Report for the Period Dec 1 1951 to Nov 30 1952. Department of State Central Files 511. 43, R59 Box 2359.
18 Section E 'Exchange of Persons (Sydney and National: Violet J. Robinson, C.A.A.) in Combined Evaluation Report for the Period Dec 1 1951 to Nov 30 1952'. In DOS RG 59 Box 2359, NARA.
19 3 February 1950, Sydney to DOS, USIE Country Paper – Aims and Objectives of the USIE Program in Australia. In R59 Department of State Central Files, Educational Exchange/ Grants (travel)/ International Exchanges, Box 2359, NARA.
20 3 May 1950, Confidential Air Pouch to DOS. Draft of USIE Country Paper for Australia – Suggested Revisions. In DOS RG 59 Box 2359, NARA.
21 2 January 1951, Sydney to DOS, Transmittal of USIE Semi-Annual Evaluation Report. DOS RG 59 Box 2359, NARA.
22 'Exchange of Persons (Sydney and National: Violet J. Robinson, C.A.A.), Extent of Program'. In FSD Dec 31, 1952 Evaluation Report. AMConsulate Sydney to DOS: Subj: IIA: Transmitting Combined Evaluation Report for the Period Dec 1 1951 to Nov 30 1952. In DOS RG 59 Box 2359, NARA [see n. 17].
23 RG 59 General Records of Department of State 1955–59 Central Decimal File 511.43/ 9–2056, NARA.
24 RG 59 General Records of Department of State 1955–59 Central Decimal File 511.43/ 9–2056, NARA.
25 6 June 1961, A.L. Moore, Private Sec, PM's Dept, to Mr E.J.B. Foxcroft, PM's Dept. In 'United States Educational USEF in Australia – Fulbright programme – Policy', A463 1963/611, NAA.
26 USEF board minutes, 28 February 1958 and 14 May 1959.
27 25 March 1958, USIS Field report, Canberra. 7. Statement to Facilitate Inspection, Section 2. International Educational Exchange Program. MC 468 Box 316 file 316– 7: 'GROUP XVI Post Reports' in CU, UoA SpC.
28 14 April 1958, McConeghey, PAO, to Les Moore, Prime Minister's Department, in A463 1963/611, NAA.
29 USEF board minutes, 22 April 1958.
30 Adele Millerd and Alice Garner. Adele Millerd interviewed by Alice Garner in the Fulbright scholars oral history project [sound recording], National Library of Australia, 2011. http://nla.gov.au/nla.oh-vn5755494.
31 USEF board minutes, 9 July 1958.
32 USEF board minutes, 26 April 1957.
33 USEF board minutes, 20 February 1957.
34 USEF, 'General Requirements and Conditions', September 1958. A1838 583/1 PART 6, NAA.
35 USEF Memo No 169 to DOS (IES). Oct 28 1953. On: Selection of American Grantees. Appendix to USEF board minutes of 26 October 1953.

36　USEF Score sheets in 'United States – Educational USEF – Policy', A1838 583/1 PART 6, NAA.

37　USEF board minutes, 23 May 1960.

38　USEF board minutes, 17 May 1962.

39　Committee on Study and Training minutes, 4 May 1959, in A463 1963/611, NAA.

40　USEF board minutes, 14 May 1959.

41　USEF board minutes, 14 May 1959.

42　28 May 1959, USEF Memorandum on 'Travel Grant Selection Procedures', and 'Proposed Terms of Reference', signed by Rossiter. In 'United States – Educational USEF – Policy', A1838 583/1 PART 6, NAA.

43　28 May 1959, USEF Memorandum on 'Travel Grant Selection Procedures', and 'Proposed Terms of Reference', signed by Rossiter. In 'United States – Educational USEF – Policy', A1838 583/1 PART 6, NAA.

44　6 June 1961, A.L. Moore, Private Sec, PM's Dept, to Mr E.J.B. Foxcroft, PM's Dept. In 'United States Educational USEF in Australia – Fulbright programme – Policy', A463 1963/611, NAA.

45　31 March 1964, Record of conversation by Loveday (EA) with Moore (PM's), re Extension of Fulbright Programme. In A1838 583/1 part 1, NAA.

46　[n.d. but est. late November 1965], K.N. Jones to N. Flentje, in A463 1964/5174 PART 2, NAA.

47　AAEF board minutes, 27 September 1965.

48　Peter I. Rose, *Academic Sojourners: A Report on the Senior Fulbright Programs in East Asia and the Pacific* (United States Bureau of Educational and Cultural Affairs, Office of Policy and Plans, 1976), p. 106.

49　Rose, *Academic Sojourners*, pp. 106–7.

50　USEF board minutes, 28 March 1962.

51　USEF board minutes, 18 July 1962.

52　Hugh Collins and Alice Garner. Hugh Collins interviewed by Alice Garner in the Fulbright scholars oral history project [sound recording], National Library of Australia, 2011.

53　AAEF board minutes, 16 May and 26 November 1991.

54　AAEF board minutes, 24 February and 26 May 1992.

4

'Mutual benefit' v. 'the needs of the country': Programming academic fields

One early autumn day in 1951, a zoologist from Harvard University, called William Brown, caught a train to the Sydney suburb of Camperdown. Sharing his carriage was a group of Australian woolgrowers. They were in high spirits, for they had just pocketed their biggest ever wool cheques. Brown lifted his trouser hems and showed them his socks. He asked them to guess what they were made of. Wool, they supposed. When he told them they were made of nylon, the woolgrowers refused to believe him. Brown told this story to a Melbourne *Herald* journalist, who interviewed him alongside four other Americans, all of them Fulbright scholars, the first to arrive in Australia since the scheme had begun.[1]

The newspaperman wove a great story out of the nylon sock incident, titling his article 'Shock for Woolmen in U.S. Clothing'. He listed all the synthetic clothes the five Americans had brought with them: 'a dozen rayon, rayon and cotton, and seer-sucker suits; half a dozen nylon shirts; several dozen pairs of nylon socks; a number of nylon ties; and various miscellaneous articles of clothing such as nylon windbreaker jackets'. This wardrobe, he warned, 'ought to make Australian woolgrowers shudder beneath the weight of their golden fleeces'.[2] Here was a cautionary tale about the future of the wool industry, 'the sheep's back' upon which Australians had relied for so long. The Americans' response to the nylon sock encounter had been to wonder 'if the Australian woolgrower really knows what is going on in the field of synthetics?' The impact of American technological advances and global economic reach could no longer be ignored: the future was here. Fulbrighters, this story suggested, were its harbingers.

The article barely touched on the Fulbright scholars' real reasons for being in Australia, for of course they had not come to dance on the grave of Australian sheep grazing. Delving into the archives, we found that Brown had come to study a tribe of ants called the Dacetini, for only on the Australian continent could three of the Dacetini's four sub-tribes be found together in one place.[3] Russell Barrett of Kansas, whose was doing a PhD at Melbourne University, which he turned into a book a few years later, titled *Promises and Performances in Australian Politics, 1928–1959.* That Barrett was in fact married to a Melbourne woman he had met in New York was possibly a factor in his applying for a Fulbright.[4] John Eberhardt was another Kansan political science postgraduate, studying the Victorian State Electricity Commission as an example of a public corporation (and one that was dismantled in a privatisation push forty-five years later). Gilbert Hardee was a rural sociologist who went on to write about farming families in North Carolina, and in the late 1960s researched Pakistani men's family planning knowledge and strategies.[5] The fifth Fulbrighter, Clayton Newton, was an Atlanta-born navy veteran and geographer who came to Melbourne to study agriculture, and ended up a specialist in defence mapping.[6]

Clearly what they were wearing was incidental to the substance of their visit. Yet such small details are indicative of deeper undercurrents in the potential of this Fulbright exchange of scholars. A vital aspect of the Fulbright Program's history is showing how the program influenced changes, especially the development of academic fields. In January 1950, before the first USEF board was named, an External Affairs officer noted the terms of the Australian–US Fulbright Agreement. One of the first expectations of the USEF in Canberra was to 'study the needs of the country for educational exchange'. This involved inviting recommendations from universities that would help identify 'the fields in which American citizens can work to the mutual benefit of the grantees and the educational system'. The BFS realised that those in universities charged with this task were likely to design their recommendations around individual Americans whose visit they particularly desired. They advised that, as this was an open competition, 'proposals should, in general, be in terms of subject categories rather than be shaped to individuals who may or may not be awarded grants'.[7]

In other words, although Australian universities could, as part of their proposals, 'suggest' the name of their preferred American candidate, the decision on who actually came remained with the United States. The suggested person was then expected to apply in the standard way through US agencies, in open competition. So there was no guarantee of that named individual being selected. Other, possibly better qualified, or preferable, applicants might turn up and be favoured by US selectors over the stated choice of the Australian host institutions.

This conflict posed a potential dilemma for administration of the Fulbright Program. Programming the US awards was a delicate balancing act. Administrators sought to meet the needs of the host country while satisfying the desires and interests and capacities of potential visitors. This was not always possible. The US-based BFS, established under the Fulbright legislation, guided global exchange policy, while bi-national commissions in the partner countries, like the USEF, were to make decisions about award selection procedures and programming policies in response to local needs. Tensions existed between them. The field of research emphases in awards reveals how these tensions could surface with regard to what we might call changing national preoccupations, and how administrators could turn 'mutual understanding' into the more utilitarian 'mutual benefit', or woollen socks into nylon ones.

All Fulbright Foundations and Commissions grappled with the problem at various times, as BFS annual reports and program reviews by US agencies pointed out. The archives on Australian programming on the US awards trace changes to the recommended fields for research and teaching over the years. These provide an intriguing snapshot of the beginning and development of disciplines in Australia, as well as of evolving national and bi-national priorities. Although Fulbright scholarships could be and were awarded in every academic field, from the outset the BFS gave particular encouragement for awards to scholars in the humanities and social sciences. This was consistent with Fulbright's original idea of building 'mutual understanding' between peoples, in favouring scholars and teachers whose research and teaching background equipped them to make sense to their hosts of their own country's history, politics and cultural expressions. State Department and BFS responses to Australian programming reveals there were enduring conflicts between US and Australian objectives and their understanding of what 'mutual understanding' might mean. An overview of evolving disciplinary developments demonstrates that principles of 'mutual benefit' were applied. These occurred within the context in which the bi-national exchange relationship was established.

Figure 4.1 American Fulbright scholar Dick La Ganza (right) and Neil Dixon examine Treloar's Hill Mine, 'Expedition to an Opal Field', *The Australian Women's Weekly*, 7 May 1958

Australia 'not ... sufficiently attractive'

Sondra Silverman (postgraduate 1961) 'fell in love with Australia and would have stayed there forever' had she been able to extend her visa.[8] Some scholars did return to become permanent residents, and generally this decision was, like the potential success of their exchange, closely tied to the field of study they pursued. What might American scholars, in the early years of the program, seek from studying in a country like Australia? Culturally Australia was considered something of a backwater, when anything was known about it at all. American GIs who had been stationed in Australia during the war knew more than most of their compatriots, and some wanted to return, but Australia was not generally perceived as a destination for academics.

In the 1950s Australia had difficulty attracting high-calibre scholars interested in studying Australian history, culture and society. Luring experts in other histories and cultures to Australian institutions was no easier. Partly this was a bias amongst US academics. Australia found that it was lower down in the pecking order of host countries for US Fulbrighters than, say, France, Italy or the UK.[9] It could not compete against its near and distant neighbours as an Asia-Pacific destination. Everywhere else in the world was closer, at a time when international travel was slow and difficult. They had to come by ship, and spend weeks at sea. Although Europe and the UK were still struggling with post-war shortages and only slowly rebuilding, the nature of academic fields meant these older nations had a cultural cachet and intellectual pull that Australia could not match. As one Australian resident in the United States put it in 1950, 'Most students apply for European education, where there are centuries of culture and art to delve into. It is not easy to think of something sufficiently attractive ... as justification for study in Australia.'[10]

Perhaps it was considered too similar to the United States to offer meaningful learning experiences. This overlooked what Australia had to offer as a region of recent European settlement and Indigenous populations, with a history of leading the world in women's suffrage, in labour politics and democratic reforms; its comparative value as a new mass migration destination and its cultural place as an Asia-Pacific outpost of British empire – all areas that would become critical fields of historical and social scientific enquiry before the end of the twentieth century. Its value to scientists, geologists, geographers, astronomers, marine biologists, zoologists and botanists may have been more obvious, but the BFS preferred to push a humanities and social science agenda. They could however promote Australia as a destination for those who lacked the language competence for living in other countries.

The lack of curiosity amongst American scholars or Fulbright officials was partly a fault of academic fields within Australian institutions. When Robert LeRoy Johnson, a lecturer in comparative literature from Kansas State University, arrived in Adelaide in September 1963 to take up his Fulbright award, he was taken aback to discover how low the status of Australian literature was in the minds of students. Coming to the end of his sixteen-month stay, he reported that 'A typical question which was asked me when I said what I was studying was, "What, you mean there is such a thing as an Australian literature?"' He found the teaching of Australian literature, generally

speaking, to be 'inadequate', and he also suffered from a serious lack of resources outside of Sydney and the ANU in Canberra.[11] The first chair in Australian literature had
only been established the year before Johnson's arrival.[12]

Fulbright awards were valuable in developing the field of Australian literature.
Visiting American scholars who were curious about Australian culture and society, by
bringing a serious, scholarly lens to their hosts' world, as well as experience in the academic development of their own 'area' studies, encouraged Australians to look again
at themselves in a new light. In 1953, for example, Professor of Education J. Franklin
Hunt came on a senior Fulbright award to study the Australian accent, and newspaper
articles photographed him recording locals speaking 'Australianese'.[13] A year later a
Canberra Times article noted that Fulbright scholars working on Australian ballads,
women novelists and the nationalist writers of the 1890s, had spurred the development of an Australian literature course in the nation's capital. Canberra University
College (CUC) had a policy of developing Australian studies, as 'particularly suitable
to Canberra' and inaugurated a full, year-long academic course in Australian literature
stimulated by four American postgraduates who were studying with T. Inglis Moore.
CUC hoped that the University of Melbourne would recognise the course as an arts
degree subject.[14]

It took some time, however, for Australian studies to be fully embedded into the
university system. Harry Heseltine, a 1953 Australian Fulbright scholar in literature, noted that the nation's first undergraduate course in Australian studies was the
University of New South Wales' offering of 1964 – and 'not before time'. In the early
1960s, Heseltine had travelled to the United States and England intending to bring
back ideas for 'our burgeoning Australian Studies course' in Sydney, and found that 'in
the interdisciplinary study of their native culture, American academics were far ahead
of their Australian counterparts'. When he returned to Australia, he found he had 'no
occasion to apply any of the ideas' he had 'garnered', because the new head of history
had 'swept Australian Studies right out of the Faculty's list of offerings'.[15] One step forward, one step back.

Participants in the exchange program like Johnson and Hunt (among many others)
played an important part in challenging the low value placed on Australian studies,
but it would be a long, uphill battle to have the field properly recognised. The 1970s
saw a fuller flowering of Australian history and literature, but the seeds had been
planted earlier, not only by American visitors' curiosity and search for understanding,
but by returning Australian Fulbright scholars who looked afresh at their own
culture(s), having experienced the comparatively unapologetic and robust American
studies scene.

It may also have been difficult to attract Americans without also promising them
additional funds. American scholars were selected for the Australian program in quite
a different way from Australian candidates. Until the late 1970s, as we have seen, a
Fulbright award for Australians was essentially a travel-only grant. For Americans the
award covered travel, tuition and living costs. This difference, which initially was due
to the specific currency arrangements under the Fulbright Act, was maintained even
after the agreement was renegotiated on a different funding basis. The rationale was

that Australians had access to myriad scholarship and university funding schemes in many eligible (and often better-resourced) institutions in the United States, whereas there were very few such opportunities for Americans wishing to visit one of the small number of Australian universities. As an External Affairs officer put it in a confidential 1963 memo, the Fulbright Program 'serves to make up, in some small measure, for the wealth of American scholarships and the scarcity of Australian scholarships'.[16] The consequence was that while Australian awards were subject to where that support could be found by individual scholars, awards to US scholars were required to fall into a range of targeted research and teaching areas considered *beneficial to Australia*, a list that the board altered slightly from year to year.[17]

Thus while Australian Fulbright applications were essentially open as to field of research or teaching, this was not quite the case for Americans seeking awards. From the late 1940s, the BFS required foundations in partner countries to develop annual proposals identifying areas of research or teaching which might benefit from the contribution of American scholars or lecturers. These were then passed on to the US-based agencies administering selection, which put out calls for applications from Americans working in those particular fields. This aspect of the process caused enduring frustration amongst Australian university people who went to considerable effort to justify their recommendations. Thirty years into the program, the USEF noted that the 80 per cent failure rate for recommendations was taking its toll on the willingness of university department heads to engage in the process.

In the first three decades of the Australian program's life, a large section of each annual proposal was devoted to the description of broad research fields or 'projects' under which recommendations for lecturers and research scholars were grouped. The USEF relied heavily for this section on suggestions from Australian universities which it sought each year, a procedure that was onerous for all concerned but also crucial to Fulbright programming decisions.

Geoffrey Rossiter's first annual report, written early in 1952, explained succinctly some of the difficulties associated with program planning in the first years of the scheme.[18] He had prepared three proposals (for 1951, 1952 and 1953) in the space of eighteen months, which had 'placed a heavy strain upon the limited resources of the Foundation secretariat'. This was a 'lengthy procedure' that entailed answering a long list of questions about each institution proposing a placement for a scholar. Universities were understaffed, and Rossiter felt it was unreasonable to request the level of detail demanded by the BFS.

Contributing to the problem of attracting appropriate scholars were the procedures USEF required. When Australian vice-chancellors received the USEF's request for suggestions of 'fields of study in which they feel that the visit of an American specialist would be mutually beneficial', they sent it on to their departmental heads. The heads' suggestions were then passed back to the vice-chancellor's office, which forwarded them to the USEF with no attempt at prioritising proposals. That is, there was no effort to coordinate suggestions according to a vision of the big picture of educational or other national needs. This tended to produce a 'distorted picture of the Australian requirements', according to Rossiter. For the 1953 program, the USEF changed tack and asked vice-chancellors to screen their department heads' proposals before submitting them to the USEF. Only three institutions followed this advice, but their recommendations had been 'notably successful'; that is, they had resulted in awards to scholars.

By this time, Rossiter had come to the conclusion that 'if the predominant educational needs of the country were to be ascertained accurately, it would be desirable for a panel of experts to be engaged continually on the problem'. This was a pipedream, of course, so the Foundation took upon itself a more proactive role when making programming decisions. The USEF supplemented the university recommendations with its own 'appraisal of the economic, social and political needs of the country', 'specific knowledge held by members of the Board', as well as Rossiter's observations based on 'periodic visits' to universities.

Rossiter explained that the USEF sought to 'provide a nicely balanced programme which not only makes provision for highly specialised fields of study but also for broader and at times more practical opportunities which are calculated to achieve the wider objectives of the program'.[19] These 'wider objectives' referred to the goal of improving mutual understanding between the two countries. One could argue that an exchange in any field would contribute to that goal merely by virtue of the individuals concerned adapting to a new academic culture and society through living there for a period of time and reflecting on their experiences upon their return. But US Fulbright policy-makers and administrators in particular considered some disciplinary areas to provide better opportunities than others for the articulation and negotiation of social and cultural differences. They wanted the mutual benefit to flow to the discipline and not just the individual. Regular discussions turn up in the program archives about the ideal balancing of sciences and humanities, and their relative worth in contributing to mutual understanding.

So a second problem was the difference in judgement between the USEF in Australia and the priorities of the State Department in the United States over what would be of benefit. Indeed the State Department was clear that 'mutual benefit' meant also to the United States, not just the needs of Australia. In 1951, the second operational year of the Australian program (and the first year in which Americans came to Australia), the State Department analysed the USEF's annual proposal (as it would continue to do every year), and claimed there was too heavy an emphasis on physical and biological sciences in the Australian foundation's list of recommended fields. It argued that 'research in the social sciences, and possibly also in the humanities, offers more advantages than are mentioned in the list submitted by the Foundation'. Given that the Fulbright goal was mutual understanding between people of the two nations, 'American acquaintance with history, social processes and developments in Australia needs enhancement through the study and research which might be conducted by American recipients of Fulbright grants'.[20]

The USEF's perspective on this was, needless to say, somewhat different. For example, Rossiter, in his first annual report, covering the same period as the State Department appraisal (1951–52), emphasised that in relation to the American awards, there were 'excellent fields of study in Australia apart from political science', particularly for postgraduate students. His advice became rather pointed here: 'it is considered that bush ballads do not provide really good opportunities for research'! (Rossiter would no doubt have been amazed to see the direction cultural history would take in later decades.) He went on to list areas in which Australian institutions could provide good research opportunities and facilities for visiting Americans: public finance – in particular, problems of federation; Australian history; forestry; zoology, entomology; agriculture and soils, irrigation; geography and geology; education.

In the next year's analysis of the Australian program, the State Department repeated its complaint about the balance of fields, noting that 'Some of the conferees on this proposal believe that it requests somewhat too many lecturers in technological subjects and too few in the social sciences and humanities'.[21] Meanwhile, in a USEF board meeting, former chief justice of the High Court of Australia (and later chair of the board) Sir John Latham tabled a letter in which he proposed the contrary, namely that 'greater emphasis be laid upon the biological and agricultural sciences'.[22] Presumably these were areas in which Australian educational institutions and society more generally needed particular support. Latham, however, also had an abiding concern about the possible propagandistic uses to which social sciences projects (especially) might be put during this politically troubling time (see chapter 5).

The contest between the USEF and BFS/State Department over programming priorities echoed some of the Cold War differences that had threatened the negotiation process. The sciences/humanities balance in the program continued to be debated throughout the decades. By the 1960s Senator Fulbright himself had something to say on this when he argued that universities beholden to government agendas tended to favour scientific over humanities projects.[23] This was in the context of robust debates about the military-industrial complex and research funding for defence projects in the United States, but had relevance to the exchange program's foci.

In 1980, at a conference held in Washington, DC on 'The Fulbright Program in the Eighties', sponsored by the BFS and the US International Communication Agency (a short-lived USIA replacement), detailed discussions were held about program objectives, procedures and future possibilities. One of the key questions raised was how exactly the program fitted with US foreign policy, or rather, how national interests (of both the United States and partner countries) were in reality 'accommodated under the rubric of binationalism'? 'The classic example', according to the conference reporters, 'found throughout Fulbright history' was to be found 'in the pressures which most Commissions feel from non-U.S. members for programs in basic and applied science and technology and the corresponding pressure on the American side for area studies, translating into social sciences and humanities'.[24] So Australia was not alone in experiencing this persistent mismatch of priorities.

In 1984 the BFS was still concerned that the Australian Foundation had too many award openings in science, and expressed surprise that some scientific collaborations had been categorised under the heading of American and Australian studies.[25] The board argued back that 'to exclude first class proposals simply because they were in the sciences, could produce negative reactions in the academic community to the detriment of the Fulbright program in Australia'. They explained that the Foundation was offering up to 50 per cent of its awards 'in support of academic work that is directly concerned with Australia or America or any aspect of relationships between them'. This encompassed not only 'the traditional aspects of Australian and/or American Studies (such as the history, literature, sociology, economy and political structure of each country or of both countries)', but 'projects in technology or the sciences where the subject of the work is of national concern in each country, e.g. environmental pollution'.[26] When we look at the fields of American scholars who visited in 1984, only five out of twenty were in the sciences; in 1985, nine out of twenty-seven. Over the same two years, Australian scientists won a total of only thirteen out of sixty awards to the United States.

It is understandable, then, that the Australian Foundation (renamed the Australian-American Educational Foundation, or AAEF, in 1964) should have rejected BFS criticism that its program was too heavily weighted towards the sciences, particularly at this time. In 1985 the AAEF board raised the 'question of quality of applications' in response to the BFS criticisms, noting that 'there had been some years when the quality of applications in the humanities was not up to scratch and the Board had not felt it appropriate to select applications that were not considered to be of an adequate standard. The principle of maintaining excellence as the over-riding criterion for selection was endorsed'.[27]

Scholars in the humanities and social sciences might, in the course of their work, address more explicitly (and publicly) the areas of difference and/or convergence between Australian and US societies. We have learnt from Fulbright scholars themselves, however, through interviews, archival research and surveys, that scientists and non-humanities scholars have been just as engaged in making sense of their host culture, and talking about their experience with their colleagues, friends and acquaintances upon their return.

Professor James Moyer's commentary on the eating habits of Australians, reported in a daily Melbourne newspaper, is one example of the way that a scholar in a technological field could interpret the host society in ways that caught the attention of a broad (not purely academic) audience. In late 1952, the NSW Institute of Technology submitted a request to the Foundation for an American Fulbright lecturer in food technology, specifically 'The Fundamentals of Processing of Fruit and Vegetables'. The Food Technology Department was, they reported, 'still very young', and needed someone who could teach graduate courses. 'There is a distinct need for courses of this nature on many of the fundamentals of the food processing industries since, for the most part, the technical personnel in these industries have acquired such specialist knowledge as they possess on the job.' Moreover, 1954 looked like being 'a year with a very big demand for teaching' in this field, especially given the likelihood of Colombo Plan student enrolments. This recommendation led to the granting of a senior Fulbright award to James C. Moyer, a professor of food technology from Cornell University, who arrived, accompanied by his wife, at his host institution in October 1954.

The following February, Moyer featured in the Melbourne daily press, when he was visiting a 'Better Food Exhibition' in the Victorian capital. In an article entitled

'Australian Appetite Amazes American Professor', Moyer was quoted exclaiming over his hosts' eating and drinking habits. The fact that Australians could eat so much and yet stay 'slim' made no sense to him, and nor did the way an 'Australian drink[s] boiling tea on a hot day, and claim[s] the hot tea cools him'. He found the Australian 'meat breakfast' 'staggering', morning and afternoon tea seemed 'unnecessary' (Americans preferred a soft drink when tired), and a three-course hot meal at midday seemed excessive for an American used to eating a light sandwich for lunch. Australians, he thought, ate 'too much potatoes and white bread'. And, he pointed out, if Australians thought they were 'underfed', they 'should be shipped immediately to southern Europe to see what underfeeding really is'.[28]

Moyer's observations, while entertaining to us today, are revealing of larger, socio-economic resonances that a scholar in a technological field could identify in the ordinary, daily habits of his hosts. Every scholar, no matter his or her area of expertise, could contribute to the development of a humanist 'mutual understanding'.

'A country's needs'

The balance of humanities and sciences was not the only issue, when it came to programming. There was another contest between USEF and the BFS, which provides another example of the different approaches that had plagued the negotiating process. In late 1951, the BFS sent the Foundation new guidelines for planning, in which they required annual programs to be expressed 'in terms of projects' rather than 'categories'. The USEF board did not respond well to this terminology. Rossiter explained that 'The Foundation feels that the suitability of the "project" approach to programme planning varies greatly from country to country and that its adoption is less profitable in proportion to the degree of resemblance between the institutions and the culture of the country concerned and those of the United States'. He went on to explain that 'It is believed that the practical benefit to be derived from the new policy will be considerably less in countries like Australia and New Zealand than, say, in Burma, the Philippines or India'.[29]

This was a subtle-ish way of saying that the Australians refused to see themselves as aid recipients – particularly as they were in the very act of positioning themselves as aid-providers in their region, in the context of the recently launched Colombo Plan. In April 1953, the board's Programme Committee, responding to the BFS's planning recommendations, proposed that 'care should be taken to avoid creating the impression that it was the intention to bring American specialists to Australia in order to solve local problems'.[30] And at the following meeting, the board agreed that it would not use the word 'projects' when writing to universities to request program or field recommendations, presumably for fear of creating just this impression.[31]

Despite its initial reluctance to embrace the new language that evoked US aid to the developing world, the Foundation did begin to frame its annual program documents

according to the BFS's required 'projects', and as it turned out, these were often jus-
tified in relation to perceived Australian 'needs' in specific areas. In April 1953, the
board started to plan the 1955 program, for it was required to do its preparation well
in advance of calls for applications, in order to have its proposals endorsed by the BFS.
It came up with several 'project areas' which it proposed to pass on to universities to
guide the submission of specific recommendations. It is hardly surprising that one
of the areas listed should be 'Australian-American Relations', given the overarching
goal of the Fulbright scheme. This would remain a focus throughout the decades
with more or less emphasis at different times. For example, by the 1980s, it was AAEF
policy to devote up to 50 per cent of awards to applicants under this heading. More
telling, perhaps, is that number *one* on the April 1953 draft list of projects was 'Migrant
Assimilation'.

The USEF had in fact already included migration-related research in the previous
year's program, before the 'Project' template was introduced, featuring among requests
for American Research Scholars 'Sub-group B' (or junior research scholars, roughly
equivalent to today's postdoctoral category). In its program document the USEF
highlighted the issue of 'Race Relations', and explained that 'The present large-scale
selective immigration, into a population which is very homogeneous in extraction,
offers opportunities for the study of the development of change of values, beliefs and
attitudes about other ethnic or national groups'. To emphasise the point, the USEF
added that 'The present situation in Australia is analogous to past phases in the history of the United States'. That this area of research should have been bumped up the
following year to the number one research priority indicates the sustained, indeed
growing, interest and concern in this early period in Australia's post-war mass migration scheme.[32]

Australian anxiety about the effects of the new mass migration policy, and a curiosity about how Americans had dealt with immigration's social and cultural impacts,
played out in all sorts of fascinating ways in the ensuing decades of the program. In
1957, the Snowy Mountains Hydro-Electric Scheme, to which thousands of post-war
European migrants were indentured for two-year labour contracts, was proposed
as an 'institution' accredited to receive Fulbright scholars. Senator Fulbright visited
the scheme in 1965.[33] Later, Fulbright scholars of both nationalities played a part in
Australian moves to dismantle the White Australia Policy, helped to develop migration studies in Australia, and explored race relations in the broader sense. One of
those was Bill Ford (postgraduate, 1958). In the United States 'I became aware of
the migrant worker', he said, 'of the sacrifices they were making' for their families,
which no one was looking at in Australia. On his return he started interviewing
workers who were immigrants, which, he says, 'no one had ever done'. Studying
industrial sociology in the United States was eye-opening. 'I could see the beginning of industry relocation ... made me aware I was living in a world of massive
change. I came home with a whole lot of things to do'.[34] From personal friendships he
made he also brought home ideas about how to bring about change in race relations
(discussed in chapter 8).

Coming after Migrant Assimilation in the draft 1955 program was Transportation, seeking scholars who might advance 'an integrated national system of Transportation', followed by Export Trade, broken down into 'marketing, merchandising, display, etc' – a domain in which Americans were considered a leading force. Trade was, of course, an area of considerable political sensitivity in the bi-national relationship, and one in which the American government and businesses had a particular interest in changing existing Australian practices and, in particular, British loyalties. After Australian-American Relations, came 'Increased Productivity', which was broadly interpreted in the context of post-war reconstruction. Last but not least came 'Comparative Studies in Music and the Fine Arts', a category which, it emerged, would struggle to capture sufficient applicant interest or award success until the 1990s.

Several months later, the draft program was revised and Increased Productivity moved up to number one, followed by Migrant Assimilation. At number four was a new priority, 'International Economic Relationships'. Literature was added to Art and Music, and Education was now included along with National Health. The final spot on the list was taken by the extremely broad 'project' of 'Pure and Applied Science'. These changes are evidence of ongoing and (one imagines) robust discussions about the merits of the various areas of research and teaching, between board members representing academia, business and government.

When board members discussed the universities' responses to the proposed 1955 fields, they noted that the number one project area, Increased Productivity, had received the largest number of proposals. But these varied widely, and included recommendations in veterinary science, accountancy, insect physiology and viticulture. Meanwhile, only one suggestion had come in under Migrant Assimilation. This shows that no matter how the board might frame its priorities, universities had their own research agendas and these did not always fit neatly into programming categories. An example of how 'a country's needs' and 'mutual benefit' was an awkward fit was the field of American studies.

American studies

With the deepening of the Cold War, the promotion of American studies became an explicit focus of US cultural diplomacy efforts.[35] This was a boon to scholars around the world studying US society, but it proved problematic, too, for what was still, in the academy, a marginal field. In the post-war period when the world was coming to terms with burgeoning US power, many academics saw American studies as an expression of that power, rather than as a spontaneously developing, legitimate academic field. In their 1965 history of the Fulbright program, Walter Johnson and Francis Colligan discussed the promotion of, and resistances to, American studies throughout the world in the 1950s and 1960s. They found that 'American literature, history and government were not yet well known as established disciplines, and even the most authentic offerings were liable to be suspected by faculty, students, or the public as being simply "propaganda".[36]

We have seen how encouraging American studies overseas was high on the agenda of the BFS from at least 1951.[37] The USEF board indicated its willingness to support scholars in American history and politics when, in the third year of the program it declared: 'Notwithstanding the Fields and Institutions included in the present proposal, the Foundation wishes to emphasize that it considers that at all times a place can be found in the program for a distinguished lecturer in AMERICAN HISTORY or AMERICAN INSTITUTIONS.'[38] However, a BFS proposal in late 1952 for the establishment of an American Studies Institute in Australia, which would hold seminars in American history and literature, caused concern among some board members.[39]

In May 1953, Sir John Latham wrote to US Ambassador Pete Jarman to suggest that the USEF 'should proceed with great caution on the subject of American studies conferences'. He feared 'It might do grave harm if the Fulbright scheme were to run the risk of being charged with passing from the field of general assistance to education as a means of promoting understanding between the USA and other peoples into that of propaganda'.[40] The American Studies Institute was not implemented, and it would be more than half a century (2007) before a US Studies Centre was established, in Sydney. However, American studies in Australia did receive a strong fillip from both visiting US lecturers, of which there were a good number in history, literature and anthropology, and from returning Australian scholars who brought back home a more nuanced understanding of US society, politics and culture, upon which they then drew in their research and teaching of Australian students.[41]

In 1964, Wisconsin historian Merle Curti, one of the founders of the American Studies Association in the United States in the previous decade, visited Australia on a Carnegie grant, and attended the first conference of the newly formed Australian and New Zealand American Studies Association (ANZASA). In 1965 he published an article on 'American Studies Down Under', in which he recognised the significant contribution to the development of the field in Australia of US-based agencies, which he identified as the Carnegie Corporation and 'the State Department, the United States Information Service, and the Fulbright-Hays programme with its Australian and New Zealand commissions or foundations'.[42] It is hardly surprising that American studies should have experienced a boost from the Fulbright Program, despite persistent fears of propagandistic intent amongst many Australian intellectuals.

The more interesting flip-side of this development is that American scholars visiting Australia encouraged the growth of *Australian* studies, which barely existed in academic circles when the Fulbright Program began. Australian history and literature struggled for air in antipodean universities in the early 1950s, resources for serious research were scarce, and a general leaning towards all things British – especially in education and cultural affairs – meant that Australians in higher education tended to devalue local cultural production, as LeRoy Johnson discovered of Australian literature in 1960s Adelaide. Johnson's experience shows that the impact of the Fulbright Program could bring value to the host country by studying its culture. Academic fields were one of the most critical aspects of the exchange program.

'To avoid the problem … of applications with marginal relevance to priority areas'

Fields of study were constantly evolving. In 1954, two new 'project' areas were added to the program proposal for 1956: Pacific Area Studies and Marketing. The Marketing project appears surprisingly early given that the first Australian chair in marketing was not created until 1965; even in the 1970s it was still in its infancy as a freestanding academic discipline. Here was one example of the Fulbright Program seeking to fill a perceived gap in the Australian educational landscape by bringing out American scholars who could help to develop a disciplinary identity. Full marketing programs had existed in US universities since the early 1920s.[43] Public administration also made its first appearance in the 1956 program, drama was added to the list of arts fields, and architecture joined building construction. In the 1956 program preparations for two years hence, law was named for the first time to the project list (even though ten American lawyers had already participated in the program), and social history too.[44] The board also discussed a recommendation by one of its members, Arthur Denning, director of technical education in NSW, that the fields of study be broadened, to embrace areas like adult education, home economics, forestry and printing.[45] These 'Special Categories' awards would support Australians working in fields lying outside traditional academic disciplines, helped to cement new research fields and foreshadowed the eventual creation of a 'Professional' Fulbright award category.

Programming emphases a decade later in the early 1960s reveal how Australian society and the language of those who studied its many aspects were evolving. The programming fields lists looked roughly similar to the 1950s lists, with a few notable changes: in 1961, 'Migration Assimilation' was dropped, and 'Social History' was replaced by 'Social Science', a catch-all embracing social work, econometrics, anthropology, Pacific history, city and regional planning (specifically problems of urban renewal). The board decided in 1961 to give a push to mathematics, in which they agreed there was a crisis in Australia. This was probably prompted by Professor Huxley, board member and vice-chancellor of ANU, who noted an 'acute shortage of teachers of mathematics at all levels', which was being 'aggravated by the increased demand for mathematicians outside the teaching profession'.[46] The other program emphasis was to be American studies – business as usual. Next came 'Secondary Education', a new entry, which might be explained by the passage in that year of the NSW Public Education Act of 1961, based on the Wyndham report of

1957, which radically reshaped secondary education in that state and had national repercussions.[47]

The maths and American studies emphases were maintained for several years. In 1964, the Foundation reported that the mathematics project had been 'entirely successful at all levels' – presumably in attracting recommendations from universities which resulted in award offers to Americans who went on to make strong contributions in the field during their exchange. Three years later, Huxley reported at a special Fulbright planning conference of board members and vice-chancellors that 'the mathematics project mounted a few years ago had had a profound effect on the teaching of mathematics in Australian schools'.[48] In contrast, the American studies project had been disappointing, mainly due to the 'difficulty of obtaining suitable lecturers'. While American studies lived on as a priority area, mathematics dropped down the list and in 1966 was replaced by engineering 'with particular reference to the development of mineral resources'.[49]

There had already been exchanges through the 1950s of geologists whose work had applications in the mining industry. These included the very first Australian Fulbrighter, Max Kennedy, on a Colorado School of Mines scholarship in 1950; Carolyn Fix, a postgraduate geologist who carried out studies in Broken Hill and was profiled in the *Barrier Miner* under the heading 'Woman Geologist Studies B. Hill'[50]; Margaret 'Peggy' Parker, another postgraduate student who, according to a *Sydney Morning Herald* article, planned 'to establish a method of using punched cards and machines to facilitate the integration and analysis of geological data, particularly coal data'. This was cutting-edge stuff, as 'machine-tabulated' punch cards were 'used only on a limited scale in the United States and at present not at all in Australia'.[51] In 1956, Francis Turner, Professor of Petrology at the University of California and 'one of the world's foremost authorities on some aspects of petrological research', came to the ANU.[52] Evidently in 1964 the board believed it was time to add further impetus to this research area. In the Foundation's description and justification of 'Mineral Resources Development' as a project in its 1967 program proposal, the status of the industry was described thus: 'Within the last two years there has been an enormous amount of interest in Australia's mineral resources. For the first time a commercial petroleum field has been brought into production and there has been sharply increased oil exploration in a number of promising areas.' Mentioning resources in Western Australia and Queensland as well, they argued that 'this aspect of Australian development is on the verge of even more spectacular expansion, and the value to the economic position of Australia is tremendous'. They saw the Fulbright exchange of 'experienced workers and academics' in the field as likely to 'play a significant part in this rapid expansion'.[53] Soon after this, the Foundation was in discussions with the Colorado School of Mines about supporting a seminar in Petroleum Exploration and Hard Rock Mining and the eventual creation of a graduate school in Australia. In 1967 it agreed to offer $8,000 towards what it was now calling 'Schools in Mineral and Petroleum Exploration.'[54]

When Senior Scholar Willard ('Bill') Lacy, who had founded the geological engineering course at the University of Arizona, came out to Queensland in 1967, he met up with an American postgraduate Fulbrighter already in the field, his former student Ken Cornelius. He collaborated with Roger Taylor, 'a towering figure in Australian minerals exploration' from whom he 'learned of the Down Under deficiency in the economics and concepts of integrated exploration, mining and metallurgy, and business philosophy in the various geology curricula'. He went on to develop the MSc at James Cook University in Northern Queensland.[55] Presumably the board would have considered the outcome of this 'project' successful in a similar way to the mathematics endeavour.

Changes to programming emphases also reflected developing regional and military concerns in Australian and American society. Directly after the familiar number one 'American studies' project in 1965 came the renamed (expanded) 'Asian and Pacific studies'. This was just two months after the first Australian troops departed for Vietnam and a fortnight after the first national service intake began training. 'Studies associated with mineral resources development' remained high on the list, followed by a new project named tentatively 'Business administration and advanced management'. The board agreed to consult Professor of Economics Russell Mathews at the ANU on the 'correct terminology' for this project title, which indicates that this was considered a new field and one of which none of the board members felt they had sufficient grasp to be sure this was the correct description. In 1966, the Foundation included 'information science' in its list for 1968. The precocity of this proposal (or at least of the use of this vocabulary) becomes apparent when we consider that the first scholar identifying with a variation of this field heading – 'information management' – did not come to Australia for another twenty years.

By 1990, the priority areas were reduced to three, and were identified as international trade issues; practitioners of the arts; and environment (science, law, and industry management). The board advised that the environment priority area 'should emphasise solutions to environmental problems as it was felt that quite a lot of research had already defined what the environmental problems were'.[56] In its response to the new program, the Council for International Exchange of Scholars (CIES) suggested a broadening of priority areas and that 'greater encouragement be given to comparative Australian-American studies'. This led to discussion about the usefulness (or not) of efforts to prioritise, given the 'overall higher standard of applicants in other areas'. Some members argued that they had chosen a 'narrow' defining of areas 'to avoid the problem, manifested in past years, of applications with marginal relevance to priority areas, being "stretched" to fit into a particular priority area category', while others thought this particular program went too far. 'American Studies' was added to the final iteration of the priority area list (it seems they were unable to let this one go), and the Arts area renamed 'Visual and Performing Arts'. The board noted that the inclusion of this particular area had 'partly been a response to the Board of Foreign Scholarships desire to encourage applications in the Humanities'.[57]

In February 1998, the board decided it would no longer include areas of program emphasis in its general award descriptions although some sponsored awards did specify fields. Thus, the Fulbright Program chose to support a breadth of fields, and also facilitated the creation of strong links between a great variety of institutions in both countries, including not only universities but (in Australia) bodies including state-based Water Boards and Electricity Commissions, the Snowy Mountains Hydro-Electric Scheme, and the Australian Council for Educational Research.

These aspects of the program have caused headaches for administrators, and ultimately make accounting for Fulbright 'impacts' almost impossible to gauge because of the great geographical and disciplinary dispersion of scholars' efforts. An important question is to what extent the US and Australian education systems have been shaped by this exchange of scholars? At the administrative or governmental level, negotiating exchange across quite different national/state/regional systems and academic cultures has required administrators to engage directly with and understand those systems. Awards and discipline fields reveal fascinating snapshots of societal and institutional change over the decades, that we explore in the following chapters.

Notes

1 'Shock for Woolmen in U.S. Clothing', *Herald* (Melbourne), 31 March 1951, found in NAA A1838 250/9/8/3 PART 1 (United States of America – Relations with Australia – Requests for Information on Fulbright Agreement). Note there was no byline.
2 'Shock for Woolmen in U.S. Clothing'.
3 See 'A Preliminary Report on Dacetine Ant Studies in Australia' [1954] at https://academic.oup.com/aesa/article-abstract/46/4/465/18205?redirectedFrom=fulltext (accessed 12 May 2018).
4 Russell H. Barrett, *Promises and Performances in Australian Politics, 1928–1959* (New York, 1959). The *Herald* article mentioned his marital status.
5 In 1956 Eberhardt published what was probably his thesis, *The State Electricity Commission of Victoria, Australia, 1918–1951: A Study of a Public Corporation* (University of Kansas, Political Science, 1956). J.G. Hardee published his *Evaluation of an Educational Program with Part-Time Farm Families: Transylvania County, North Carolina, 1955–1960* (Raleigh, Dept. of Rural Sociology, North Carolina State) in 1963 and later produced, with Mohammad Azhar, *Change and Differentials in Men's Knowledge of Attitude Towards and Practice of Family Planning in Pakistan during 1960's* (Islamabad, Pakistan Institute of Development Economics, 1977).
6 Newton's career is briefly outlined in an obituary at www.obitcentral.com/obitsearch/obits/ks/ks-cowley20.htm (accessed 16 August 2012).
7 [n.d. – c. January 1950], 'Summary of P.L.584 – Fulbright Act', handwritten notes by an unnamed External Affairs officer, in A1838 250/9/8/7 PART 1, NAA.
8 Sondra Farganis, née Silverman, response to Survey, La Trobe University, 2011.
9 First USEF Annual Report, 1952 in 'United States of America – Relations with Australia – United States Educational Foundation – General', A1838 250/9/8/4/2 PART 2, NAA, p. 18.
10 Extract from 12 August 1950, letter from Lawrence Power, New York City, to Edgar Russell, Port Pirie, South Australia. In 'United States of America – Relations with Australia – Requests for Information on Fulbright Agreement', A1838 250/9/8/3 PART 1, NAA.

11 Robert LeRoy Johnson, 1963 postgradute scholar, US Scholar report, in A463 1963/
    611, NAA.
12 Norman Abjorensen and James C. Docherty, eds, *Historical Dictionary of Australia*,
    4th edn (London and Lanham, 2014), p. 237.
13 Articles on J. Franklin Hunt's research included: 'Australianese', *Advertiser* (Adelaide),
    2 October 1953, p. 2; 'An American Praises W.A. Speech', *West Australian* (Perth), 24
    July 1953, p. 5; 'American Check On Our Accent', *Advertiser* (Adelaide, SA: 1931–
    1954), 1 October 1953, p. 3.
14 'University College Course in Australian Literature', *Canberra Times*, 19 March
    1954, p. 2; 'Wide Interest in University Literature Course', *Canberra Times*, 30 March
    1954, p. 2.
15 Harry Heseltine, *In Due Season: Australian Literary Studies: A Personal Memoir*
    (Melbourne, 2009), pp. 106–11.
16 15 May 1963, 'Confidential – Patrick Shaw to the Minister (via the Secretary) re
    Cabinet Submission: US Proposal to Extend the Fulbright Programme'. In A1838 583/
    1 part 1, NAA.
17 USEF board minutes, 1950–51.
18 First USEF Annual Report, pp. 15–16.
19 First USEF Annual Report, p. 16.
20 'Department [of State]'s Analysis of the First Year Program in Australia (for the
    academic year 1951–52), II Discussion' in MC 468 Box 114, Bureau of Educational and
    Cultural Affairs Historical Collection (hereafter CU), University of Arkansas Special
    Collections (hereafter UoASC).
21 BFS. Dept Analysis of the 3rd Yr Prog in Australia (Acad yr 1953–54). MC 468 Box
    114, CU, UoASC.
22 USEF board minutes, 25 May 1953.
23 J. William Fulbright, *The Arrogance of Power* (New York, 1966).
24 Summary of Conference Proceedings, 'The Fulbright Program in the Eighties',
    sponsored by the Board of Foreign Scholarships and the US International
    Communication Agency, Washington, DC, 16–17 October 1980, p. 7.
25 AAEF board minutes, 2 August 1984.
26 AAEF Information Booklet, 9th Edition, July 1984, Sect. 2.3, p. 5, cited in AAEF board
    minutes, 2 August 1984.
27 AAEF board minutes, 25 July 1985.
28 'Australian Appetite Amazes American Professor', *Argus* (Melbourne), 1 February
    1955, p. 1.
29 Draft annual report for year 1952, p. 14. A1838 250/9/8/3 Pt2, NAA.
30 USEF board minutes, 27 April 1953.
31 USEF board minutes, 25 May 1953.
32 There is a rich literature on this subject, but titles of particular interest include
    Nicholas Brasch, *Australia's Immigration Policy: 1788–2009* (Sydney, 2009); John
    Higley, John Nieuwenhuysen with Stine Neerup (eds), *Nations of Immigrants: Australia
    and the USA Compared* (Cheltenham, UK and Northampton, MA, 2009).
33 'US Senators in Wagga Tomorrow', *Daily Advertiser* (Wagga Wagga), 25 November
    1965, p. 3; 'Senators Begin Visit to Wagga', *Daily Advertiser* (Wagga Wagga), 27
    November 1965, p. 1; 'Senators Impressed By Our Friendliness – and Our Bread', *Daily
    Advertiser* (Wagga Wagga), 29 November 1965, p. 3.

34 G. W. (Bill) Ford and Alice Garner, *Bill Ford interviewed by Alice Garner in Fulbright scholars oral history project*, National Library of Australia, 2010.

35 On new priority given to American studies, Walter Johnson and Francis Colligan, *The Fulbright Program: A History* (Chicago, 1965), pp. 68–72.

36 Johnson and Colligan, *Fulbright Program*, p. 120. See also Robert Walker, ed., *American Studies Abroad* (Westport, CT, 1975), pp. 5, 9, 23. Also, Walter Johnson, *American Studies Abroad: Progress and Difficulties in Selected Countries. A Special Report from the United States Advisory Commission on International and Cultural Affairs*, July 1963, pp. 8–9, 21–2.

37 Johnson and Colligan, *Fulbright Program*, p. 46.

38 Bureau of Educational and Cultural Affairs Historical Collection (CU) – Series 3. Binational Foundations and Commissions – Program Proposals, in University of Arkansas Special Collections, CU, MC 468: Box 114. Capitalisation in original.

39 24 December 1952, 'Establishment and Operation of Institutes for American Studies Conferences or Similar Projects'. Printed document of 8 pp. sent from USEF to Casey via N. Deschamps (External Affairs), in 1952 United States of America – Requests for information on Fulbright Agreement, A1838 250/9/8/3 PART 3, NAA.

40 Latham to Jarman, 21 May 1953, in Papers of Sir John Latham 1856–1964 (bulk 1890–1964) [manuscript] – MS 1009 – NLA – Series 68 Box 105: Australian-American Relations 1946–63. In a draft report on the February 1953 USEF meeting, External Affairs officer Noël Deschamps explained to his minister that 'Sir John Latham, in a written comment, expressed his fear that this scheme, if carried out, would be understood and represented in many quarters as merely subsidised American propaganda and might defeat its own object. Mr. Rossiter [Executive Officer of USEF] reported that this view was not shared by the Australian Vice-Chancellors' Committee to whom he had submitted it and who were enthusiastic'. In NAA 'United States of America – Relations with Australia – Requests for Information on Fulbright Agreement' in A1838 250/9/8/3 PART 2, NAA. For more on Latham, see Alice Garner and Diane Kirkby, ' "Never a Machine for Propaganda"? The Australian-American Fulbright Program and Australia's Cold War', *Australian Historical Studies*, vol. 44:1 (2013), pp. 117–33.

41 See scholars' reports in pamphlet, USEF, *The Fulbright Programme: The First Eight Years and the Future* (Canberra, 1958).

42 Originally published in *Exchange*, the article was reprinted as an introduction, with a postscript by Norman Harper, to Norman Harper, ed., *Pacific Circle: Proceedings of the Second Biennial Conference of the Australian and New Zealand American Studies Association* (St. Lucia, Qld., 1968), pp. 4–5.

43 Robert B. Ellis and David S. Waller, 'Marketing Education in Australia before 1965', *Australasian Marketing Journal*, vol. 19:2 (2011), pp. 115–21.

44 USEF board minutes, 29 June 1956.

45 USEF board minutes, 29 October 1956.

46 USEF board minutes, 12 September 1961.

47 USEF board minutes, 29 November 1961.

48 From Record of the Sept 23 1967 Special Conference called by the AAEF, in Australian-American Educational Foundation Background Papers for Review Meeting, 3 December 1976, AAFC archives.

49 USEF board minutes, 13 July 1964. On program for 1966.

50 'Woman Geologist Studies B. Hill', *Barrier Miner* (Broken Hill, NSW: 1888–1954), 27 May 1954, p. 2.

51 'Analysis Of Geology Data Done By Cards', *Sydney Morning Herald*, 13 May 1954, p. 4, Section: Women.

52 USEF board minutes, 1 September 1954.

53 UM312 1966/217.

54 AAEF, 28 November 1966 and 3 November 1967.

55 Allen W. Hatheway ad Lothar M. Klingmuller, 'Willard Lacy', A Paper in the AEG Website *Biography* Series, 27 July 2005. Lacy had given Ken Cornelius a positive reference in his Fulbright application, describing him as a 'prodigious worker'. Summary of 1964/65 US candidates, in 'United States Educational Foundation in Australia – Fulbright programme – Policy', A463 1963/611 NAA.

56 AAEF board minutes, 28 November 1990.

57 AAEF board minutes, 26 May 1992.

5

'Meeting [our] domestic Communism problem': Cold War governance and the public university

Geoffrey Rossiter's term of employment as executive officer of the Australian Fulbright Program (1950–64) coincided neatly with Robert Menzies' term as prime minister (1949–66) of the L-CP government. While this provided a stability of policy and direction for the USEF, the neat symmetry also captures the overlap between politics, governance and educational exchange that characterised the Fulbright Program.

Just as the Fulbright Program was being set up in the late 1940s and initiated in the 1950s, the United States became increasingly immersed in its Cold War with the USSR. Devised in late 1945 in a short-lived burst of liberal internationalist optimism, the Fulbright Program had now to be implemented in an environment of deepening distrust, superpower struggle and high nationalist fervour.[1] What did this mean for the program and the Australian universities which provided the candidates for awards and which, as publicly funded institutions, had an important place in national policy making?[2]

As the United States sought to secure allies in its conflict and a new European war threatened, the first five years of the Fulbright Program were particularly fraught. When, in 1948, the French government signed a Fulbright exchange agreement with the US government, the Communist newspaper *L'Humanité* responded by publishing an article claiming that 'every informed man' knew that American professors and students were, 'for the most part … current or future agents of the American information services'.[3] Some historians, looking mainly at Fulbright partnerships with European countries, have similarly seen the program as becoming 'merely another weapon in the crusade against Communism'.[4] Did this mean that in the context of the hardening Cold War, the Australian-American Fulbright Program was being moulded to serve US or Australian government, foreign policy objectives, its scholars exploited for political purposes? Perhaps the more pertinent question is whether the Australian program did at times succumb to deliberate interference, and if so, when and how?

During these tumultuous Cold War years, the Australian Fulbright Program was considered to be an effective arm of the United States' 'soft power' approach in the Asia-Pacific region. Despite this, contained within its core was the program's need to be independent of government if it was to succeed. Academics going on exchange programs were not and did not wish to be confused with public servants, government agents, parliamentarians or political actors, whatever their own individual political views. Managing the tension between adherence to government-imposed policy and funding, and avoidance of becoming simply an instrument of government, was a constant challenge for program administrators. It was particularly marked in this initial period of Australia's program when it was susceptible to the descending force of global Cold War geopolitics.

The pattern of juggling political pressure to conform, against the maintenance of an independent identity, is recognisable now with historical hindsight as a distinguishing feature of Fulbright history. This was an intense period of legislative and political activity against the perceived threat of domestic Communism in both Australia and the United States. This timing, as well as a striking crossover between key figures involved in both the Fulbright Program's administration and leaders in anti-Communist activism in Australia, reveals a complex interplay of forces that cannot simply be characterised as interference.

Avoiding propaganda

The incoming L-CP government of Robert Menzies in December 1949 was ideologically committed to defeating Communism both domestically and abroad. Its success at the polls was partly due to a crippling strike by coalminers supposedly orchestrated by the Communist Party of Australia (CPA) and damaging to the ALP. In February 1950, a US information officer reported from Sydney that the new L-CP government was 'committed by platform to destroy Communism in Australia. How America has met and is meeting her domestic Communism problem has become a matter of serious study by Australian officials'.[5] National defence was a priority and soon the Australian government signed two new treaties with the United States: the ANZUS Pact in 1951, and SEATO in 1954. These treaties formed an alliance for the mutual defence of the signatories, that in reality, drew Australia deeper into the military orbit of America's Cold War, first in the Korean War (1950–53) and a decade later, into war in Vietnam.

Ideological battles raging in this period and a hot war in Korea were shaping factors on the Australian Fulbright Program's administration and programming. The deepening Cold War accompanied the two governments' drawn-out negotiation of the terms of the exchange agreement through the late 1940s and the program's first five years of operation. When the scheme was finally in full swing, in 1953, Cold War concerns were already at a peak.

It is undeniable that the US government engaged in propaganda during the Cold War and that it exploited activities including information, cultural and educational exchanges, in its struggle to win the hearts and minds of people throughout the western and non-aligned world.[6] Recent scholarship exploring American anti-Communist propaganda in Europe, however, is a caution about the limits to the success of such 'public/cultural diplomacy'. Especially in areas which had strong anti-American cultures, the 'penetration and impact of such policies were sometimes less than expected.[7] Propaganda was not a subtle tactic and not workable as a tool of persuasion and manipulation when local resistance was strong. If this was true of mass or popular culture, was it not also and perhaps even more true among students, teachers and scholars, who were wary of the United States and claimed intellectual freedom as a core tenet? Australia's Fulbright Program illuminates this point.

It seemed that Australia might well be following the United States' anti-Communism path. One of the first acts of the new government was to introduce a bill to ban the Communist Party of Australia. Prime Minister Menzies presented the Communist Party Dissolution Bill to the House of Representatives on 27 April 1950. Percy Spender, the new minister for External Affairs, had sat on the sub-committee which drafted the Communist Party Dissolution Bill, during which time his departmental staff began to keep a file on 'Subversive Activities – Proposed United States legislation'.[8] Spender was *ex officio* a member of the new Fulbright board.

Suspicions about the Fulbright Program's stated goal of 'mutual understanding' might well have swelled in the breasts of Australian sceptics, Communists and fellow travellers upon discovering that several Australian public figures prominent in investigations into and campaigns against the Communist Party had been named as Fulbright board members between 1950 and 1953. According to the terms of the Agreement, US Ambassador Jarman was honorary chairman, with veto power, and in naming the three other Americans on the board he chose two foreign service officers – employees of the US government – and one American resident in Australia, a private businessman, not an academic or public official. Spender and Jarman then together chose the three (later four) Australians.[9] One of them was Victorian chief justice and chancellor of the University of Melbourne, Sir Charles Lowe.

The day after Menzies introduced his anti-CPA bill into the House of Representatives, Justice and now Fulbright board member Lowe, submitted his 242-page, handwritten 'Report of the Royal Commission Inquiring into the Origins, Aims, Objects and Funds of the Communist Party in Victoria and Other Related Matters' to the Victorian Parliament.[10] Justice Lowe made no specific recommendations, and his conduct of the inquiry was widely praised as even-handed (including by Communist Party lawyer Ted Hill).[11] Yet the voluminous findings in the report would furnish plenty of material useful to the anti-Communist press. One editorial declared, for example, that Lowe's report supplied 'justification for the most drastic and sweeping purge of the "Red" element in our national life'.[12] This proved useful the following year to those drafting the new anti-Communism bill the Menzies government was bringing in, this time to change the constitution by referendum.

Spender was closely involved in regional campaigns to eradicate Communism. A month before the first Fulbright board meeting, Spender travelled to a meeting of Commonwealth foreign ministers in Ceylon, where work had begun on the scheme offering material and technical aid and training to developing countries in the Commonwealth (and later, beyond). The Colombo Plan's key goal was to shore up support for the Free World in regions considered vulnerable to Communism. Spender played a key role in the set-up of the scheme and made regular public pronouncements explaining its purpose.[13]

After the CPA and ten unions, with former minister Evatt as the barrister leading the case, successfully challenged the constitutionality of the CP Dissolution Act, the anti-Communist membership of the Fulbright board was strengthened by the appointment of former Chief Justice, Sir John Latham. He had been the sole dissenting judge when six out of seven judges on the Full Bench of the High Court annulled the CP Dissolution Act. Latham was a well-known anti-Communist, going back to his inter-war years as a conservative parliamentarian. As Federal Attorney-General in 1926, he had amended the Crimes Act to enable the declaration of 'revolutionary and seditious' organisations as unlawful, a move aimed at the Communist Party.[14] Following the High Court decision in 1951, Latham went against judicial protocol and advised his old colleague Menzies on the wording of the government's next attempt at banning the Party: the 1951 Referendum Bill.[15] Then, upon retirement in late 1952, Latham was invited to join the Australian Fulbright board, soon after giving a speech in Brisbane in which he praised the 'role of US in fight against Com etc'.[16] Latham took on the Fulbright directorship with gusto, eventually became chairman of the board, and remained there until 1961.[17]

Latham's Fulbright invitation had come from Richard Casey, the new minister for External Affairs replacing Spender, who was sent to Washington as ambassador in early 1951. When Casey had been the Australian minister to Washington (1940–42), he befriended Dean Acheson, then assistant secretary of state.[18] Before becoming minister, Casey was already well known for his calls for purges of Australian Communists and fellow travellers. Even though he claimed to be appalled by Senator Joseph McCarthy's tactics in the United States, his May 1952 accusation that the Australian public service was a 'nest of traitors' invited comparisons with the infamous red-baiter and he cultivated CIA activities in Australia.[19]

McCarthy was at this time attacking the US State Department for harbouring fellow travellers and promoting un-American material in USIS libraries abroad. Foreign service officers in the field – two of whom always sat on the Australian Fulbright board – were on notice. The detailed reports embassy and consular officers sent to the State Department from Australia over this period reveal the extent to which Cold War thinking and strategies shaped their working lives. In their despatches, they described their goals, operational environment and the extent and success (or otherwise) of a range of activities in their USIE (Information and Exchange) work. In a confidential despatch of February 1950, Sydney-based officer Thomas Alexander outlined the 'basic aims and objectives of the USIE program' in Australia. The first goal was 'To acquaint Australians with all facets of American life, in part to the end that Australia may understand America and her role of leadership against Communism and thus be induced, as a South Pacific partner, to share responsibility in the cause of international peace'.[20]

So, Alexander's information work was not simply about acquainting Australians with the 'American way of life', but was explicitly directed towards ensuring their support for US Cold War foreign policy. Although he was not specifically discussing the Fulbright Program here, Alexander was outlining the general approach to information and cultural work that informed the team's day-to-day labours – a small, multi-tasking team stretched over a vast continent.[21]

These officers were involved not only in selling the American story to their number one 'priority target group' – 'middle class, white collar workers' who could be influenced by 'dramatic cultural programs such as art, theater and student exchange'[22] – but also in coordinating behind-the-scenes efforts to undermine Communism within Australian unions. In January 1951 they revised their priority targets and Labor unions and politicians were given top slot.[23] Declaring that 'Communist power in the unions must be broken', the strategy was to support anti-Communist labour officials, 'pumping them with hard facts, methods and ideas they can use'.[24] In July 1952, US officers reported having arranged publication and distribution of political leaflets accredited to local groups (or fronts) and which were designed to be (they explained) ' "in key" as to printing style, typography, and paper-stock with regular indigenous Commie [*sic*] and anti-Commie leaflets'. They argued, with no apparent sense of irony, that this was necessary because 'No American source can have this impact. Indeed, any American source strongly weakens the impact of any leaflet, since it strengthens the Commie theme that America is meddling in internal Australian affairs, and trying to tell Labor what to do'.[25]

Central to President Truman's 'Campaign of Truth', which shaped USIS officers' modus operandi from April 1950, was the claim that only a liberal democracy could guarantee its citizens intellectual and personal freedom from interference by the state. The problem for this particular liberal democracy was, of course, how to sell such a message without appearing to tell people what or how to think. Information (or propaganda) advocates acknowledged that educational exchange had a role to play here, but they also considered it a less effective weapon than other, 'faster' strategies available.

In his 1950 report, Alexander envisaged 'Exchange of Persons', including Fulbright awards as well as the more politicised State Department Leader and Specialist grants, as 'the most glamorous USIE program in Australia'. He also argued that, despite Australian interest in such opportunities, exchanges would make a smaller contribution to the key USIE 'objectives' in Australia than the 'purely cultural and information aspects'. He considered that 'three months of full operation of press, motion pictures, radio, and libraries might make more qualitative impact on Australian thinking and of course infinitely more quantitative, than say, fifty Australians and "leaders or specialists" visiting in America for a year'.[26]

This was one salvo in a lively and sometimes acrimonious debate in the United States throughout this period over the relative merits of 'fast' and 'slow' approaches to cultural diplomacy, a debate to which Senator Fulbright addressed himself from time to time, always defending the long-term benefits of exchange. So, while the Fulbright Program lay within the fast-growing web of Cold War cultural diplomacy, it was treated as something of a different beast from more overtly politicised, sharply targeted campaigns, for it would not reliably serve short-term foreign policy agendas.

The close involvement of these early Fulbright board members, Australian and American, in anti-Communist campaigns is undeniable. This did not necessarily mean, however, that the exchange program itself was distorted or politicised. Although there were significant pressures on the program to reinforce US government foreign policy goals in partner countries, there were some strong protective forces working against politicisation of the Australian program, ensuring that the exchange scheme retained its educational integrity in the eyes of academics. This may not have been true everywhere in the Fulbright world.

As Fulbright's bill wended its way through congressional processes in 1945–46 and the wartime accommodation between the United States and the Soviet Union gave way, ideological differences re-emerged in new and ugly forms. With Truman's administration developing its Soviet containment strategy along the lines of diplomat George Kennan's famous 'X' telegram of February 1946, supporters of educational and cultural exchange started to fear that the Fulbright scheme's 'mutual understanding' goal might be undermined by short-term foreign policy aims. So Fulbright sought to build in some protective mechanisms against politicisation of his program, ensuring, for example, that a national board of educationalists (the US BFS) would oversee general program policy; that administration would be split between the State Department and several non-government agencies specialising in student and academic services, as well as bi-national commissions or foundations in partner countries; and that selection would be carried out primarily by academics. The administrative architecture could never be completely watertight, but it denied a concentration of power in the hands of any one organisation or government department.[27]

We have seen in an earlier chapter, how the Australian–US Fulbright Agreement was painstakingly negotiated by the Chifley ALP government, specifically by Evatt's External Affairs staff, over a period infamous for difficult Australian–US diplomatic relations. A litany of misunderstandings, mutual suspicion and frustration marked these three years (1946–49) of haggling over Fulbright terms – years which saw the Czech oslovakian coup, the Berlin blockade, the Chinese revolution and, in Australia, the seven-week NSW coalminers' strike. Despite some knotty areas of disagreement, however, Evatt, his secretary John Burton and officers, along with Treasury, Post-War Reconstruction and Office of Education staff, managed to carve out an agreement on the exchange program with Acheson and the State Department, that was more favourable to Australians than it may have been had they been less stubborn about specific clauses. The nature of this agreement would become important as the Cold War deepened domestic tensions both in Australia and in the United States.

The Americans' strongly expressed desire to see the scheme in operation may have, on the one hand, raised suspicions amongst some Australians that it represented a new form of imperialism. On the other hand, as discussed in detail in chapter 1, it opened up some room for the Australian negotiators to push for a greater say in local Fulbright administration than the Americans initially wanted to give. And so the Australian negotiators *did* push, much to the annoyance of the State Department, with whom Evatt was already highly unpopular. External Affairs' desire to negotiate the Fulbright Agreement as equal partners with the United States was seen as apiece with Evatt's jockeying for greater Australian influence on the international stage, which the US government found irritating, and even 'embarrassing'. The 'mutual understanding' that the program proposed to nurture was not much in evidence during this crucial establishment period. US and British suspicions of security leaks attributed to External Affairs staff further undermined the relationship.[28]

External Affairs' determination to ensure a meaningful Australian say on the local administration of the Fulbright Program – to make it as truly 'bi-national' as possible despite the great disparity in wealth and power between negotiating nations – stood the program in good stead in the Cold War context. American officials could not ignore the Australians' strong conception of an educational partnership and a meaningful, two-way exchange.

This last point is a crucial one, because the Fulbright Program was an educational scheme, and it had therefore to gain the respect and interest of the academic community in Australia – students, lecturers and researchers. This was a community that US foreign service officers and some Australian anti-Communists characterised as 'pinkish' and, more often than not, anti-American.[29] According to one US foreign service officer, higher education in Australia was an area 'where doctrinaire Marxism makes inroads'.[30] This anti-Americanism was as much due to deep-rooted intellectual connections to Oxbridge, as it was to any political tendencies. At the same time, this was also a community for whom the free exchange of ideas was a core professional value. All this made for tricky territory for anyone tempted to use the new exchange program for bald political purposes.

US information officers reflected quite regularly in their reports on Australian intellectuals' resistance to US government messages. In a 1951 report sent to Washington from Sydney, one officer noted that 'cultural leaders' through whom USIE connected with the Australian public, though 'friendly', nevertheless 'recognize themselves and USIE immediately to be respectively "buyer" and "seller" and the normal resistances in such circumstances prevail'. This resistance was compounded by a 'suspicion of anything a government tells him, be it his own or American' and complicated, the officer claimed, by 'an envy of America and a sensitiveness caused by his feeling of inferiority'. As a result, the officer advised against 'the direct approach', unless used 'with full knowledge of the Australian personality'.[31]

So, even though US foreign service officers who sat on the Fulbright board were using highly politicised, anti-Soviet language in their confidential reports to the Department of State, along 'Campaign of Truth' lines, and though Spender was making explicit links between the new Colombo Plan and the fight against Communism in Asia, this strong ideological speak was absent from the Fulbright board minutes and from public statements about the program in Australia. The neutrality of the language of the Australian Fulbright board records, concerned solely with the mechanics of the program's administration, is striking compared to the hyperbolic public statements emanating from both US and Australian governments at the time. The fact is, the board members – and the Foundation's first executive officer, Geoffrey Rossiter – knew their academic market. In the higher education world, ideals of academic independence and freedom of political expression were alive and well – even if under threat and often observed more in the word than the substance of action.[32]

Figure 5.1 Professor Zelman Cowen, Dean of the Faculty of Law, University of Melbourne, with Sarawakian student Abang Bohari bin Datu Abang Yan who was studying law under the Colombo Plan, 1955

In 1952, US Information officers claimed in despatches that their new, harder-hitting approach to Campaign of Truth efforts in Australia was proving effective in curbing Communist influence in the unions. This vigorous and targeted campaign may, however, have backfired, if pursued in the world of potential Fulbright applicants. The Melbourne-based US public affairs officer noted 'considerable concern among the university "intellectuals" over what they consider or term the "anti-communist hysteria" in the United States and its effect on academic freedom'.[33]

The Cold War university

On 13 September 1951, the Political Science Society of the University of Melbourne held a public meeting on the looming Communist Party Dissolution Referendum. A thousand students overflowed into the aisles and pressed against the walls to hear three professors, all of whom, for different reasons, counselled a 'No' vote.[34] The meeting's convenor, MacMahon Ball, warned of a more general threat to 'independent thinking'.[35] Professor Pansy Wright argued that 'We are being asked to grant powers proper to a despotic State, but not proper for a democracy', while Professor R.M. (Max) Crawford thought repressing the Communist Party would only create more 'sympathisers', and doubted the ability of 'even judges and statesmen' to determine with any certainty whether someone was a Communist or not. Professor Zelman Cowen, dean of law, acknowledged that he had supported Menzies' earlier (and overturned) Communist Party Dissolution Bill, but argued that the constitutional changes proposed in the referendum went too far and would threaten basic civil liberties.[36] Sympathy for Communism was not always the basis for opposition to the referendum, as the arguments of the University of Melbourne professors made clear.

The chancellor of the university, Sir Charles Lowe, was on the Fulbright board. At the University Council meeting following the debate, he expressed concern about the use of university property for events (like this one) that might be seen as partisan. A highly publicised outcry ensued, with the Student Representative Council warning that 'No group of people has the right to deny us our right to express ourselves'.[37] Lowe, appalled at the public response to his statement, claimed he was seeking only to protect students from professors' abuse of 'prestige and authority', and declared that the university 'should provide a forum in which all views can be discussed but [was] never a machine for propaganda'.[38] So, the meeting's supporters and Lowe were, in essence, levelling similar charges at each other, each claiming to be reacting against some form of 'propaganda' or limitation on free speech.

Notwithstanding his public opposition to the referendum, Zelman Cowen won a Fulbright award to the United States, in 1953. This was Cowen's second trip across the Pacific, and it gave him (among many other things) a disturbing, close-up view of the effects of the Cold War on academic freedom.[39] He was particularly impressed by the actions of his friend and mentor Erwin Griswold, dean of the Harvard Law School, who 'stood firm' against McCarthyist attacks on freedom of speech and the fifth amendment, at a time, as Cowen put it, 'when strong men turned to jelly'.[40] Cowen would later publish a biographical piece on Latham, in which he criticised the Chief Justice's dissent on the High Court case, implying that his anti-Communism skewed his legal reasoning in this matter.[41]

Professor Crawford, the Professor of History at Melbourne University, kept a file on the 1951 university referendum debate that included his colleague, political scientist W. MacMahon Ball's defence of the meeting. In 1958, Crawford was granted a Fulbright Senior Scholar award, even though, nine years earlier, he had encountered difficulties obtaining a visa to enter the United States to take up a CCNY grant, apparently because of his past involvement with Australia-Soviet House. Crawford, like Cowen, featured on the newly created Australian Security and Intelligence Organisation (ASIO)'s 'D' list of academics, whose political affiliations were unclear, but who were at the very least considered 'free-thinkers' and who were therefore being watched.[42]

Crawford had sought to overcome the US visa hurdle with the help of his colleague at Melbourne University, historian Norman Harper, a well-connected Americanist and another early Australian Fulbrighter. While in Chicago on a joint Fulbright/Carnegie Corporation-funded trip, Harper wrote to Colonel Charles Spry, director of the still young ASIO, in Crawford's defence. This was in March 1951, the same month the High

Court struck down the CP Dissolution Bill.[43] Harper was still overseas at the time of the referendum, but he was a regular correspondent through the 1950s and beyond with American and Australian Fulbrighters, and also with US foreign service officers – consuls general, public and cultural affairs officers. These connections, as well as his intellectual and personal interest in foreign affairs, point towards another element in this story: the role of the United States Information Service (USIS, and, from 1953, USIA) in Australia in supporting the administration of the Fulbright Program and other exchanges between Australia and the United States, in making American literature and films available to the Australian public (and teachers) in a time of severe import restrictions, and (of special relevance to the referendum question) in bolstering anti-Communist activism in Australian unions.[44]

This tapestry of links illustrates how the Fulbright scheme brought higher education into the orbit of foreign policy, as well as the extent to which debates about (and attacks on) Communism were central to the experience of both administrators and participants in the scheme. At the same time, even this cursory depiction reveals the complexity of positions, individual and institutional, that warn us against making any simplistic assumptions about the Fulbright Program's role in the Cold War.

Resisting politicisation

In early 1953, as the Republican Eisenhower administration came to power, political developments in the United States began to threaten more directly the image of the Fulbright Program in Australia. At this time a struggle was taking place in the United States over the appropriate administrative home for educational exchange. The head of a proposed new information agency (USIA) to be carved off from the State Department, sought to retain educational exchange as a 'hard core' to lend the propaganda program 'greater strength and greater credibility'.[45] Senator Fulbright and others opposed this move, arguing for educational exchange to remain with the State Department.[46] In July 1953, in a televised Senate Appropriations Committee hearing, Republican Senator Joseph McCarthy attacked the Fulbright Program directly, as part of a broader assault he had been waging on the State Department, which he accused of being riddled with Communists and fellow travellers.[47]

In a case that made the front page of *New York Times*, the American Civil Liberties Union protested the State Department's rescinding of a Fulbright scholarship which had been granted to a Brooklyn College classics professor, Napthali Lewis, to go to Italy. Despite the fact that there was no evidence that Lewis had any Communist background, his wife, Helen Block Lewis, a psychoanalyst, had refused to testify to the House UnAmerican Activities Committee, or HUAC, about her possible past membership of the Communist Party. Senator McCarthy believed cancelling the scholarship was an excellent idea.[48] Senator Fulbright stood up to McCarthy, stressed the independence of the BFS from the State Department, and, according to BFS member and historian Walter Johnson, mounted the 'first successful resistance to McCarthy within the government since his [McCarthy's] premier appearance on the national scene in 1950'.[49]

Board members reading US Fulbright grantees' reports coming into the Canberra office in 1952–53 could not ignore the impact of McCarthyism. One grantee reported that Australians regularly asked him why 'you let McCarthy get away with it?'; another scholar noted a 'common misconception [that] McCarthy is the most important person in the United States'; a social worker reported that Australians were most interested in 'Household appliances, clothes, and book-burnings or witch-hunts', and a research scholar in government and constitutional law noted that 'many of the more thoughtful Australians are just now more interested in and fearful of America's Internal Security program and her foreign policy'.[50] Australian newspapers were full of articles critical of McCarthy and the sensationalist Senate committee hearings then being conducted.

At this point former Chief Justice Latham joined the USEF board. We have briefly outlined some of his contributions to anti-Communist campaigns in his political and judicial career. There is much more to Latham, however, than this. Before the First World War, Latham had taught philosophy and law at Melbourne University, so the academic world was familiar to him. He was also a confirmed atheist and founding member of the Rationalist Association in Victoria. In the later 1950s, even while president of the Australian Association for Cultural Freedom, which established the magazine *Quadrant* under the editorship of Catholic convert and fervently anti-Communist poet (and Fulbright scholar!) James McAuley, Latham helped keep the competitor publication, left-wing literary magazine *Meanjin*, from folding, by talking to Prime Minister Menzies, and, later, to Melbourne University Vice-Chancellor George Paton.[51] He was not alone among anti-Communists to consider McCarthy's techniques as beyond the pale.

Latham had a long-standing interest in scholarly exchange, and was surely aware of debates in the United States over the relationships between information programs and educational exchange.[52] When the BFS communicated to the Australian Fulbright Foundation its hopes for 'the establishment of an Institute for American Studies conferences to conduct seminars on certain aspects of American studies', to be financed out of Fulbright funds and 'which might be attended by both American and Australian nationals',[53] Latham led the resistance to this proposal. He understood that if the program were tainted with the accusation of being propagandistic, at a time when Australians were intensely interested in and, for the most part, appalled by McCarthyist developments in the US, its future would be thrown into question.[54]

At its next May meeting, the USEF board resolved to inform the State Department that some members 'entertained fears' that holding American studies conferences might be read 'in some quarters, as an instrument of propaganda rather than a bona fide academic objective'.[55]

Early the following year, the new US ambassador, Amos Peaslee, reported that the board continued 'to look with suspicion upon any suggested procedures or activities, the implementation of which might give rise to criticisms of using the Fulbright program for propaganda purposes'.[56] One proposal it rejected concerned the 'utilization of rejected applicants', whom the embassy hoped to approach for public speaking engagements.[57] That Latham's concern for the program's integrity was being fed by political developments in the United States is suggested by a November 1953 *Argus* article in which he criticised American-style committees of inquiry, hoping that 'we'll not find ourselves led into any such methods', while declaring that 'it could easily happen'.[58] So it turns out that the Fulbright Program had in Latham a committed protector against politicisation, even while he continued to engage in anti-Communist activism, notably in his work for the Australian Committee for Cultural Freedom from 1954. Anti-Communism could be subtle in its strategy.

Meanwhile, Richard Casey, minister for External Affairs, and *ex officio* a Fulbright director, was actively developing Australian propaganda strategies to shore up anti-Communism in Southeast Asia. He saw the Colombo Plan as an essential element in this effort.[59] Ironically, this probably acted as another protective factor for the Fulbright Program in Australia. In the board minutes (as discussed in the previous chapter) we see a resistance to BFS suggestions, delivered via the State Department, that Fulbright annual programming be organised in terms of 'projects'.[60] This was the language of foreign aid – the language of the Colombo Plan – and the Australian government did not want to see itself as a passive recipient of US largesse. Casey was seeking to position Australia's identity in the Asia-Pacific region as somewhere 'between the Cold War power blocs and the values they appeared to represent' – a kind of *juste milieu*.[61] Just as Evatt and his staff had insisted on negotiation as 'equals', Casey's External Affairs department resisted being lumped in with other, less developed countries that they themselves were targeting with 'psychological warfare' strategies.[62] This increased Australian sensitivity to anything resembling propaganda flowing from the US end into Fulbright board discussions.

Another protective factor lies with the Fulbright scholars themselves. We have ample evidence that the political pressures on the program we have described did not determine the quality of scholars' experiences or reactions in Australia or the United States, and that the Fulbright Program in Australia could distinguish between political activism and academic activity.[63] Most spent a year or more overseas on exchange, time to make up (or unmake) their own minds about their host society and culture in the context of day-to-day living and working. Indeed, many younger Fulbrighters lived in International House accommodation and met and befriended and argued with scholars from all over the world, offering them an exhilarating range of political, religious and social perspectives, on the United States and on their home countries. Their very varied experiences could never be squeezed into the straitjacket of USIS 'country objectives'.

The Fulbright Program was not devised primarily as a vehicle for propaganda (or its euphemism 'information'), as were some other schemes like the Department of State's Leader and Specialist program, Voice of America or USIS films.[64] It was not a simple instrument of State Department policy. Nevertheless in the Cold War battle for the hearts and minds of intellectuals and scholars, the goals of 'mutual understanding' enshrined in the Fulbright Program of international educational exchange were undoubtedly at risk of collapsing into the more limited unilateral goals of US foreign policy. It could indeed be hard to tell the difference. It seems the Australian Fulbright

Program, certainly in its very earliest years, and thanks to the persistence of Australian External Affairs negotiators who won a fairer Australian representation on the board, was better prepared to navigate these boundaries. It steered a course clear of crude manipulation, even though it was subjected to pressures and may even have been vulnerable to CIA penetration.[65] As a scheme, it illustrated the 'complex mix of public and private organisations' operating from the 1940s onwards in which anti-Communism was rarely a crude mechanistic tactic.[66]

The philosophy of liberal internationalism and academic freedom on which the Fulbright scheme was founded, combined with the rejection by most Australian public officials of McCarthy-like tactics and a refusal to be cast as recipients of US foreign aid or propaganda, meant a solid foundation stone was laid. In these crucial initial years, the Australian Fulbright Program succeeded largely in maintaining a level of independence from overt interference from either the US (State Department) or Australian (LC-P coalition) government. Tensions were not absent and did not abate however. Issues of government interference resurfaced constantly over the life of the program which, with its dependence on government funding, sat awkwardly in an increasingly hardline, bitter campaign against domestic Communism.

In 1959, the *New York Times* reported on another distinguished professor who had been refused a Fulbright award on the dubious grounds of 'loyalty'. The screening committee had recommended history professor Bert J. Loewenberg of Sarah Lawrence College in Mississippi to the BFS who instead awarded the grant to the committee's second-choice candidate. Academic groups along with the American Civil Liberties Union mobilised widely to demand a review, which found the BFS policy contained worrying opportunities for loose and secretive interpretation. Although there were 'no overt prescriptions of political or social orthodoxy, or of conformity', the requirement that candidates should be 'associated with desirable personal qualities … and identifiability as a pleasant type of American citizen' were potentially excluding individuals whose views might not be in line with the government's. The BFS policy on loyalty and disloyalty was subsequently changed.[67]

Universities were deeply affected by Cold War battles. The Cold War climate enhanced political interest in the national importance of higher education. For example, Cold War anxieties 'focussed attention on the role that universities might play through their science and technology expertise and research'.[68] It thus ushered in a period of increased government funding for universities. This was true of both US and Australian institutions.[69] The federal government embarked on an expansion of the higher education sector and began to pour money into institution building. The Cold War also 'paved the way for increased government scrutiny and policy control of all aspects of university life … [in] debates about science and technology and the humanities and academic and student subjectivities and power relations'.[70] Pressure was brought to bear on those who were employed in the sector. Australian higher education histories often touch on the Cold War pressures that were placed on university personnel and policies, though a full systematic investigation has yet to be undertaken.

Australian universities underwent substantial change in the post-war period. Commonwealth-funded scholarships for students from poorer backgrounds, and ex-servicemen's scholarships for an older (and more experienced) group, opened up educational opportunities to a broader pool of students.[71] There was also an expansion in tertiary education as part of the ALP government's post-war reconstruction plans, which included the establishment of the modern Commonwealth Scientific and Industrial Research Organisation (CSIRO) (by legislation in 1949) and the ANU (by legislation passed in 1946). The L-CP government continued this expansion, setting up a Commonwealth committee of inquiry into the universities in 1950.[72] The Murray Report was preoccupied with the Cold War and the economic and strategic standing of Australia. 'Through discursive repetition of phrases such as "the free world", a "democratic country", "the nations of the West" throughout the Murray Report, Australian universities are repositioned as institutions at the forefront of Cold War competition for economic, scientific and military supremacy. They are constructed as essential contributors to the defence of Western democratic government and knowledge production.'[73]

The Fulbright scheme is rightfully positioned as part of this expansion of tertiary educational opportunity. The exchange scheme played a valuable role in the growth of tertiary education and research. The new national university (ANU) was to become an important pivot in the educational exchange of scholars between Australia and the United States in providing and receiving scholars for the scheme. The first scholars to arrive under the Fulbright Program in Australia coincided with the first academics to arrive at ANU. The founding vice-chancellor of ANU, Douglas Copland, who had been suggested for the USEF/Fulbright board, was an economist who had been selected as the Rockefeller Foundation's Australian and New Zealand representative on the Laura Spelman Rockefeller memorial (fund) in 1925. He had forged links with the international community when he visited 'key universities, business schools, agricultural colleges, research institutes, government departments and banks in the United States of America, Canada, Britain and Europe'. Through this work, Copland had created opportunities for overseas scholars to visit Australia and for Australians to study abroad. Copland was an adviser to the wartime ALP government 1941–45, and at war's end was appointed Australian minister to China. He attended the first session of the United Nations General Assembly. Copland urged closer economic ties with the United States, and was 'outspoken on government policy', although trying to exert influence was 'not always popular with the government'. He left ANU in 1953 to become high commissioner to Canada.[74]

The Fulbright Program also became a major, if unobtrusive, player in the reorientation towards the United States of intellectual elites in post-war Australia. The Fulbright Program facilitated the emergence of the United States as a destination for future academic and intellectual leaders, replacing British universities and reorienting Australian higher education institutions towards the United States, widening the resources pool and the recruitment of talent. In 1974 Fulbright Senior Scholar to Australia Henry Albinksi recognised this transformation when he said that the British tradition that had dominated Australian universities for so long had also 'depressed the flowering of a vigorous intellectual atmosphere'. Reorienting this culture towards the US model brought 'a far more professional and even personal cosmopolitanism among Australian university faculties'.[75] This was an influence on Australian academic life in which the Fulbright Program had surely played a significant part. Peter I. Rose, in his 1976 *Academic Sojourners* report based on a series of interviews with Fulbright scholars, noted in his section titled 'The Americanization of the Australian University' that 'One after another of those interviewed claimed that the character of Australian academic life had been changing from a British orientation to an American one'. This view, he pointed out, 'was heard over and over from coast to coast'.[76]

Influence also went the other direction, although perhaps more at the individual level. 'I was ahead of the curve on interdisciplinary work when I returned to America in '66', a scholar reported, 'because ANU was less discipline bound than most American institutions of comparable intent'. She returned to acquire a teaching position 'and I was perceived as a bit of an academic rebel because of my criticisms of tradition bound disciplines'. Her years at ANU 'both spoiled me when I went back home and gave me an edge (in the sense that I saw ahead of time where the academy would be going)'.

'ANU was ... a rare moment of discovery', to this American Fulbright student, 'as so many graduates (esp. in the social sciences and humanities) ... who could not find many doctoral possibilities in Australia, were ready to engage ANU'. These students and the staff 'brought a maturity and set of lived experiences that made Australian education in general and ANU in particular a perfect intellectual storm'. She could not know then 'how important it would be for me', but she later recalled that 'my sub-sequent career moves benefitted in a way not clear at the time. I learned the value of doing traditional philosophy so that i could elevate the impact of my more narrow studies. i certainly learned the value of talking with all kinds of folk at the university on what i was interested in and why and solicited answers about their own work. i truly learned about collegiality'.[77]

Universities – especially the ANU, which was the solitary university funded by the Commonwealth – were vulnerable to interference from the government. The ANU Research School of Social Sciences and the Research School of Pacific Studies were regarded as 'fairly red'. As early as 1948 the registrar of the ANU was 'trying to avoid the Liberal Party and the Country Party zeal for witch hunting' even while they were in Opposition. By 1951, two years into its period in government, ASIO began 'a systematic appraisal of all academics whose files contained "adverse reports"'. Such harassment and surveillance was by no means confined to the ANU, and neither was ASIO's attention confined to academic appointments nor to academics per se. As one historian has said, 'ANU was sometimes placed in situations that undermined its avowed commitment to uphold academic and political freedom, notably its practice of volunteering the names of applicants to ASIO for security screening'.[78]

At first ASIO had concentrated on scientists in the CSIRO. Historians have shown how ASIO monitored staff at the University of Melbourne, drawing up a list of names and classifying those whose loyalty was in doubt. There were four categories: known members of the Communist Party; suspected members; sympathisers; and those for whom there was insufficient evidence to place them into one of the other catergories. In 1951 there were sixty-three names, two-thirds of them in this last category.[79]

The surveillance was extensive and primarily targeted reformers, radicals and progressives.[80] Charles Spry, who was appointed as the director-general of ASIO, was concerned about universities appointing staff who, as he told the prime minister, were 'likely to infect students with subversive doctrines'. He also argued that travelling to foreign countries was likely to mean them being refused entry, which would reflect adversely not only on the university employing them but also on the government. For his part, Menzies wanted to limit the employment of staff who might be either Communists or sympathisers, yet he also acknowledged that this made it difficult to maintain academic freedom. Publicly he acknowledged the difficulty. Privately he supported Spry's interventions in Vice-Chancellor Douglas Copland's appointments of staff at the ANU.[81]

So while there was resistance to politicisation and support for the preservation of academic freedom, this may not have protected Fulbright candidates from being (secretly) vetted on their political affiliation. The Fulbright Program's complex positioning in being partly run by the State Department meant it was frequently caught up in efforts by the State Department to influence decision-making, even in Australia.[82] While the USEF could select and offer awards, successful candidates depended on the State Department for visas to travel. When playwright Arthur Miller was named on a Distinguished Visitor wish list in 1960, the board ruled his candidacy out before any steps could be taken, presumably on the basis that he was politically too hot to handle;[83] in any case, even if approved by the board, he may not have been granted a visa. There were other occasions when successful recipients, such as Melbourne historian Max Crawford in 1958, had to be defended against charges of Communism to the head of ASIO before they could get a visa to take up their award. Postgraduate Sondra Silverman who wanted to stay on in Australia had her request to extend her visa denied. This was in part due to her deliberate flouting of the dress rules at her university college that led to her being brought before the Fulbright board and in part to her left-wing political activities which were documented in the file kept on her by ASIO.[84] After Silverman's departure in 1966, her partner and fellow anti-Vietnam War activist, Australian academic Robin Gollan, arranged a trip as a visiting scholar to universities in the United States and Canada, but was denied a visa by the State Department.[85] Gollan's brother was head of the Australian Communist Party and it was presumably these affiliations that led to his ban from the United States. Ultimately the Fulbright program could not escape the Cold War, governments controlled the visas which enabled scholars to travel on exchange, whether they were on awards or not.

Notes

1 Walter Johnson and Francis Colligan, *The Fulbright Program: A History* (Chicago, 1965) explored the ways Cold War politics impinged on the program. Whitney Walton, *Internationalism, National Identities, and Study Abroad: France and the United States, 1890–1970* (Stanford, 2010) acknowledged the political pressures on the program and the assumption among many French, particularly on the Left, that it was

merely a tool of American foreign policy but revealed the story was more complicated than this.

2 Noam Chomsky, Laura Nader, Immanuel Wallerstein, Richard Lewontin and Richard Ohmann, eds, *The Cold War and the University: Towards an Intellectual History of the Postwar Years* (New York, 1997).

3 'Quand M. Yvon Delbos se fait contrôler par l'ambassadeur d'Amérique', *L'Humanité* [n.d.] May 1949, cited by Walton, *Internationalism, National Identities, and Study Abroad*, p. 234, n. 30.

4 Richard Pells, *Not Like Us: How Europeans Have Loved, Hated, and Transformed American Culture Since World War II* (New York, 1997), pp. 63, 62.

5 31 December 1952, FSD from Sydney to Washington DC. 'Subject: IIA: Transmitting Combined Evaluation Report for the Period Dec 1 1951 to Nov 30 1952'. RG59 511.43 Box 2359, NARA.

6 US Foreign Service Despatches [FSDs] from Australia over this period, in NARA State Department Records Series RG59, support this claim. See also Kenneth A. Osgood, 'Review Essay: Hearts and Minds: The Unconventional Cold War', *Journal of Cold War Studies*, vol. 4:2 (2002), pp. 85–107; Paul A. Kramer, 'Is the World Our Campus? International Students and U.S. Global Power in the Long Twentieth Century', *Diplomatic History*, vol. 33:5 (2009), pp. 783, 796–7; Frances Stonor Saunders, *The Cultural Cold War: The CIA and the World of Arts and Letters* (New York, 2000); Scott Lucas, 'Campaigns of Truth: The Psychological Strategy Board and American Ideology, 1951–1953', *The International History Review*, vol. 18:2 (1996), p. 279; Giles Scott-Smith, *The Politics of Apolitical Culture: The Congress for Cultural Freedom, the CIA and Post-War American Hegemony* (London and New York, 2002), p. 61.

7 Simona Tobia, 'Introduction: Europe Americanized? Popular Reception of Western Cold War Propaganda in Europe', *Cold War History*, vol. 11:1 (2011), p. 2.

8 David Lowe, *Australian Between Empires: The Life of Percy Spender* (London, 2010), pp. 128, 118. The External Affairs file is at A432, 1950/838, NAA.

9 The board's bylaws were altered to bring the membership to eight on 26 April 1954 (USEF board minutes).

10 'Wrote Seventy-Thousand Word Report in Longhand', *Advertiser* (Adelaide), 1 May 1950, p. 1.

11 Newman Rosenthal, *Sir Charles Lowe: A Biographical Memoir* (Melbourne, 1968), pp. 133–6 and J.R. Poynter, 'Lowe, Sir Charles John (1880–1969)', *Australian Dictionary of Biography*, National Centre of Biography, ANU, http://adb.anu.edu.au/biography/lowe-sir-charles-john-10865/text19285 (accessed 20 July 2012).

12 'May Day', *Advertiser* (Adelaide), 2 May 1950, p. 2.

13 The Cold War rationale is plainly stated in 'Brief for Cabinet for Commonwealth Conference, Colombo', Canberra, December 1949, reprinted in David Lowe and Oakman, eds, *Australia and the Colombo Plan 1949–1957 (Documents on Australian Foreign Policy)* (Canberra, 2004), pp. 22–33. It is possible that the Fulbright Program, already operating in several countries, inspired the educational component of the Colombo Plan. On the Colombo Plan see Daniel Oakham, *Facing Asia: A History of the Colombo Plan* (Canberra, 2004); David Lowe, *The Colombo Plan and 'Soft' Regionalism in the Asia-Pacific: Australian and New Zealand Cultural Diplomacy in the 1950s and 1960s* (Geelong, 2010).

14 On Latham's career and anti-communism, see Zelman Cowen, *Sir John Latham and Other Papers* (Melbourne, 1965) and Clem Lloyd, 'Not Peace but a Sword: The High

Court under J.G. Latham', *Adelaide Law Review*, vol. 11:2 (1987), pp. 175–202. Volume 3 of novelist (and Fulbright alumnus) Frank Moorhouse's *Edith* trilogy puzzles over Latham's High Court dissent in 1951. *Cold Light* (Sydney, 2011).

15 Lloyd, 'Not Peace but a Sword', p. 202.

16 Casey proposed to Jarman that Latham join the board in November 1952. A1838 250/9/8/4 PART 3, NAA.

17 USEF board minutes, 15 July 1959.

18 W.J. Hudson, *Casey* (Melbourne, 1995), p. 135.

19 ' "Nest of Traitors" in Government Service', *Sydney Morning Herald*, 28 May 1952, p. 1; and Hudson, *Casey*, p. 242; Frank Cain, *The Australian Security Intelligence Agency: An Unofficial History* (Ilford, UK, 1994).

20 3 February 1950, FSD, Sydney to Department of State: 'USIE Country Paper – Aims and Objectives of the USIE Program in Australia'. RG 59 511.43 Box 2359, NARA.

21 1 February 1954, FSD, Canberra to Department of State, 'Semi-Annual Report of the International Educational Exchange Program', Group XVI Post Reports, MC 468 Box 316 file 316-7, Bureau of Educational and Cultural Affairs Historical Collection (hereafter CU), University of Arkansas Special Collections (hereafter UoASC).

22 3 February 1950, 'USIE Country Paper'. RG59 Box 2359 NARA.

23 2 January 1951, USIE Semi-Evaluation Report, Sydney to Department of State. RG59 511.43 Box 2359, NARA.

24 22 January 1952, FSD from USIE Sydney – Semi-Evaluation Report, signed Donald W. Smith, American Consul General. RG59 Box 2359, NARA.

25 23 July 1952, FSD, AmConsul Sydney to DOS. Re: Transmitting Advance Narrative Reply, FY-1953 USIS Mission Prospectus. RG59 Box 2359, NARA. Underlining in original.

26 3 February 1950, 'USIE Country Paper'. CU, UoASC: MC 468 Box 316 file 316-7.

27 On the senator's realisation of the need for a Board of Foreign Scholarships 'to protect the program from political interference and short-term policy considerations', see Randall Bennett Woods, *Fulbright: A Biography* (Cambridge, 1995), p. 134.

28 On Evatt's unpopularity with the Americans see John Murphy, *Evatt: A Life* (Sydney, 2016); Laurence Maher, 'Downunder McCarthyism: The Struggle against Australian Communism 1945–1960 Part One', *Anglo-American Law Review*, vol. 27:3 (1998), pp. 352–4. On suspicions about External Affairs: Phillip Deery, 'Decoding the Cold War: Venona, Espionage and "the Communist Threat" ', in Peter Love and Paul Strangio, eds, *Arguing the Cold War* (Melbourne, 2001), pp. 113–14; on Evatt embarrassing the United States at the United Nations, see 3 February 1950, USIE Country Paper (n. 20). Also Neville Meaney, 'Australia, the Great Powers and the Coming of the Cold War', *Australian Journal of Politics and History*, vol. 38:3 (1992), pp. 327–8.

29 The descriptor 'pinkish' was used by Richard Krygier, founder of the Australian Committee for Cultural Freedom, in a letter to Pearl Kruger of the American Committee, 18 December 1951, in Records of the Australian Association for Cultural Freedom, MS 2031, Box 2, NLA. Also 31 December 1952 FSD, American Consulate Sydney to Department of State. Subject: IIA: Transmitting Combined Evaluation Report, RG 59 511.43 Box 2359, NARA, and 1 February 1954 FSD, 'Semi-Annual

Report', CU, UoASC (see n. 21). On anti-Americanism in Australia see Brendon O'Connor, 'Anti-Americanism in Australia', in Vol. 3: *Comparative Perspectives of B.O'Connor, Anti-Americanism: History, Causes and Themes*, 4 vols. (Westport, CT, 2007); Ann Capling, '"Allies But Not Friends": Anti-Americanism in Australia', in Richard A. Higgott and Ivona Malbasic, eds, *The Political Consequences of Anti-Americanism* (New York, 2008).

30 The 'Marxism' reference was in a 31 December 1952 Foreign Service Despatch, American Consulate Sydney to Department of State. Subject: IIA: Transmitting Combined Evaluation Report for the Period Dec 1 1951 to Nov 30 1952. In NARA RG 59 511.43 Box 2359.

31 USIE Semi-Evaluation Report, 2 January 1951, Sydney to Department of State. RG 59 511.43 Box 2359, NARA.

32 On Australian threats to academic freedom, see Fiona Capp, *Writers Defiled: Security Surveillance of Australian Authors and Intellectuals, 1920–1960* (Melbourne, 1993); Phillip Deery, 'Scientific Freedom and Post-War Politics: Australia, 1945–55', *Historical Records of Australian Science*, vol. 13:1 (2000), pp. 1–18.

33 Combined Evaluation Report for the Period Dec 1 1951 to Nov 30 1952. RG59 511.43 Box 2359, NARA.

34 '1,000 Students Hear Professors', *Argus* (Melbourne), 14 September 1951, p. 5. See also Fay Anderson, *An Historian's Life: Max Crawford and the Politics of Academic Freedom* (Melbourne, 2005), pp. 232–5; Peter McPhee, 'Pansy': *A Life of Roy Douglas Wright* (Melbourne, 1999), p. 98; and Zelman Cowen, *A Public Life: The Memoirs of Zelman Cowen* (Melbourne, 2006), pp. 176–8.

35 Macmahon Ball, n.d. in 'Correspondence re referendum on the Communist Party of Australia', Papers of R.M. Crawford, 1944–1970, Box 29, 7/189, University of Melbourne Archives.

36 All three quotes from '1,000 Students Hear Professors'. See also Anderson, *Historian's Life*, pp. 232–5.

37 '"Hands Off", Say Students', *Argus* (Melbourne), 6 October 1951, p. 44.

38 '"Hands Off", Say Students'.

39 Another Fulbrighter who left for the United States in 1953 was the economist Heinz Arndt. He had been a vocal opponent of the CP Dissolution Bill in 1951, according to Liberal MP William McMahon. Peter Coleman, Selwyn Cornish and Peter Drake, *Arndt's Story: The Life of an Australian Economist* (Canberra, 2007), pp. 116–18.

40 Cowen, *A Public Life*, pp. 188–9. In a letter to Griswold after the referendum meeting, Cowen wrote that he could not imagine 'a more appropriate occasion for a professor of Public Law to express himself than upon one involving the merits of a change in the Constitution'.

41 Cowen, *Sir John Latham and Other Papers*, p. 48.

42 See McPhee, 'Pansy', p. 96. Capp, *Writers Defiled*, pp. 92–3, notes that Mac Ball, on the other hand was on the 'C' list, for Communist sympathisers. On ASIO's surveillance of university researchers see Cain, *ASIO, Unofficial History*, pp. 172–3.

43 Letter from Norman D. Harper to Colonel Spry, dated March 21, 1951, written from University of Chicago Illinois ('Norman Denholm Harper', A6126 144, NAA); Vice-Chancellor John Medley had written earlier in Crawford's defence to Whitney Shepardson of the Carnegie Corporation of New York, in November 1949 (NYCR91-A6 Series III Grants. Box 128 Folder 1: Crawford R.M, Carnegie Corporation of New York Records).

44 Papers of Norman Denholm Harper, UM: 1986.0050 and 1987.0037.
45 *Hearing on Overseas Information*, part 2, 863, 1046, quoted in Johnson and Colligan, *Fulbright Program*, p. 81.
46 Richard T. Arndt, *The First Resort of Kings: American Cultural Diplomacy in the Twentieth Century* (Dulles, 2005), pp. 261–3. When the USIA was created in June 1953, it didn't retain educational exchange on US soil, but in the field its Cultural Affairs officers, attached to US embassies, were involved in both information and exchange programs. Thus, arguments over the relationship between exchange and information would re-ignite periodically for decades. Johnson and Colligan, *Fulbright Program*, pp. 76–81.
47 Johnson and Colligan, *Fulbright Program*, pp. 55–8; Arndt, *First Resort of Kings*, pp. 257–60; Wilson P. Dizard Jr., *Inventing Public Diplomacy: The Story of the U.S. Information Agency* (Boulder, 2004), pp. 56–8.
48 Frederick Graham, 'Professor Loses Fulbright Award after Wife Balks at Red Inquiry', *New York Times*, 20 June 1953, p. 1.
49 Johnson and Colligan, *Fulbright Program*, pp. 102–3; Arndt, *First Resort of Kings*, pp. 234, 262.
50 The first two reports are in A1838 250/9/8/4/2 Part 3, NAA and the last two in A1838 250/9/8/4/2 PART 2, NAA. Only a small number of grantee reports have survived from the early 1950s and 1968. Most were destroyed by the Australian-American Educational Foundation Fulbright (AAEF, the successor to USEF) in 1970. AAEF board minutes, 5 June 1970.
51 10 August 1959, Christesen to Latham requesting help for *Meanjin*, and 15 September 1959, Christesen to Latham, thanking him for having apparently saved *Meanjin*, in Papers of J.G. Latham, MS 1009, National Library of Australia; Fulbrighters Sydney Rubbo and Max Crawford sat on the *Meanjin* committee at this time.
52 Latham had publicly advocated the mind-broadening benefits of educational travel for Australians during the war: 'Education and War', Professor John Smyth Memorial Lecture (Melbourne, 1943), pp. 19–20.
53 USEF board minutes, 25 February 1953.
54 Latham to Jarman, 21 May 1953, in 'Australian-American Relations 1946–63' file, Papers of Sir J.G. Latham, Series 68 Box 105, NLA.
55 USEF board minutes, 25 May 1953.
56 1 February 1954, FSD, American Embassy Canberra to Department of State CU, UoASC.
57 USEF board minutes, 26 October 1953.
58 'Don't Fall Into Smear Trap', *Argus* (Melbourne), 20 November 1953, p. 6.
59 Daniel Oakman, 'The Politics of Foreign Aid: Counter-Subversion and the Colombo Plan, 1950–1970', *Pacifica Review: Peace, Security and Global Change*, vol. 13:3 (2001), pp. 255–72.
60 USEF board minutes, 25 May 1953: 'in explaining the Foundation's objectives […] the term "project" should be avoided.'
61 Oakman, 'Politics of Foreign Aid', p. 268.
62 Oakman, 'Politics of Foreign Aid', p. 259.
63 Interviews conducted by Alice Garner with Australian Fulbright alumni in 'Fulbright Scholar Oral History', NLA. Online survey of 162 American and 185 Australian alumni (2010–11); Sondra Farganis in interview with Diane Kirkby June 2017,

transcript, p. 11; see also Sally Ninham, *A Cohort of Pioneers: Australian Postgraduate Students and American Postgraduates Degrees 1949–1964* (Melbourne, 2011).

64 See for example, Giles Scott-Smith, *Networks of Empire: The US State Department's Foreign Leader Program in the Netherlands, France, and Britain 1950–1970* (Brussels, 2008); Nicholas Cull, *The Cold War and the United States Information Agency: American Propaganda and Public Diplomacy, 1945–1989* (Cambridge, 2008); and Giles Scott-Smith and Hans Krabbendam, *The Cultural Cold War in Western Europe, 1945–1960* (London, 2003).

65 An American Fulbright alumnus recounted that while on his Australian exchange in 1968, he was approached by a 'CIA guy' who asked him to 'rat on' other Americans; he politely 'declined' (private email communication with authors, 3 February 2012). In 1973, a US national security operational instruction forbade the use of Fulbright grantees for CIA cover, implying it may have been used in this way previously (4 September 1973, Operations-General: Restrictions on Operational Use of Certain Categories of Individuals' from US Digital National Security Archive online).

66 Scott-Smith and Krabbendam, 'Introduction: Boundaries to Freedom', in Scott-Smith and Krabbendam, *Cultural Cold War*, p. 3.

67 Louis Joughlin, 'The Selection of Fulbright Scholars', *American Association of University Professors Bulletin*, vol. 46:1 (March 1960), pp. 8–17, 14. Joughlin provides an exhaustive account of the review of BFS.

68 C. Campbell, 'Cold War, the University and Public Education: The Contexts of J. B. Conant's Mission to Australia and New Zealand, 1951', *History of Education Review*, vol. 39:1 (2010), pp. 23–37.

69 Chomsky *et al.*, *The Cold War and the University*.

70 Catherine Manathunga, 'The Role of Universities in Nation-Building in 1950s Australia and Aotearoa/New Zealand', *History of Education Review*, 45:1 (2016), pp. 2–15.

71 Robin Gollan, *Revolutionaries and Reformers: Communism and the Australian Labour Movement 1920–1955* (Sydney, 1975), pp. 196–7.

72 Marjorie Harper, 'Copland, Sir Douglas Berry (1894–1971)', *Australian Dictionary of Biography*, National Centre of Biography, Australian National University, http://adb.anu.edu.au/biography/copland-sir-douglas-berry-247/text17371, published first in hardcopy 1993 (accessed 29 July 2017). Further research in Copland papers, MS 3800 NLA.

73 Manathunga, 'The Role of Universities in Nation-Building'; K. Murray, *Report of the Committee on Australian Universities* (Canberra, 1957), pp. 7–9.

74 Harper, 'Copland, Sir Douglas Berry (1894–1971)'; Copland papers, MS 3800 NLA.

75 Henry Albinski, *Politics and Foreign Policy in Australia: The Impact of Vietnam and Conscription* (Durham, NC, 1970), pp. 142–5.

76 Peter I. Rose, *Academic Sojourners: A Report on the Senior Fulbright Programs in East Asia and the Pacific* (United States Bureau of Educational and Cultural Affairs, Office of Policy and Plans, 1976).

77 Sondra Farganis, response to Survey, La Trobe University, 2011.

78 Geoffrey Gray, '"A great deal of mischief can be done": Peter Worsley, the Australian National University, the Cold War and Academic Freedom, 1952–1954', *Journal of the Royal Australian Historical Society*, vol. 101:1 (June 2015), pp. 25–44.

79 Gray, '"A great deal of mischief can be done"'. See also Capp, *Writers Defiled*, p. 93.

80 Anderson, *Historian's Life*.

81 Gray, '"A great deal of mischief can be done"'.

82 The Bureau of Cultural and Educational Affairs (CU) was based in Department of State, and worked with the other agencies, including IIE, to implement the program. BFS had policy oversight but CU was closely involved in implementation.
83 USEF board minutes, 21 November 1960. Listed along with four other desired scholars, 'It was decided not to support the request for Mr Arthur Miller for the time being' while inquiries were to be made into the others.
84 Sondra Farganis interview; Discussion over women students' opposition to dress rules at dinner ANU archives. ANUA 207/2 Minutes, ANU Governing Board, 1960–5, Minutes of meeting 2 May 1962, 6 June 1962; Sondra disciplined by Fulbright board for incident 18 July 1962, 12 Sept 1962 USEF (Fulbright) minutes; Sondra Joyce Silverman-ASIO file, 1962–66, National Archives of Australia (NAA) A6119, 2384.
85 Robin Gollan Papers, MS9372, Box 1, NLA, Correspondence, 1965–66.

6

Education, or 'part of our foreign policy'?:
At war in Vietnam

Late on the afternoon of 25 August 1964, officials in the Australian Prime Minister's and External Affairs departments scrambled to change arrangements they had made for the signing of the new treaty between the United States and Australia. This executive agreement was to replace the original 1949 Fulbright Agreement and enable the continuation of the scheme into the future. Federal Executive Council had approved Paul Hasluck, minister for External Affairs since April 1964, to be the government's signatory to the agreement, alongside the American ambassador, William Battle. This followed the precedent of the original Fulbright Agreement of November 1949 which had been signed by then External Affairs Minister Evatt, alongside US Ambassador Pete Jarman. On this occasion, however, and 'at the last minute', Prime Minister Menzies was persuaded to attend, and to sign in Hasluck's place.[1]

Five years earlier, in August 1959, when Richard Casey held the External Affairs portfolio, he had advised officials planning the program's tenth anniversary celebration that they might invite Evatt along, to acknowledge his 1949 role and to lend a bi-partisan tone to the event. The prime minister, on the other hand, he claimed, 'would not want to be bothered'.[2] External Affairs Minister Hasluck, however, now thought having Menzies sign the new treaty would be a 'nice compliment to Battle' and would also 'ensure the Prime Minister's personal interest in the Agreement'.[3] It seems Hasluck was responsible for getting Menzies to attend the signing and for persuading Menzies to sign in his place.[4]

Why might Menzies be asked, and now be bothered, in 1964? The short answer is that it was a mark of how significant the US–Australian relationship had become to Australia's defence and economic policy over the previous fifteen years. More importantly, it showed the Australian government's ambition to have this continue into the future. Having the prime minister sign this second agreement added symbolic weight to the event, and by extension to the Australian–American relationship the program sought to strengthen. Menzies' decision in 1964 to step in and sign the new agreement reflected the determination of his government to have continued access to the United

States, to US institutions of higher learning, building on the benefits that were perceived to flow from the ANZUS alliance. Australia was now more deeply immersed in the US orbit and saw strategic advantage to drawing the United States further into defending regional security. The value placed on the program by the Australian government is demonstrated by its decision to commit to co-funding, and in the prime minister's actions in signing the agreement. Emphasising the bi-national commitment and the value attached to the renewal of the existing educational exchange relationship matched the government's declaration of shared foreign policy goals and its cultivation of the US alliance. As the minister for External Affairs in that government, Paul Hasluck fervently espoused the Domino Theory, and was a keen supporter, even urger, of military intervention in Vietnam.[5]

On 7 August, just weeks before the signing of the new agreement, the US Congress had passed the Gulf of Tonkin Resolution, which effectively gave President Lyndon B. Johnson permission to employ conventional military force in South Vietnam. It was a key moment leading to the escalation of the American commitment in Indochina. Six days later, Menzies informed parliament that his government was seeking to increase US commitments in Southeast Asia.[6] In the same week, Australian officers in External Affairs and the Prime Minister's Department were finalising discussions with US State Department officials about the draft educational exchange agreement, and preparing press releases for the signing.[7]

While these developments in educational exchange and Southeast Asian intervention were not openly connected by those involved, the coincidences of timing and personnel involved invite questions about the positioning and significance of this government-funded educational exchange program in the broader foreign policy context at that time.

Australia was seen by the US Embassy in 1959 as being 'in a sensitive area of the world' which meant the United States should give Australia every assistance 'to develop its latent potential and enhance the status of the free world in Asia'. Five of the first ten countries to sign up to the Fulbright Program were in the Asia-Pacific region – China, Burma, the Philippines, Australia and New Zealand. By the mid-1960s twenty-seven countries across the world had signed agreements but only Australia and New Zealand among the western nations now joined the United States in fighting the Vietnam War. Their goal was to secure the defence of their region.[8] Under the Menzies government, Australia became the United States' keenest ally in Vietnam, actively and uncritically supporting military intervention in the hope of retaining a strong US presence in Southeast Asia over the long term.[9] That policy continued under Menzies' successors following his retirement in 1966, so much so that even Hasluck, unwavering supporter for US policy in Vietnam, would blanch, with many others, at the full implications of Prime Minister Harold Holt's 'All the Way with LBJ' statement during the president's visit to Australia.[10]

The Australian-American Fulbright exchange thus demands a particularly close scrutiny over this period, leading up to and resulting in the new Fulbright Agreement of August 1964, and the changes that came about as a result.

Machinery of the program and implications of renegotiation

Under the terms of the new agreement, the Canberra-based, bi-national body administering the Australian side of program, the USEF, known colloquially as the Fulbright Foundation, was to be replaced by a new 'Australian-American Educational Foundation' (AAEF). This name change signalled to the world that the Australian government would now co-fund the scheme, to the tune of AU £90,000 (US$180,000) per year for five years. Australia was one of the earliest Fulbright partner countries to take this step, soon after five northern European countries and Taiwan, and was the first in the Southern hemisphere to do so.[11] Symbolically and practically the co-funding heralded a change in the power dynamic of the agreement. Up until then, the program funding, though in Australian currency, was seen by all involved as American money because it was owed to the US government under the Lend-Lease Settlement Act of 1946. Now that the debt had been honoured and those funds had dried up, the exchange scheme could be reconfigured as a genuinely bi-national affair.

The future of the Australian program had been under discussion since its tenth anniversary celebration in 1959, when the bi-national board moved to investigate possibilities for its continuation beyond 1964, and published a report including supportive statements from former scholars.[12] In March 1960 the board discussed a resolution drafted by its chairman, Sir John Latham, calling for the two governments to begin discussions about the program's future, and declaring the possibility of its ending 'a great misfortune'.[13] The US ambassador then wrote to the minister for External Affairs along similar lines in April.[14] In August, an External Affairs memo on the future of the program noted that while several other countries had already extended their Fulbright agreements, they were able to draw on US surplus disposals in local (non-US) currency, which it seems was not an option for Australia. So far, there had been no instance of US dollars being appropriated for Fulbright exchanges by Congress.[15]

It seems that nothing happened for a while, because in February 1961, US Ambassador William J. Sebald wrote a letter to deputy assistant secretary for Far Eastern Economic Affairs, Avery F. Peterson, proposing that an informal approach be made to the Australian Department of External Affairs officer who sat on the USEF board, to initiate the next step in discussing the program's continuation. 'I suggest "informally"', he explained, 'because we obviously would not want to risk a formal turn-down on a venture of such great mutual importance'. He believed that the program had had 'a direct and desirable influence on U.S.-Australian relations' and that 'We are not yet at the stage in our relations where we can take each other so much for granted that we do not need a constant exchange of Americans and Australian in the non-official and non-commercial field'.[16]

The timing was fortuitous, for the following month (March 1961), Senator Fulbright and Representative Wayne Hays (D-Ohio) submitted a bill to Congress designed to streamline the various pieces of federal legislation dealing with educational exchange into one all-encompassing Fulbright-Hays Act (or Mutual Educational and Cultural Exchange Act). The bill was debated and passed in July, and signed on 21 September

1961 by President Kennedy.[17] It superseded numerous earlier pieces of US legislation, including the original 1946 Fulbright Act. Among other things, the Fulbright-Hays Act enabled congressional appropriations in US dollars for the purpose of international exchanges, so that Fulbright programs were no longer restricted to drawing on foreign currencies owed to the US government by partner countries.[18] This meant that when the US$5 million initially set aside to fund the initial Fulbright exchange finally ran out, the Australian–American program might – if both parties agreed – be continued, with appropriations from US Congress and Australian Federal Parliament in US dollars and Australian pounds.

The passage of the Fulbright-Hays Act, along with some informal pressure by US Ambassador Sebald, nudged things along at the Australian end, and when P.R. Heydon, first assistant secretary of External Affairs, wrote to the secretary of the Prime Minister's Department in April 1961 about the program's future, he gave reasons why a 'sympathetic reaction' from the minister to its continuation might be desirable. Aside from the program's effectiveness in 'fostering Australian/United States understanding', he argued that 'Our relations with the United States will continue to be of a special character which should be developed over the widest area', and – last but not least – that President Kennedy 'attached high importance to cultural and educational exchanges and Senator Fulbright is Chairman of the Senate Foreign Relations Committee'.[19] The link he made here between educational exchange and foreign policy considerations could not be clearer – a link that would prove troubling in ensuing years.

By mid-1962, the Department of State was working on a draft proposal, which it sent to the Australians for consideration in December.[20] Department of State officials seem initially to have been unsure whether the Australians would agree to contribute to the continuation of the program, but in January 1963, not long after Menzies had promised a first, as-yet-unspecified contribution to US efforts in Vietnam, American foreign service officer Edward Ingraham wrote about the Fulbright Program to the US chargé d'affaires in Canberra, William Belton, that 'The details of the matter are still not clear to me, but it looks as if the problem of continuing the program will not be so difficult as we had feared'.[21] On 8 February, Max Loveday of External Affairs, planning an inter-departmental meeting on the matter, suggested to the minister (now Sir Garfield Barwick[22]) that, given the program had been financed since 1949 'on "American" funds, Australia could cut a bad figure if she now refused to join in on a 50–50 basis to continue the programme'. Furthermore, the Americans had informed him that West Germany and Austria had recently agreed to contribute to continued Fulbright Programs, and that the State Department was actively looking into the pos-sibility of allocating moneys obtained from the disposal of US agricultural commod-ities under PL480 in Pakistan, to put towards the Australian program.[23] A week later, Loveday reported with some surprise that the State Department, in anticipation of a positive response from the Australians, had 'already' converted US$250,000 worth of Pakistani rupees into Australian dollars, in readiness for a new educational exchange treaty.[24]

Loveday had expressed momentary concern about the Pakistani PL480 origin of the funds in his earlier, 8 February, letter, wondering whether there might not be 'financial, and even political implications' of the US decision to use Pakistani rupees. Might Pakistan be 'annoyed' about this? As it turned out, he had no time to pursue this line of questioning, given that the United States acted so quickly to convert the rupees. But then, the question reared its head again, two months later.

On 9 April, Loveday wrote to Patrick Shaw (Loveday was acting assistant secretary, in Shaw's place) on a question of particular relevance to the Fulbright negotiations, which had now formally begun. The memo's intriguing subject was: 'Should C.S.I.R.O. Accept Research Money Derived from U.S. PL480 Deals?' It concerned an amount of US$200,000 earmarked for Australian research by the US government, money that originated from certain PL480 deals in other countries. Loveday noted a recent article in *Time* magazine listing recipients of US economic and military assistance, and wondered whether the Australian 'receipt of these "once-removed" U.S. research funds would be noted down in the sort of lists from which *Time* would get its information'. He came to the conclusion that the research money should be accepted, given that the Australian position – 'if we had wanted to present ourselves as rigidly independent of aid' – was 'already compromised'. Having already accepted American military aid (he didn't specify in what form or when), 'even though we are trying to argue that it is only technically so', it would be pointless now to refuse this offer to CSIRO which was, he argued, 'a good defensible use of money'. Unfortunately he did not indicate the nature of the research the US$200,000 would support.

Loveday realised that this question was relevant to the educational exchange negotiations under way, because, as he explained to Shaw, 'Some sort of parallel will occur when the Fulbright question comes up for debate', given that the American share of the program funding also derived from PL480 sources.[25] As it turned out, the rupee conversion does not seem to have caused any headaches – perhaps because the conversion was a *fait accompli* well before the new agreement was signed. But Loveday's sensitivity to possible critiques of government funding for certain kinds of research foreshadowed vigorous public debates on this subject in the coming years. This concern had been presented forcefully back in January 1961 by President Eisenhower in his Farewell Address to the Nation, in which he warned of the growing power of the 'military-industrial complex', and in 1966, Senator Fulbright would address it too, in his book *The Arrogance of Power*. Loveday understood that in taking on the co-funding and administration of the renewed exchange program, the Australian government would need to tread very carefully in the zones where higher education, foreign policy and defence needs crossed over.

The negotiations

Although there was somewhat less haggling over wording by the negotiating parties than had been evident in the 1946–49 inter-governmental discussions, there were several matters requiring careful reconsideration, now that the Australian government was contemplating co-funding the scheme. One question that preoccupied the public servants hammering out a new agreement was this: which Commonwealth department should have primary responsibility for the program? Though this may sound like a bureaucratic argument of little interest, in fact it called for an articulation by politicians and public servants of the exact nature of the program and where it sat in relation to foreign policy. For this reason, the documents repay our close attention.

In late 1961, long before official negotiations began, a draft report on the continuation of the program was circulated amongst Fulbright board members and External Affairs officers. An early version kicked off with some very broad statements about the value of educational and cultural exchange in the field of international relations – a section that was most likely written by Geoffrey Rossiter, now in his eleventh year as the Foundation's executive officer. An External Affairs officer who read this draft, possibly Assistant Secretary Max Loveday, made some critical remarks in the margins, which illuminate some of the dilemmas posed by this program.

The draft began slightly awkwardly in the passive voice: 'It has long been realized that the real solution to the problems which face the world today is greater understanding between nations.' In the margins, the External Affairs officer wrote: '*Could be debated.*' The report went on: 'Modern diplomacy can no longer afford to rely on political and economic relations alone.' '*Did it ever?*' came the retort in the margins. The draft writer then proposed that 'the greatest hope for international understanding lies in educational and cultural relations which, in the last two decades, have assumed an important role in the foreign affairs of many countries'. Comment: '*Questionable.*'

The report was intended to drum up support amongst parliamentarians and other interested parties for ongoing funding of the program. Perhaps the Foundation's executive officer thought arguments along these lines would convince politicians who might be reluctant to spend money on educational exchange for its own, scholarly sake. Evidently the External Affairs officer thought differently, and his comments seem to have hit home. In the final draft, although some comments on the place of educational exchange in the foreign relations domain appeared in the 'Transmittal Letter' written by the US ambassador, the main section reporting on the program's achievements to date focused much more on educational benefits than on international relations.[26]

Essentially, the dilemma was this: how to sell the program and thus ensure its longevity? Did emphasising the foreign policy aspect of the program serve or damage it? In April–May of 1963, External Affairs officers tossed this around as they prepared a submission seeking in-principle approval from Cabinet for the program's continuation with Australian funding, and the matter finally reached ministerial ears. In August 1963 we find a revealing exchange of letters between Prime Minister Menzies and Sir Garfield Barwick, minister for External Affairs, over the appropriate departmental home for the renegotiated scheme.

Menzies wrote to Barwick on 5 August to say that although he understood that External Affairs – the only Commonwealth department represented on the USEF board until now – had a 'rightful interest in the wider context of participation and relations with the United States', he was 'not easily persuaded' that it should have administrative responsibility for the Fulbright Program. He argued that the scheme was 'concerned strictly with education, and educational institutions' and that 'the rationale of our participation is an education benefit'. This being the case, the Education Division of the Prime Minister's Department should have 'functional responsibility' for the renegotiated scheme. And so, he proposed that the Cabinet submission be prepared jointly with his department.[27]

Several drafts of this letter sit in the Prime Minister's Department archives, along with memos from the departmental secretary, E.J. Bunting, who probably wrote the drafts before seeking Menzies' approval to send. These documents suggest that Bunting and his colleague Les Moore's desire to take responsibility for the Fulbright Program was partly driven by a sense that External Affairs was dipping its toes into areas that lay outside its proper jurisdiction, in this case Education. Bunting argued that External Affairs 'exhibits a tendency to buy into matters even to the extent of a small wing in the department, merely because those matters happen to have an educational aspect'.[28] The letter to Barwick that he drafted for the prime minister was as much about territoriality in the public service, then, as it was about the best home for the Fulbright scheme. While we might see this as petty bureaucratic bickering, it does help us to understand something about the positioning of the Fulbright Program in politicians' and public servants' thinking, and the degree to which its functioning might be affected by changing political circumstances, domestic and international. It also echoes the long-running arguments over the distinction between education and information programs in State Department circles in the United States.

In his reply to the prime minister, Barwick concurred that the 'principal rationale' for the Australian–American Educational Foundation was the 'educational benefit' it offered, and agreed that the Cabinet submission on the program's continuation be put jointly by their departments. Although External Affairs would have a continuing interest in the program because it concerned relations with the United States, Barwick reassured Menzies that his department did not want to 'involve itself in the education of Australians'. He then took up a larger question raised by Menzies, concerning overlapping departmental interest in various international training schemes.

Barwick argued that unlike the Fulbright Program, other training schemes under the External Affairs umbrella 'are not, in my opinion, a matter of education policy but of international aid policy as part of our foreign policy'. He listed some of their aims, including assistance to under-developed countries, establishing Australian contacts with 'future leaders in developing countries' and presenting 'a favourable picture of Australia in other countries'. 'The emphasis', he argued, 'is on the national interest of the country and not on the individual'.[29] The Fulbright Program, with its focus on individual academics pursuing their own study or research projects, did not fit this model.

Barwick had probably seen a long document prepared a week earlier by three External Affairs staffers. On 21 August, officers Loveday, Throssell and Truscott produced a long memo responding to their Secretary Tange's request for 'a critical examination of Australian training programmes to delineate respective Departmental responsibilities'. In this document, schemes were classified according to three 'main purposes': (1) Achievement of foreign policy objectives; (2) The Development of Education as an end in itself; and (3) The Development of a particular aspect of Australian research. They placed the Fulbright Program under the second purpose, bundled up with fellowships to the UK and 'the more highly developed countries of the Commonwealth'. 'Foreign policy implications', they noted of these Development of Education schemes, 'are of a general nature not requiring general oversight'; foreign policy was served here 'by freely operating exchanges of scholars'.[30]

In contrast, the Colombo Plan and SEATO fellowships were listed under the first category, primarily serving 'foreign policy objectives'. This differentiation between educational schemes echoes the separation we saw in the USIS despatches of the 1950s, in which State Department Leader and Specialist grants were discussed in an openly political way, compared to a more restrained or neutral language around the academically focused Fulbright awards.

The External Affairs document on training schemes recommended that 'In accordance with the Prime Minister's wishes', the successor to the Fulbright Program be shifted to the Commonwealth Office of Education in the Prime Minister's Department, and that the Cabinet submission being prepared be suitably amended. The submission was delayed by Australian federal elections in November, much to the frustration of the Foundation board, but discussions resumed early in 1964.

In February 1964, the question of the essential nature of the exchange program came up yet again. In a letter to Lawler of the Prime Minister's Department, Ralph Harry of External Affairs asserted his department's ongoing interest in the program, claiming that it was 'not solely educational in its objects but is basically a cultural exchange scheme'. He supported his argument with quotes from an unspecified document, declaring that ' "a primary factor in selection" of persons for awards "is the potentiality of the candidate to further understanding between his country and the United States of America" '. On this basis, Harry argued that the Prime Minister's Department in its administration of the scheme 'must take into account the interests of the Department of External Affairs and those of the USA'.[31] In his response, Lawler, while agreeing that External Affairs should 'have a continuing knowledge of activities under the scheme', drew Harry's attention to the earlier correspondence between Barwick and Menzies, pointing out that 'Fulbright is NOT a cultural exchange scheme'.[32] So, the matter was not entirely resolved in the minds of all public servants who would be involved in running the new program.

Finally, after many inter-departmental memos and telephone calls, Submission No. 88 ('Proposal to Establish a Joint Australian-American Educational Foundation') was put to Cabinet, and discussed on 19 March.[33] E.J. Bunting, secretary of the Prime Minister's Department, took notes on the meeting. Barwick, in his last month as External Affairs minister, presented the submission. The notes are brief but intriguing, and it is possible that they only record the essential features of the conversation and not the detail.[34] The abbreviations are as they appear in the document:

Barwick – introduces – successor to Fulbright – a fund of £[180,000] jointly over
　　5 years
Holt. No objec'n – but should be new scheme.
P.M. It is a new scheme
Hasluck The name "Fulbright" disappears
Holt. Tax qn – there should be exempn of US tax as well as of Aust tax.

P.M. That seems fair enough – should cut both ways

Hasluck. Admn of this scheme shld be divorced from the general academic brotherhood.

Agreed.[35]

What exactly did Hasluck mean by 'the general academic brotherhood'? After the departmental discussions at the time reinforcing the notion that the program was primarily academic rather than narrowly focused on foreign policy objectives, this comment comes as something of a surprise. Then again, Hasluck was probably not aware of the conversations that had been going on around departmental responsibility for the new Fulbright Program, for he was still minister for Defence at this stage and would have been focusing his energies on the problem of Australian military involvement in Indonesia, Malaysia and, increasingly, Vietnam. Given what we know was to come with campus protests against the Vietnam War, it is tempting to read his 'brotherhood' comment as broadly critical and even dismissive of academics.

Another reading, and one that Hasluck's biographer Geoffrey Bolton proposed, was simply that Hasluck thought a public service acting without fear or favour was best suited to this kind of administrative work, and would 'deflect any suggestion of favouritism or bias or pettiness that might arise if it were administered solely by academics'.[36] This makes sense when we consider that Hasluck knew the university world from the inside: he had been an academic historian at University of Western Australia (UWA), before Prime Minister John Curtin lured him to External Affairs back in 1941, and in the early post-war period Hasluck returned to UWA as a Reader, and wrote two volumes of the official history of Australia in the Second World War.[37] Later, he called upon academics – including scholars who were on the other side of the fence politically – to carry out studies for him when he became minister for Territories.[38]

Hasluck assumed the External Affairs portfolio on 24 April 1964, and as already noted, it was he who encouraged Menzies to sign the new agreement four months later, in August. The records concerning the administrative arrangements developed after the new agreement was signed in August reveal that the Australian–American Educational Foundation continued to rely heavily on the support and advice of academics. Indeed the Office of Education (Prime Minister's Department) made a point of increasing the number of academics on selection committees, and saw this is a deliberate shift from previous arrangements.[39] The matter seemed to be settled.

This year also marked the last for Executive Officer Geoffrey Rossiter. After fifteen years with the USEF, Rossiter moved on to take up the position of warden of Burton College at the ANU. In July 1965 he handed the reins to Frank Willcock, who came from a position as administrative public relations officer at UWA. Willcock was forty-eight at the time of his appointment, and a family man. He had a BA from the University of Sydney, a BL from the University of New England, Armidale, had been a schoolteacher from 1939 to 1951 (excluding War Service with the RANVR), a public relations officer with Ford Motor company in 1952, a partner in an advertising agency, and then a high school teacher again from 1955 to 1961, before his post at UWA. This combination of academic and public relations experience would have made him an appealing proposition to a bi-national board of directors mixing scholarly and business worlds. He was offered a five-year contract.[40] He stayed in the position until 1973, through what was a tumultuous time for the AAEF. The introduction of military conscription for young men in November 1964, followed by the escalation of Australia's war in Vietnam from 1965, provoked demonstrations and protests on campuses across the country which worsened as the war dragged on into the early 1970s. The unrest had profound effects on many of those involved in the program, on scholars at home and abroad, as well as administrators and bi-national board and selection committee members.

A higher patriotism?

The escalation of US and Australian military engagement in Vietnam after the Gulf of Tonkin Resolution brought the Fulbright Program and its relationship with government under fresh scrutiny. The central goal of the program, now articulated explicitly (in the wording of the 1961 Fulbright-Hays Act), was to build 'mutual understanding' between the people of the United States and other nations, with the specific aim of assisting 'in the development of friendly, sympathetic, and peaceful relations' across the globe. The exchange of scholars was still in the forefront. What might 'peaceful relations' and 'mutual understanding' signify for scholars in this tumultuous period, when military engagement by both countries, in alliance, faced growing criticism? For the Fulbright Program's administrators and grantees, serious and sustained political protest on university campuses and in the streets threw up many challenges, as well as opportunities to question actively the significance of their exchange. Charles McCoy was a Fulbright Senior Scholar in Political Science to Monash University in Melbourne in 1966. On his return to the United States he became a member of a radical group formed within the American Political Science Association seeking to displace connections to the CIA and to encourage members to look critically at their nation's political systems and its weaknesses, particularly at the war in Vietnam, which was 'no mistake'.[41]

Senator Fulbright's own trajectory over these years provides a companion story. As chair of the Senate Foreign Relations Committee, Senator Fulbright had played a key role in shepherding the Gulf of Tonkin Resolution through the US Senate in 1964. Some four months after the Resolution, and just before the new Australian-American Educational Foundation (AAEF) board was named in Canberra, Senator Fulbright began to express doubts about US military involvement.[42] These doubts would grow as he learnt more about Indochinese history and politics, as well as about the details of US military strategy in the region, until he became recognised as America's leading dissenter on the war.[43]

His speeches to universities and his public statements as chair of the Senate Foreign Relations Committee articulated very clearly the dilemmas that lay at the core of the educational exchange program's intersections with the world of foreign policy. On the one hand, he continued to believe in the potential of the program to build understanding across national borders; on the other, he realised it had to be protected more actively from political manipulation, not least by his own government's secret service.[44]

Senator Fulbright's interventions in the public debates over Vietnam, especially from early 1966, added a powerful voice to the growing protest movements. Though his name was no longer officially attached to the Australian program, he was still seen by many as its spiritual founder and defender. Two weeks before the Australian co-funding agreement was signed in August 1964, Lucius D. Battle, then US assistant secretary for Educational and Cultural Affairs, wrote to the senator to thank him for his support in achieving this milestone.[45] Many still thought of their awards as 'Fulbrights' regardless of the wording on the letterhead of their scholarship offer. 1958 Fulbright alumnus and plant pathologist Noel Flentje was chair of the South Australian regional selection committee when the new AAEF came into being in 1964. The nitty-gritty of the new administrative set-up now had to be worked through, and this involved a voluminous correspondence and much inter-departmental discussion about selection processes and related matters. On 26 November 1965, Professor Flentje agreed to remain on the South Australian selection committee but took the opportunity to raise a few matters of concern, including his 'own sadness that the name of Fulbright has been dropped from the competition'. He understood that financial arrangements had changed, but thought the Fulbright name was 'well accepted' and he 'personally hoped that this name would have been retained'.[46]

On the day that Flentje wrote his letter, Senator Fulbright had indeed just landed in Canberra, along with his Foreign Relations Committee aide Seth Tillman and a contingent of three other senators, accompanied by their wives and some staff. They planned to spend several days in Australia on their way to New Zealand to attend the 11th Commonwealth Parliamentary Association conference. The timing of this short visit meant that the senator was able to attend the AAEF board meeting in Sydney where the new funding arrangement was, naturally, the major item on the agenda (see Figure 6.1).[47]

Fulbright's short visit to Australia, like the signing of the new agreement the year before, brought the foreign policy objectives of two governments and the Fulbright Program together, coalescing more starkly this time around the issue of the war. Coming just months after the United States and Australia had escalated their military intervention, Fulbright's presence in Australia sparked considerable media interest.

Fulbright arrived as a recognised critic of the Johnson administration, 'a senator at odds with his President' over escalation of the war.[48] When his party touched down at Fairbairn RAAF base in a 'lumbering C118', for President Johnson had denied them the use of an Air Force One jet,[49] Fulbright agreed to a short press conference. Journalists were annoyed when Fulbright admitted that he was 'unaware of Australia's commitment', though he knew Australia was 'supporting' the United States. His suggestion that Australia had only a 'very small contingent of troops' –1,000 compared to the United States' 160,000 – caused hackles to rise so high it prompted an apology from an External Affairs Department official.[50] Journalists prodded him to reveal his own views on the war, and whether he would like to see a moratorium on the bombing,

Figure 6.1 Senator Fulbright at Australian board meeting, Sydney, 1965

to which he replied he would like to stop it if he could, 'But I don't wish to go into it at this time'.[51] External Affairs official Max Loveday was overheard saying to the visitors as they left the media scrum: 'I must apologise for the Press'.[52]

The state president of the Returned Services League (RSL) in New South Wales fulminated 'God help the Yanks, us and the rest of the world' if the rest of the Senate committee was as ill-advised as Senator Fulbright.[53] The next day the *Canberra Times* pointed out that, proportional to the size of the population Australia's contingent was indeed as large as the United States'.[54] Two days later the *Montreal Gazette* reported that 'Australians are boiling mad' at Senator Fulbright, that 'patriotic blood was running high as Australians hastened to tell the senator' the extent of Australia's commitment of troops and equipment.[55]

Fulbright had hit a nerve amongst Australians as he exposed the delicacy of the balance of power in the Australian–US alliance. Prominent Sydney-based journalist Alan Reid said that Fulbright seemed to be confirming the ALP view 'that the Menzies government was relying too heavily upon an Australian-US alliance with the US Administration rather than upon an alliance with American people as a whole'.[56] The issue was taken up in the national newspaper, the Murdoch-owned *Australian*, which months earlier was also the only paper to condemn the government's decision to send a battalion of troops and which, among the press, was 'the only blatant critic of Government policy'.[57] An editorial in the *Australian* argued that the doctrine that Australia needed US protection in defence required a 'measure of subjugation of national self-interest' that had 'long been implicit in Australian government policies'. The case of Vietnam was 'the most striking recent example of the doctrine in action' and arguments for it had shown it to be invalid. To have 'a US politician of Fulbright's stature' comment in a way that supported critics within Australia 'may come as a shock to the Government' but should be taken seriously.[58]

This last was a dig at the Australian government which the ALP was criticising for 'its hawkish, sychophant[ic]' capitulation to the United States, a position the ALP argued was encouraging US failure in Vietnam rather than showing initiative in encouraging the United States to find an alternative solution.[59] The Australian (and New Zealand) governments had been able to influence the United States' decision in 1954 when the United States first considered military intervention in Indochina as France was losing its war with the Viet Minh. Then, for the first time, Australia and New Zealand had to choose between the diverging British and American views on what should happen in regard to Indochina, and they sided with Britain.[60] Much had changed in the ensuing decade as the ANZUS and SEATO treaties cemented. Both countries, still under conservative governments, now leaned away from the British (or European) position and towards the US policy of military intervention. Australia began supporting the United States with advisers in Vietnam in 1962.[61]

When in April 1965 Menzies announced the Cabinet's decision to send an infantry battalion, immediately the ALP's opposition to military intervention effectively ended what had until then been a bipartisan policy of support for US involvement, even bombing, in Vietnam.[62] The decision to send combat troops prompted the emergence of new protest groups and it extended opposition to the war beyond the traditional peace organisations, A protest of '300 people, mostly women' outside the US Consulate in Melbourne soon after Fulbright's visit, was dismissed by the US Consul as being so small as to indicate majority understanding 'of the real issues in our joint struggle against communist aggression'.[63] But in Sydney 2,000 people marched and there had been a large protest in Melbourne that attracted approximately 10,000 people.[64] It was an indication of the direction public opinion was taking. On arriving in Australia, Fulbright stepped into that division.

Fulbright's comments rankled the Australian press corps, riled the RSL, and nearly caused a diplomatic incident. An official from the US Defence Department claimed Fulbright had not intended offence.[65] The Johnson administration tried to make amends. Talks were held between the US Embassy and the Department of External Affairs and the embassy issued a press release that was widely distributed. The prime minister's office had been informed that 'The President wants the Government of Australia to know that he appreciates deeply the dedicated and generous support and gallant efforts' being made, by the government and also including the Australian people.[66] The Washington-based UAP correspondent noted that this message 'followed quickly on the statement by Senator Fulbright in Australia that Australia's contribution in Vietnam was small'. Meanwhile, the same article reported that *The Washington Star* had 'attacked' Australian journalists for criticising the senator and defended him thus: 'Senator Fulbright's appraisal of the Australian effort might have been blunt but it was honest.'[67] The senator spoke out again in New Zealand offering a 'frank admission that the US had opposed more nationalist movements than it should because of "errors of judgment" '.[68]

Fulbright's comment to the Australian press was no doubt an ironic tilt at US policy but also at the nature of the ANZUS alliance that was unwelcome to supporters of the alliance. This, too, was a criticism of the Johnson administration, over its 'More Flags' policy. The number of troops committed by their allies was, to the United States, less significant than that they were showing the flag in support. Only Australia and New Zealand and some Asian countries joined the battle. Only Australia did so with alacrity. Even then it was only a battalion. Revealing this failure was bound to have reverberations. Back on home soil, the alliance and the size of Australia's troop commitment was a subject Fulbright would return to a month later and then again several years later, with more determination, in a speech he made at Washington University in St Louis, Missouri, in 1969.

In the simple physical act of travelling that long distance across the Pacific in 1965 Fulbright had performed the trans-Pacific relationship between Australia, New Zealand and the United States, which was the core of the ANZUS alliance. His trip however also played a role in fomenting stronger opposition to US government policy on involvement in the Vietnam War being joined by Australia as party to that alliance. To that extent his journey was not dissimilar to the trajectory of Fulbright scholars whose crossing of the Pacific under the program of exchange brought them new insights and deeper knowledge of their own country, as well as that of their exchange country. The direct influence of ideas is hard to track and pin down but Fulbright scholars themselves can help us gauge the influence of Senator Fulbright's interventions in the public debates over Vietnam, especially from early 1966, when he added a powerful voice to the growing protest movements.

Soon after Fulbright returned to Washington he declared the war to be morally wrong, and expressed regret at his own role in supporting the Gulf of Tonkin Resolution.[69] In February, the senator chaired public, televised hearings into the Vietnam War. A few months later, Senator Fulbright gave the Christian Herter lectures at the School of Advanced International Studies at Johns Hopkins University. These lectures were later published as *The Arrogance of Power*, which became a bestseller. In the context of his wide-ranging and tough examination of the effects of US power, and of US foreign policy in Vietnam in particular, the senator explored the possibilities of and dilemmas posed by educational exchange. Addressing the matter of Fulbright scholars as 'ambassadors', and academics' potential discomfort with that role, he argued that scholars should not hold back from constructively criticising their own government, and even argued that this was a 'higher form of patriotism'.[70]

'Freely operating exchanges of scholars'

Professor of Political Science Henry Albinski (US Senior Scholar 1974) pointed out in his book on the impact of the war in Vietnam on Australian politics and foreign policy, that the Australian anti-war movement 'absorbed a disproportionately high number of educated and professional people … academic persons, members of the artistic community, and university students'.[71] Members of this group, of course, were the same to benefit from the educational exchange that was the Fulbright Program. Not surprisingly, we find many opponents to the war amongst the Fulbright alumni. Australian academic protests began with staff and students at the ANU in 1965.

In November 1967, a 'Statement on the War in Vietnam by Australian Scientists' appeared in the *Australian Journal of Science*. The petition had been signed by 677 Australian scientists, registering their 'deep concern and revulsion at our country's involvement in this war' and in particular the Australian government's expenditure of 'vast sums of money and effort dedicated to the destruction of food and the depletion of the necessities of life in a region of the world where the two greatest threats to humanity, excessive population growth and food shortage, exist side by side'. The petitioners identified themselves with colleagues in the United States and the United Kingdom who had taken a similar public stand, and called for the cessation of bombing in North Vietnam and adoption of U Thant's proposed preliminary negotiation steps.[72]

At least forty-five of the signatories had already held Fulbright awards in the previous seventeen years, and more would go on to win them. Here was one example of 'mutual understanding' between scholars of different nations which did not serve short-term national interests (as perceived by the governments of the day). This was surely the kind of informed criticism by scholars, working across national boundaries, and fed by a desire for world peace, that the senator had envisaged. Their letter qualified as that higher patriotism he called for. Sometimes – particularly during this period of the 1960s and 1970s – scholars' protests took more challenging forms, which program administrators were forced to deal with and think carefully about. One young Fulbright scholar, an Australian architect who was also a political cartoonist publishing work with strong political messages, found himself under investigation by the FBI because his cartoons upset the US government. There were undoubtedly many – both Australians in the United States and vice versa – during those years who participated in the anti-war movement.[73]

When the program funding was severely cut in 1967, at least partly, it seems, triggered by President Johnson's rage at Senator Fulbright's ongoing and effective public opposition to the war in Vietnam, the BFS changed its tone and began to question openly the perceived relationship between educational exchange and foreign policy. Professor of History (and 1960 Fulbright Distinguished Visitor to Australia) John Hope Franklin was now president of the BFS, and he was prepared to go hard in defending the program. In its Annual Report of 1967–68 the board criticised the congressional cuts to educational exchange, arguing that 'The program has been, *and has to be seen to be*, more independent of political control and judgments than any other overseas activity of the U.S. Government'. Not only this, but 'Educational exchange should not be thought of or measured merely as an "instrument of foreign policy," although it appears to us that both the Congress and the Department [of State] sometimes take this view'. The BFS sought to differentiate the Fulbright Program from other more instrumentalist aid programs, and declared that, 'We are not project oriented. We believe highly specialized kinds of training are the responsibilities of others. And we hope to make the quality of the grantees and the validity of educational efforts our main criteria'.[74] This statement is reminiscent of the Australian-US board's reluctance in the early 1950s to accept the State Department and BFS's preferred 'project' termin-ology in their planning documents, for suggesting politicised aid.

The election of Republican President Richard Nixon in 1968 extended the war, and increased the protests. Meanwhile Australia began to wind down its commitment. Four years later, the Labor government of Gough Whitlam ended conscription, brought the final troops home to end Australia's involvement, and almost brought the alliance, too, to an end. Historian James Curran argues that the relationship between Australia and the United States 'veered dangerously off course and seemed headed for destruction' as 'these two titans … clashed over the end of the Vietnam War and the shape of a new Asia'.[75] Whitlam had held a US State Department Leader scholarship. Now, as prime minister, his vision for redefining Australia's foreign policy left Nixon 'enraged and hell bent on tearing apart a strained alliance'.[76] As the Whitlam Labour government pursued a more independent policy, and aroused antagonism amongst conservative establishment forces in Australia, so its position became more precarious. When the governor-general dismissed Whitlam from office in 1975, evidence soon surfaced of CIA interference in Australia's domestic politics.

The Fulbright Program was in one sense complementing the more formal defence and security ties between the two countries. And yet, as an exchange program whose participants were individual academics and students pursuing their own research, it could never really be contained politically, by either government. Individual Australian and American scholars, young and not so young, from a broad range of academic and a few non-academic fields, were being sent to many different institutions across the United States and Australia. They had very varied experiences which sometimes lasted several years, as well as encounters which required individual choice and decision-making. 'The skies opened up for so many of us in the '60's.'[77]

Even if governmental representatives sat on the bi-national board and selection committees, they were balanced out by academics, and once the scholar departed, had little prospect of controlling what any individual might do or say. Greg Dening, who went to Harvard in 1964 to study anthropology and was later to become professor of history at the University of Melbourne, participated in various protests and knew his name was on an ASIO file. Having been given explicit instructions by his superiors not to participate in the moratorium on the war being held in Washington, DC, Dening found a way to circumvent the orders by walking counter-clockwise on the other side of the street from the marchers, where, he recalled, he was repeatedly offered cans of gasoline and invited to set fire to himself.[78] Whatever 'foreign policy implications' there were in the exchange program, as Australian government officials noted of all such education schemes in 1963, they were generally served 'by freely operating exchanges of scholars', not by government oversight.[79]

Infiltration by the CIA into the program might have influenced some decision-making, although evidence is not apparent in the Australian records and this is hard to document. Some US scholars reported being approached by CIA operatives and rejecting the invitation to spy on their fellow-academics. A postdoctoral fellow in genetics who was not personally involved in the anti-war protests remembered 'being accosted at a Fulbright gathering' by a man he called 'the CIA Guy', who basically wanted him 'to rat on other American students'. He subsequently discovered 'the CIA Guy' was known and amusingly dismissed by other students and staff.[80] Government surveillance and even manipulation did not necessarily have the anticipated effect.

When Albinski observed in 1974 that the British tradition in Australian universities had suppressed vigour in academic life, he also said that intellectual debate 'could have carried over into … involvement in social and political controversy'. He consequently noted that the influence of US academic culture on Australian universities had 'created a more congenial and receptive climate for academics' to engage in public life, and this had consequences that were not always in tune with official conceptions of the exchange partnership.[81] So, while governments saw the signing of a new Fulbright Agreement in 1964 as an endorsement of the strategic relationship between the two countries, the exchange scheme in operation often nurtured forms of 'mutual understanding' between scholars and the peoples of the two nations, that subverted or openly critiqued official discourse. The conflict posed a dilemma for individual researchers that almost brought the program into crisis. Many academics and students began to consider very deeply what it meant to be an informal 'ambassador' as part of the program.

Notes

1 28 August 1964, Department of State Telegram from Canberra to Secretary of State. RG 59 Box 390, NARA.

2 14 August 1959, Hutton (Mins, Melb) to McMillan, E A, Canberra. Subject: 'Fulbright Foundation. Your 989 of 3rd August'. In 10302 1960/204, NAA, 'United States Educational Foundation'.

3 On the signing decision from a handwritten note dated 27 August 1964, 5.15pm, in margins of a typed note to Mr Harry of Department of External Affairs, in A1838 583/ 1 PART 2, NAA.

4 27 August 1964, Department of External Affairs Minute Paper for Executive Council. A1838 583/1 PART 2, NAA.

5 Garry Woodard and Joan Beaumont, 'Paul Hasluck as Minister for External Affairs: Towards a Reappraisal', *Australian Journal of International Affairs* vol. 52:1 (1998), p. 67.

6 Gregory Pemberton, *All the Way: Australia's Road to Vietnam* (Sydney, 1987), pp. 212–13.

7 A463 1964/774 PART 2, NAA.

8 See Christopher Hubberd, *Australia and US Military Cooperation: Fighting Common Enemies* (Aldershot, UK, 2005); and Andreas Daum, Lloyd Gardner and Wilfred Mausbach, eds, *America, the Vietnam War and the World* (Cambridge, 2003).

9 James Curran, 'Beyond the Euphoria: Lyndon Johnson in Australia and the Politics of the Cold War Alliance', *Journal of Cold War Studies*, vol. 17:1 (Winter 2015), pp. 64–96.

10 Woodard and Beaumont, 'Paul Hasluck as Minister for External Affairs', p. 67.

11 US Board of Foreign Scholarships, Annual Report, 1970, p. 9. Note that Australia's commitment for 1969 was US$229,600 (which included some accrued credit from before the US cuts), compared to Germany's US$668,000 and Iceland's US$ 1,137. This gives some indication of the variety of Fulbright inter-country agreements in place.

12 10 December 1959, Casey to Rossiter cc McMillan – will ask departmental officers 'to begin preliminary enquiries as to methods which might be adopted to ensure continuation of the Foundation's activities'. 10302 1960/204, NAA, 'United States Educational Foundation'.

13 USEF board minutes, 9 March 1960.

14 19 August 1960, US Public Affairs Officer LeVan Roberts [to?] the Ambassador, on: Continuation of Fulbright Program in Australia Beyond 1964 in Folder: 13-A.2a FULBRIGHT PROGRAM in AUSTRALIA, 1961–62 Desk files, NARA RG59 Entry 5421 Box no 6, NARA.

15 16 August 1960, External Affairs memo for the Assistant Secretary, Division:1, on 'The Future of the Fulbright Program in Australia'. A1838, 583/1 Part 6, NAA.

16 1 February 1961, Official-Informal letter; RG 59 Entry 5421 Box no 6, NARA.

17 The Mutual Educational and Cultural Exchange Act of 1961, or Public Law 87–256 (75 Stat. 527), signed by President Kennedy on 21 September 1961.

18 Walter Johnson and Francis Colligan, *The Fulbright Program: A History* (Chicago, 1965), p. 306.

19 27 April 1961, P.R. Heydon to Secretary, PM's Department. A463 1964/774 part 1, NAA.

20 A1838 583/1 part 1, NAA.

21 13 January 1962, Letter from Edward C Ingraham (Office of Southwest Pacific Affairs, Department of State) to 'Bill' (William Belton, Chargé d'Affaires, US Embassy in Canberra). Marked 'Official Informal Secret'. RG 59 Entry 5421 Box no 5, NARA.

22 Sir Garfield Barwick, the Liberal Member for the NSW seat of Paramatta, served as Attorney-General (1958–61) and Minister for External Affairs (1961–64) in the Menzies Liberal government. He went on to become the longest serving Chief Justice of Australia, and gained notoriety for giving formal written advice to Sir John Kerr supporting his decision to dismiss Prime Minister Whitlam in 1975.

23 8 February 1963, External Affairs memo from Loveday to Minister via Mr Shaw. Re: US Proposal to Extend Fulbright Programme. In A1838 583/1 Part 1, NAA.

24 14 February 1963, Handwritten note recording a conversation with Mr Lamm from US Embassy, signed M.L. [Loveday]. His emphasis. In A1838 583/1 Part 1, NAA.

25 9 April 1963, External Affairs memo – Loveday [Acting Ass Sec] to Shaw. In A1838 583/1 Part 1, NAA.

26 'Report on Continuation of the Program' in 'Australian-American Educational Foundation – Policy', A1838 583/1 Part 1, NAA. The earlier Draft Report is in the same NAA file.

27 Letter from the Prime Minister to Sir Garfield Barwick, Minister for External Affairs, 5 August 1963. A1838 583/1 Part 1, NAA.

28 1 August 1963, Prime Minister's Department. Memo to the Prime Minister by E.J. Bunting (Departmental Secretary) on 'Proposal for a Joint Australian-American Educational Foundation (Submission No. 743)', in 'Proposed joint United States of America/Australia successor to Fulbright Scheme – Policy', A463 1964/774 Part 1, NAA.

29 28 August 1963, Sir Garfield Barwick Minister for External Affairs, to the Prime
    Minister, Mr Menzies. In A1838 583/1 Part 1, NAA, NAA.

30 21 August [1963], International Training Schemes – Departmental Jurisdiction. In
    A1838 583/1 PART 1, NAA.

31 14 February 1964, R L Harry (Ext Aff) to Lawler (PM's Department). In A463 1964/
    774 PART 1, NAA. The quotes from the unnamed document may have come from BFS
    policy statements, given that Australia is not specifically mentioned.

32 2 March 1964, Prime Minister's Dept Note for file. PJL.PH. In A463 1964/774 PART 1,
    NAA.

33 Cabinet Submission No. 88 11 March 1964 – joint submission by Barwick (EA) and
    Gorton (Education and Research – PM's Dept). Notes on Cabinet submission 13
    March; 19 March Decision no. 118 in favour. A4940, C3817, NAA.

34 According to the NAA fact sheet on Cabinet notebooks: 'The notebooks are not,
    nor are they intended to be, a verbatim account of Cabinet's discussions. While
    notetakers may record the discussion in any way they wish, and while the personal
    views of individual Ministers on particular issues may be recorded, by their nature the
    notebooks provide an incomplete record of the discussions.' In 'Cabinet Notebooks –
    Fact Sheet 128' at www.naa.gov.au/collection/fact-sheets/fs128.aspx (accessed 20
    June 2014).

35 19 March 1964, 8.30 p.m. Notes on Cabinet Meeting re Submission no. 88 on 'Joint
    Aust/US. Educational Foundation'. In 'Notetaker E J Bunting – Notes of meetings 18
    December 1963 – 15 April 1964', A11099 1/65, NAA.

36 The authors contacted Nicholas Hasluck in the hope he might throw some light
    on his father's use of this term. He then discussed it with Geoffrey Bolton who was
    writing a biography of Paul Hasluck. Nicholas Hasluck wrote a considered reply to
    our query based on their discussion. Email communication with Alice Garner, 2
    June 2012.

37 Paul Hasluck, *The Government and the People, 1939–1941* (Canberra, 1952) followed
    by *The Government and the People, 1942–1945* in 1970.

38 Hasluck's son Nicholas noted in an email to the author that 'Menzies and Hasluck
    respected many academics but not all. In Hasluck's case the respect is borne out by
    the fact that he engaged various academics to undertake important reviews in Papua
    New Guinea such as the report of Prof David Derham from Melbourne University
    Law School on the legal system' (see Paul Hasluck, *A Time for Building: Australian
    Administration in Papua and New Guinea, 1951–1963* (Melbourne, 1976), pp.
    349–56) 'and the report of three ANU academics including Prof Oscar Spate on
    economic development (*A Time for Building*, p. 140), even though Spate was a former
    communist and a well-known man of the left in the 1950s'. Email communication, 2
    June 2012.

39 N.d. but probably late November 1965 (in reply to a 26 November 1965 letter),
    K.N. Jones (1st Ass Sec, PM's Dept) to Professor Noel Flentje. 'In reconstituting the
    Committees we have increased the proportion of academics on them.' In A463 1964/
    5174 PART 2, NAA.

40 Biographical information from AAEF minutes, 13 July 1965.

41 John Playford, 'Political Scientists and the CIA', *Australian Left Review* (April–May
    1968), pp. 14–28, p. 24.

42 Randall Bennett Woods, *Fulbright: A Biography* (Cambridge, 1995), pp. 662–3.

43 William C. Berman, *William Fulbright and the Vietnam War: The Dissent of a Political Realist* (Kent, 1988); Haynes Johnson and Bernard Gwertzman, *Fulbright: The Dissenter* (London, 1969).

44 On Fulbright's efforts to gain oversight of CIA policies through the Senate Foreign Relations Committee, see Woods, *Fulbright*, pp. 430–1. Note 4 September 1973 Operations-General directive titled 'Restrictions on Operational Use of Certain Categories of Individuals' prohibited the 'Operational use' of 'Fulbright grantees'. US *Digital National Security Archive* online (found at NARA Maryland).

45 13 August 1964, letter from Lucius D. Battle to Senator William J. Fulbright. In NARA RG 59 EDX-Educational and Cultural Exchange – AUSTL Box 390.

46 25 November 1965, Noel Flentje, University of Adelaide, to K.N. Jones, 1st Assistant Secretary, Prime Minister's Department. In NAA A463 1964/5174 PART 2.

47 AAEF Board Minutes 29 November 1965, p. 4, Item 7. Changes to Bi-National Agreement Received copy of proposed amendments …; the visit is discussed at further length in Diane Kirkby, 'Making Australians Boiling Mad: the Fulbright Controversy over Australia's Vietnam War,' presented to Australian Historical Association conference, Canberra, July 2018.

48 A.D. Rothman, 'A Senator at Odds With His President', *Sydney Morning Herald*, 25 November 1965, p. 2; this article was also published in the *New Zealand Herald* (Auckland), 29 November 1965, p. 1; on Fulbright's relationship with Johnson see Woods, *Fulbright*, pp. 385–6, 490.

49 Woods, *Fulbright*, pp. 390–1.

50 'US Senators Arrive', *Canberra Times*, 26 November 1965, p. 3; Airgram, 'Visit to Australia of Senator Fulbright and Members of Senate Foreign Relations Committee', Fulbright papers, MS 9561.

51 'US Senators Arrive', *Canberra Times*, 26 November 1965, p. 2.

52 Told in more detail in Kirkby, 'Making Australians Boiling Mad'.

53 'Critics Rebuke US Senator', *Canberra Times*, 27 November 1965, p. 3.

54 'Critics Rebuke US Senator'.

55 'Fulbright Angers Australians', *Montreal Gazette*, 27 November 1965, p. 4.

56 Alan Reid, 'Clueing Up Fulbright', *The Bulletin*, 4 December 1965, p. 11.

57 Trish Payne, *War and Words: The Australian Press and the Vietnam War* (Melbourne, 2007), p. 92.

58 'Our Right to Independence', *Australian*, 1 December 1965, p. 8.

59 Henry Albinski, *Politics and Foreign Policy in Australia: The Impact of Vietnam and Conscription* (Durham, NC, 1970), pp. 44–5.

60 Roberto Rabel, *New Zealand and the Vietnam War: Politics and Diplomacy* (Auckland, 2005), p. 20; J.G. Starke, *The ANZUS Treaty Alliance* (Melbourne and New York, 1965); see also Gregory Pemberton, 'Australia, the United States, and the Indochina Crisis of 1954', *Diplomatic History*, vol. 13:1 (January 1989), pp. 45–66.

61 Michael Sexton, *War for the Asking: How Australia Invited Itself to Vietnam* (Sydney, 1981, reissued 2002); Pemberton, *All the Way*, pp. 147, 158–63; Glen St.J. Barclay, *Friends in High Places: Australian-American Diplomatic Relations since 1945* (Melbourne, 1985).

62 John Murphy, *Harvest of Fear: A History of Australia's Vietnam War* (Sydney, 1993), pp. 132–3.

63 'Peace Rally Attack', *Australian*, 6 December 1965, p. 2.

64 '2,000 in Vietnam Protest Rally', *Sydney Morning Herald*, 14 December 1965, p. 5; see also Murphy, *Harvest of Fear*, pp. 140–1.
65 'Fulbright Defended', *Australian*, 1 December 1965, p. 7.
66 Memo, M.R. Booker, Dept. External Affairs, Telephone Conversation with Doyle Martin, US Embassy, Subject: 'Senator Fulbright's Visit', 2 December 1965, File no. 250/9/9/15, in Senator Fulbright and other U.S. Senators, File A463 1965/4885, NAA.
67 'Thanks for Sir Robert', *Australian*, 3 December 1965, p. 7.
68 'A Christmas Truce in Vietnam', *Guardian*, 9 December 1965.
69 Woods, *Fulbright*, pp. 401–2.
70 J. William Fulbright, *The Arrogance of Power* (Harmondsworth, 1966), p. 35. It was no. 9 on the *New York Times* bestseller list in March 1967. 'In and Out of Books', *New York Times*, 26 March 1967, p. 270.
71 Albinski, *Politics and Foreign Policy in Australia*, p. 142.
72 'Statement on the War in Vietnam by Australian Scientists', *Australian Journal of Science*, vol. 30:5 (November 1967), Advertisement, p. xlvi. We thank the Australian Academy of Science for supplying Alice Garner with a copy of this.
73 See Ross Bateup, and Ann Turner, Ross Bateup interviewed by Ann Turner for the Comic artists and illustrators oral history project, NLA, 1988. Another scholar who was active in the anti-Vietnam protest movement in both countries was 1970 scholar in Political Science (and later author) Arnold Zable. See Arnold Zable and Alice Garner, Arnold Zable interviewed by Alice Garner in the Fulbright scholars oral history project, NLA, 2010.
74 Annual Report of the BFS, 22nd year, 1967–8, 'Toward Mutual Understanding … a Report on Academic Exchanges', p. v and *passim*.
75 James Curran, *Unholy Fury: Whitlam and Nixon at War* (Melbourne, 2015).
76 Curran, *Unholy Fury*.
77 Sondra Farganis, response to Survey, La Trobe University 2011.
78 Sally Ninham, *A Cohort of Pioneers: Australian Postgraduate Students and American Postgraduate Degrees 1949–1964* (Melbourne, 2011), p. 48.
79 21 August [1963], International Training Schemes – Departmental Jurisdiction. In A1838 583/1 PART 1, NAA.
80 US scholar in private email communication with authors, Friday, 3 February 2012.
81 Albinski, *Politics and Foreign Policy in Australia*, pp. 142–5.

7

'Experience is the only teacher': Academic ambassadors interpret 'mutual understanding'

In 1968 a young American postgraduate student from Yale found 'Melbourne [Australia] was not a good place for an American to be'.[1] The war in Vietnam had exposed the reality that academics were not truly ambassadors for their country. This was highlighted in November 1967, when the *New York Review of Books* (*NYRB*) published an exchange of letters between Senator Fulbright and distinguished professor of English and American studies at Amherst College, Leo Marx. Marx had twice been a Fulbright lecturer, first in Britain in 1956 and then in France in 1965, and he now had a seat on the US national Fulbright selection or 'nominating' committee.[2] Two months earlier he had written to the executive secretary of the Committee on International Exchange of Persons to tender his resignation from the nominating committee, which was later published by the *NYRB*. Making clear his respect for the Fulbright Program, his belief in its 'essentially constructive nature' and its contribution to 'mutual understanding and good will', as well as his appreciation for the 'hard work, skill and devotion' of those administering the scheme, Marx explained that he could no longer ignore a troubling element at its heart, namely 'the ambiguous relationship between the Fulbright scholar and our government'. The American Fulbright scholar abroad, he argued, was regarded 'with some justice, as a semi-official representative of this country, its values and goals'.[3] In the context of the war in Vietnam, this position, he felt, was no longer tenable for those who disagreed strongly with their country's foreign policy.

Marx hoped his resignation from the Fulbright selection committee might spark an 'organized boycott of government activities' by intellectuals, in protest against US foreign policy in Southeast Asia. He was responding to an article published earlier that year in the *NYRB* by MIT linguistics professor and activist Noam Chomsky, titled 'The Responsibility of Intellectuals'. Chomsky challenged readers to ask themselves 'What have I done?' when they 'read each day of fresh atrocities in Vietnam—as we create, or mouth, or tolerate the deceptions that will be used to justify the next defense of freedom'.[4] George Steiner, a humanities scholar at New York University, wrote to the editor in response to Chomsky's article, acknowledging his 'deep personal perplexity', and wondering how exactly he and others should respond. 'What *action* do you urge or even suggest?' he asked. Should not Chomsky, for example, quit MIT, an institution renowned for its heavy involvement in military research? Chomsky replied at length, justifying his choice to stay with the university system, as well as his radical decision to withhold a portion of his income taxes in protest at the government's military spending.[5]

When Leo Marx decided on his own choice of action, he sent a copy of his resignation letter to Senator Fulbright, not only because the senator was the initiator of the exchange program, but because Fulbright was known to be an influential and articulate opponent of the ongoing military intervention in Vietnam. Fulbright replied that while he understood and sympathised with Leo Marx's concern about the dilemma facing Fulbright scholars, and acknowledged that 'the American lecturer abroad is in a broad sense a representative of his country', he hoped that such a lecturer 'would not feel inhibited in expressing constructive criticism of his country's policies if he were so moved'. Fulbright asked whether Marx thought that he, Fulbright, 'should resign from the Senate because I too thoroughly disapprove of our government's policy in Asia?' He agreed that these were not easy decisions, but urged continued efforts to change policy from within the system.[6] Marx responded that of course he did not think that Fulbright should leave the Senate, particularly as the senator (unlike most academics) was in a position to shape policy. But Marx drew a distinction between politicians and academics. He noted the special position of the intellectual who, when travelling overseas under government auspices, effectively lends 'dignity and benignity of the scholarly community to government policy', regardless of his own personal political views.

Eight months later, Leo Marx wrote again to the *NYRB* to attempt a refinement of his position. He had received some letters whose writers had argued that they, as Fulbright scholars, were 'left entirely free to express critical opinions of American foreign policy'. Marx agreed this was true, but countered that 'that very fact places the scholar in an awkward position', and gave an example to illustrate:

> Let us suppose that the scholar appears in a symposium on American foreign policy in Paris, and that he takes a forthright position against our intervention in Vietnam. At the same time the audience knows that he is in France under the auspices of the government that is waging that savage war. 'See', the American government in effect is saying to the French audience, 'we are so deeply committed to the cause of freedom that we sponsor our critics'.
>
> At this moment, to repeat, the scholar finds himself in an awkward, not to say false, position. He has been allowed to say what he thinks, to be sure, but his presence serves to advance quite another, dubious proposition. While he is saying that the war is wrong, his role implies that on balance the actions of his government serve the cause of freedom.[7]

Here was a new perspective on Fulbright's memorable (and still fresh) claim in his bestselling *The Arrogance of Power*, that 'To criticize one's country is to do it a service and pay it a compliment. It is a service because it may spur the country to do better than it is doing'. Fulbright went further: 'In a democracy dissent is an act of faith'. To illustrate his point, Fulbright recounted the story of an American poet, Ned

O'Gorman, sent to Brazil by the State Department, whose officers advised him to avoid difficult questions from the public on the US intervention in the Dominican Republic by saying he was 'unprepared' to answer them. O'Gorman, who later described himself as 'gorged to sickness with embassy prudence' and 'hell bent for clarity', decided to answer all questions honestly. Audience applause was 'long and loud' but the embassy man chastised him. Fulbright's take on this? 'It escapes me totally why American diplomats should not be proud to have American poets and professors and politicians demonstrate their country's political and intellectual health by expressing themselves with freedom and candour.'[8]

It was this last equation, precisely, that troubled Marx – the idea that his or other scholars' critique might be used, in effect, as government PR, thus twisting the intention and undermining the power of their protest. The year previously Richard Kostelanetz had urged: '[S]top insisting that the scholars be cultural ambassadors; American students are gregarious enough to be fine emissaries without being self-conscious missionaries.'[9]

Marx's articulation of this paradox reveals the dilemma scholars involved in the Australian–US exchange faced and prompts questions about how they understood the ambassadorial expectations attached to their position. The Vietnam War and the student protests of the 1960s and 1970s brought about a particularly intense questioning of the meaning of educational and cultural diplomacy, with special relevance for Australian and American exchanges. But these questions had preoccupied some scholars and administrators to some degree from the beginning of the program.[10] Finding a connection to *people* regardless of their government was one of the benefits returning scholars lauded. Examining ambassadorial expectations for those receiving awards, and what scholars have made of them at different times, illuminates the pitfalls of seeing scholars as representative of their own country.

'Tactful visitor'/'scientific observer'/'100% patriot'? Defining ambassadorship

When a Fulbright scholar is selected today, she or he must sign a Fulbright Scholarship Agreement which outlines the terms and conditions of the award. Under the heading 'Rights and Responsibilities', an American scholar must agree 'to act as a goodwill ambassador for the United States in Australia', and to 'make use of any opportunity to extend knowledge about the United States among colleagues and in social contexts in Australia so as, on completion of the scholarship, to be considered as having been a worthy representative of the United States abroad', while the Australian scholar agrees to the same in the other direction.[11] There is absolutely no doubt here as to the ambassadorial expectations that accompany the award, even if there is no stipulation here as to what form the scholar's 'knowledge about the United States' might take.

In three crucial clauses before this 'Goodwill ambassador' paragraph, however, the agreement addresses directly the thorny problem of balancing scholars' 'personal and intellectual freedom' with what it describes as the 'free, non-political character of the educational exchange program'. While the agreement acknowledges that scholars, as private citizens, have the right to disagree with their government's 'political or for-eign policy positions', the clause on 'Political views' stipulates that scholars 'should be aware that political utterances or activity while abroad can, in certain circumstances, draw the program into the political arena' – something the administrators and funding bodies wish to avoid. This clause then concludes with a telling phrase, namely that 'This is a matter for individual judgment and self-discipline, and no ironclad rule can be laid down'.

This careful articulation of the complicated nature of an informal ambassadorial role in the award paperwork is a far cry from the early days of the program, when, though these issues were certainly discussed by scholars and administrators, relatively little concrete guidance appeared in scholarship documentation. It is also the fruit of decades of debate, particularly sharp in the 1960s and 1970s, and again more recently, around the meaning of cultural diplomacy in the educational world.

The original Fulbright Act (P.L. 584) of 1946 made no explicit reference to an ambassadorial role for Fulbright scholars – indeed it did not even refer to 'mutual understanding' as a goal.[12] Fulbright certainly envisaged that program participants would act in some sense as interpreters of their cultures abroad and of their host cul-ture upon return, but the way he and his biographer have told the story, the senator knew that in order to get his bill passed without adverse attention, he could not afford to arouse the suspicions of isolationist congressional colleagues by using the language of international peace or idealism. When introducing the first version of his bill, he did refer to the proposed use of credits from the sale of surplus property abroad for educational exchange as serving the 'promotion of international good will', but this was apparently vague enough not to cause concern, and did not appear in the final text of the Act.[13]

Once the bill was passed, however, and the newly formed BFS began to set policy, the senator's goal of international understanding came to be articulated more fully, for example in selection and programming guidelines. The term 'mutual understanding' featured prominently in the United States Information and Educational Exchange Act (or Smith-Mundt Act) of January 1948, which, though it governed other US gov-ernment exchanges, had some areas of administrative crossover with the Fulbright Program, and played an important part in publicly identifying educational exchange with cultural diplomacy and thus promoting the notion of scholarly ambassadorship.[14]

The Australian–US executive agreement of November 1949 adopted this language, stating clearly the two governments' common desire 'to promote further mutual understanding between the peoples' of their two countries, 'by a wider exchange of knowledge and professional talents through educational contacts'.[15] Although it did not mention ambassadorship specifically, the wording of the agreement implied that individual scholars were expected to contribute actively to this furthering of mutual understanding. When, in 1961, the Fulbright Act was rolled into the Fulbright-Hays Act, broadening considerably the scope of US government-initiated educational and cultural exchanges, the preamble described the Act as providing for 'the improvement and strengthening of the international relations of the United States by promoting better mutual understanding among the peoples of the world through educational and cultural exchanges'.[16]

So, mutual understanding became the *phrase du jour* in the world of educational exchange in the first decades of the global Fulbright Program. But just what did it mean on the ground, for scholars and for program policy-makers and administrators? The term could be interpreted in many different ways, which – as we have seen in Leo Marx's case – sometimes proved problematic. If seeking mutual understanding entailed the scholar's active representation of his or her own nation, culture and people to the hosts, how, and by whom, would the boundaries of this role be defined?

The BFS was conscious of this problem from the beginning. As early as 1949, in public presentations and circulars to partner agencies and commissions abroad, the BFS informed applicants of the overarching 'international understanding' goal, but also sought to ensure that scholars didn't misunderstand their role and imagine themselves to be in any sense *official* representatives of their country. In a key document entitled 'Selected Approved Policies and Principles', used by Australian External Affairs officials to guide their establishment of the USEF in Canberra in early 1950, the BFS explained, under the heading 'Privileges and Responsibilities of Grantees', that:

> The fact that grantees have received awards under the Fulbright Act will not be interpreted as conferring on them diplomatic or other official status during the term of their award.

And furthermore:

> The Board of Foreign Scholarships will welcome publication of results of research performed under Fulbright grants, but authors must take care to avoid any impression that the US Government or any agency thereof has endorsed the conclusions or approved the contents.[17]

The scholars' representational obligations, then, were given clear boundaries early on in the scheme's life. Despite this, there was still room for uncertainty. For what did it mean to be an informal or unofficial ambassador? Unlike government representatives on foreign soil, who had strict protocols to guide their behaviour in a range of social and political contexts, Fulbright scholars had to work things out for themselves, plunging into social situations in which they were expected somehow to explain their country and their people.

We can obtain a fair indication of the ways Fulbright administrators envisaged scholars contributing to mutual understanding from the questions that appeared on their final report forms. In 1953, American scholars coming to the end of their Australian exchange period were asked the following questions: 'During the course of your stay in your host country, how much opportunity did you have for more informal social contacts, such as visits to homes?' Were these contacts 'important in furthering international friendship and understanding', and did they think the Fulbright Program was realising this goal?

Scholars were then asked to list any 'misconceptions' held by Americans about Australia, and vice versa, and asked 'In what ways, if any', they might have 'contributed to clearing up any of these misconceptions' during their award period. The importance of this last question was highlighted by the request that the writer 'Please be as specific as possible' in answering it. Clearing up misconceptions was supposed to work in two directions: scholars were expected not only to make sense of their home country to their hosts, but to return home ready to challenge generalisations or assumptions about the place and people they had come to know.

Questions like these continued to appear on report forms into the early 1960s, but a discernible change in focus and format occurred in the mid-1960s. While we have a good collection of final scholar reports by Americans in the early–mid 1950s and the 1960s, unfortunately we have been unable to source more than a couple of Australian reports of a similar nature. Australians were supposed to submit reports to one of a range of administrative agencies in the United States, whose archives have proved difficult to access, while Americans submitted to one central body, the USEF in Australia, making them easier to locate. Unfortunately, USEF and its successor AAEF made the regrettable decision to destroy most of their scholar files in the early 1970s, but some copies of reports survive in the Australian External Affairs Department and Office of Education archives.

In a striking difference between Australian and American recipients, the Australian scholars we interviewed mostly had no memory of submitting a report during or after their US exchange. Perhaps the US agencies were not particularly assiduous in chasing them up, or perhaps alumni have simply forgotten. It seems that few felt any pressure to act as ambassadors for Australia, and that they were mostly left to their own devices once they arrived in the United States. Because Australian Fulbrighters were recipients of a travel grant only, their dependence on university-funded scholarships meant they often identified more strongly with the university or organisation funding the bulk of their exchange. More significantly perhaps, there was a reluctance among Australian government and educational bodies to engage self-consciously (or to encourage scholars to engage) in the kinds of cultural diplomacy that were fast developing in the United States. Take, for example, the USEF board's refusal in February 1955 to try to articulate 'the basic philosophy of the people' of Australia for the purposes of an orientation and information brochure being put together by the State Department for American grantees.[18] They were not (yet) prepared to 'sell' an Australian way of life or way of thinking – though this attitude would change in decades to come.

In contrast, the Americans who came to Australia under Fulbright auspices, who were granted a full scholarship with travel, tuition and maintenance included, tended to see themselves as Fulbright scholars first and foremost. This had implications for their self-perception as ambassadors – both for the United States and for the program itself. It was this which led to the crisis among American intellectuals in the mid-1960s, a crisis not fully shared by their Australian counterparts. That makes American scholars' efforts to interpret or enact mutual understanding in Australia of particular interest.

Through the decades, some scholars have taken on the ambassadorial task with gusto, while others have expressed discomfort, confusion, or reluctance to assume such a role. The USEF's executive officer, Geoffrey Rossiter, articulated the ambassadorial dilemma early in the first decade of the Australian program, when he commented on reports submitted by young American Fulbrighters under his watch in Australia. He told the board in 1956 that, based on recently submitted scholar reports, many visiting postgraduates seemed 'confused' about the nature of their responsibilities.

> Although they came to engage in academic pursuits they had been informed of the fundamental purpose of the programme in promoting better understanding between the people of the US and those of other countries. Some had neglected their research and studies in the interests of being 'ambassadors of goodwill'. Some grantees had suggested that, particularly with postgraduate students, it was desirable to place greater emphasis upon academic responsibilities, since students with no serious academic purpose bring discredit on the programme and on American academic institutions.[19]

This confusion was surely provoked, at least in part, by the prevailing public discourse back home, solidifying around Cold War visions of a divided world, explored in chapter 5. Central to this discourse was a concern with the ways the United States should justify its power and influence to people of other nations.

In May 1951, President Truman wrote to the BFS chairman Walter Johnson to praise the Fulbright Program for being 'effective in combatting Communist lies and distortions about social, economic and political conditions and objectives in the participating nations'. This followed on a resolution passed by the BFS, which claimed the program had 'demonstrated that persons speaking to persons are an effective means of explaining the ideas and aspirations of America to other nations and of these nations to America'.[20] The wording of the BFS resolution was much less aggressive than Truman's, but the message was surely not lost on scholars being selected. When the Fulbright Program came under direct attack from Senator McCarthy in July 1953, as part of his broader onslaught on the State Department,[21] one of the many negative consequences was a series of long delays while American applicants' loyalty was checked before award offers could be made, delays that jeopardised the proper functioning of the worldwide program for some time.[22] Pressure was building on all sides.

Scholars were asked to explain themselves, but not always in the way they may have expected. For many American scholars participating in the first years of the Australian program, their ambassadorial role required them to explain the excesses of McCarthyist anti-Communism to hosts and colleagues who read the US news in horror.[23] In other words, scholars quite often found themselves in defensive mode, which encouraged some honest reflection on the nature and pitfalls of this ambassadorial role. Anti-American sentiment already had strong roots in the Oxbridge-oriented Australian university world, and congressional witch-hunts made visiting Americans' task of explaining their country all the more challenging.

Drawing on his Western Australian experience, one lecturer in education advised future American scholars in 1953 that 'Life will probably be happier for the future grantee if he assumes the role of "tactful visitor" or "scientific observer" rather than that of "100% Patriot"'. He had found that Australians reacted 'quickly and sometimes violently to criticism of any sort' and warned his compatriots about the Australian press, who liked to push for trouble-making comparisons between Australia and the United States.[24] A US postgraduate student in Child Welfare found in 1954 that 'one of the greatest hazards to "understanding" in the first few months of one's stay in a foreign country is the matter of when and what opinions to express'. She had often been encouraged to give an opinion when she felt that she had 'insufficient basis for forming one', and feared that her honest opinion might 'not be well received'. She came to the conclusion that 'experience is the only teacher in learning how to handle this'. While she liked to encourage frank questions and comments about the United States during Q&A sessions at her public talks, she had learnt it was wise 'to make it plain that any opinions [she] expressed were those of one person and not Americans in general'.[25]

American scholars were not only called upon to explain the excesses of McCarthy, but to counter damaging stereotypes about American people and life. Most scholars felt these stereotypes and 'misconceptions' were primarily created and perpetuated by Hollywood and the press. John Rose Faust, for example, observed in 1953 that 'while Americans and Australians already have very much in common', it was 'essential for Americans traveling overseas to see their country as others see them, and also help Australians to see the United States in its true perspective rather than as pictured by Hollywood and Australian newspapers'. Newspapers, he argued, were doing a 'great deal of harm', by playing up 'the sensational stories (crime, corruption, and vice) McCarthyism, etc.', while movies misrepresented American life. In the same year, social work lecturer Mrs Georgie Travis, a divorcée who wished she had worn her old wedding ring and packed a black hat rather than a red one, to avoid social misunderstanding, felt she may have countered popular stereotypes simply by being herself:

> I assume that acquaintance with a middle-aged social worker who still washes on the board at home and worries about the rent on the house and deplores the films, and who seems to be relatively sound professionally may have helped to overcome a Hollywood idea of Americans!

Charles Hartshorne, an American philosopher in Melbourne in 1952, thought that it was useful for Australians to see 'that some Americans are neither soldiers, business men, nor Hollywood actors and actresses, but persons with whom they may share universal cultural interests or a love of nature'. And in an effort to counter the popular Australian notion that 'all of America is like Hollywood and the colored pictures of American magazines', entomologist Barbara Ann Stay 'tried not to emphasize American consumption goods'. She hoped her own presence may have helped to 'lend variety' to her hosts' conception of 'the typical [American] countryman'.[26]

Despite these efforts, in the eyes of Rossiter and some USEF board members in Australia, US scholars were above all ambassadors for the educational institutions from which they came, the American educational system more generally, and for the Fulbright Program itself as an educational scheme. Australian academics tended to hold a low opinion of American schooling and universities. No matter how good-natured visiting Fulbrighters might be, or how willing they might be to talk publicly or socially about their home country, if they were not intellectually impressive, or if they did not apply themselves seriously to their proposed research project, they would, unwittingly perhaps, confirm the prevailing Australian impression of US educational institutions. This would imperil a scheme whose success relied on the perception that a US educational exchange experience was worth having.

Through the 1950s, there were frequent USEF board statements along these lines. For example, in October 1953, the Foundation suggested 'respectfully' to the State Department that in the previous two years, 'too much emphasis may have been placed upon filling the quota of awards, rather than concentrating upon the quality of the candidates', and went on to explain why this was a problem:

> In some academic circles here, it is a fact that the standard of American edu-
> cation, particularly at the college and university level, is regarded as open to
> question, even though this attitude may be without justifiable foundation. In
> view of this, the Foundation believes that it is of the utmost importance that the
> academic standing of visiting grantees, particularly in the lecturer and advanced
> research scholar categories, should be of the highest order possible.[27]

Some nine months later, it returned to this problem, though this time it was about visiting postgraduates: 'All members of the Board agreed that unsatisfactory students did the programme much harm and that immature students did not get as much from their visit as might be desired.'[28] And in early 1956, Rossiter noted that it was becoming hard to place some American students, particularly those who applied for a Fulbright in their senior college year, as 'many heads of department took the view that students of this type did not have the background or experience to undertake postgraduate work at any Australian university'.[29] This was, above all, a problem of negotiating two very different academic systems – a problem to which we will return elsewhere. But it also resonated in the context of the Australian-based Foundation's particular conception of (educational) ambassadorship.

Program administrators and policy-makers were not always on the same page regarding the form scholars' ambassadorship should take. While Rossiter was concerned that some scholars were neglecting their educational work and thus running down the program's reputation, a key board member was taking a very different tack. Robert J. Boylan was a US public affairs officer and USEF treasurer from 1955 to 1957. In a confidential report submitted to the USIA in Washington in September 1956, he complained about the decision-making of the Australian Fulbright Program.[30] Boylan seemed to suggest that returning Australians would make the most effective ambassadors for the United States. These academics inhabited 'large State universities

Figure 7.1 Peter Hamilton tapes the American ballad 'The Yellow Cat' sung by visiting Fulbright researcher Dr John Greenway, 1957

with strong doubts of the United States' ability in foreign affairs', institutions which were, Boylan claimed, 'the dominant influence of [*sic*] the political and economic leaders of tomorrow'. In them 'we have potentially able defenders of United States domestic and perhaps foreign policy'.[31]

Sydney violinist Ernest Llewellyn encountered this official assumption at the end of his 1955–56 Fulbright award at the Juilliard School of Music in New York. The administering agency for research and Senior Scholars, the Conference Board of Associated Research Councils, sought to determine the impact of his award when it asked him, 'In what important respects has your stay in the United States changed or confirmed the opinion of American life and people which you held prior to your visit?'[32] Llewellyn answered in language that satisfied the requirements of the form. 'My stay in the United States', he wrote, 'has confirmed my previous impression that it has become the world center of music in all forms – performing and teaching. My main source of information prior to my coming here, were the American artists visiting Australia … In every way these artists, without exception, have been wonderful ambassadors for the United States and have presented truthful and attractive pictures of the American way of life'.[33] Here, he endorsed the overarching goal of the scheme, in words that would ring positively in the ears of the program managers. In long, regular letters home, Llewellyn's wife Ruth painted a more nuanced picture of their daily life; while mostly positive and upbeat, she did explore some of the grittier aspects of living in a poor neighbourhood in New York – details that did not appear in her husband's final report. Llewellyn's is one of the few Australian scholar reports from this period that has been preserved and we have managed to locate – thanks to a rich personal archive donated to the National Library of Australia. Other evidence is found in publications by the USEF where returning scholars report.[34]

There is no denying then, that the Australian Fulbright Program was under pressure to support short-term US foreign policy goals, especially at this time. This had implications for ideas about scholarly ambassadorship, forcing a preoccupation (from the USIA/State Department perspective) with selling (or buying) the American 'free world' story. Nevertheless Boylan's vision of fostering awardees as academic ambassadors was by no means universally embraced (as he himself admitted), neither by his colleagues on the board, nor by all scholars. As we have explored in another chapter, the board regularly made clear its refusal to endorse any activities or approaches to programming that smacked of government propaganda.

Pressures of this kind on student programs would grow in ensuing years, with the early 1960s seeing the State Department and USIA develop a joint campaign abroad known as 'Emphasis on Youth'. The coordinator of this campaign in Australia was Public Affairs Officer LeVan Roberts, who over the same period sat on the Fulbright board in Canberra.[35] We can see echoes of the campaign in the scholar report forms over this period, which sought a much higher level of detail than before about scholars' social activities.

In the 1950s, scholar report forms had asked for details of public speaking and informal socialising opportunities, and sought examples of misunderstandings being 'cleared up' by scholars. In 1964, the report form went further, asking the scholar to:

> Please describe some instance in which you think may have contributed to the accomplishment of this [mutual understanding] objective. You may recount, for example, occasions on which you participated in school and community activities, assisted with local civic projects, wrote for local publications, participated in cultural or professional meetings, traveled within your host country, addressed or spoke informally to local audiences, or participated in informal social activities with your hosts. Describe the reception accorded your efforts and the individuals and groups with whom you were associated.[36]

An extraordinarily high level of detail was being requested here. The Department was virtually requesting the submission of a social diary.

Things would soon change. As campus protest movements grew in strength and breadth in the 1960s, with battles raging over political, intellectual and personal freedoms, foreign policy and militarism, Fulbright administrators inevitably had to reconsider, and re-articulate, the ambassadorial expectations of program participants. Students and academics were questioning much more vigorously the way government programs were impinging on research practices and limiting academic freedom, for example. Indeed Senator Fulbright himself contributed to public debates on this subject, and, as we have seen in the correspondence with Leo Marx, was all too aware of the dilemmas facing scholars who had trouble balancing their conflicting role as ambassadors for and yet potential critics of their own country. Sondra Silverman's experience at the ANU is illustrative. She challenged both governments and university policies in her own and her host country. Although she found it hard to extend her award, she succeeded in continuing her postgraduate work despite the board's disapproval of her disruptive behaviour.

In 1963, the US Advisory Commission on International Educational and Cultural Affairs (created under the Fulbright-Hays Act of 1961) reported its concern to Congress that the USIA's supervision of cultural affairs officers who were involved (often very closely) in the administration of the Fulbright Program on non-US soil, might not be 'in the best long-term interest of the program'.[37] When Charles Frankel of Columbia University published a Brookings Institute report on cultural and educational diplomacy three years later, he criticised (among other things) these same administrative arrangements which opened the door for political pressures to be brought to bear on the Fulbright Program, and at the very least provoked accusations of propagandistic intent from observers in partner countries.

In 1966, student magazine *Ramparts* made disturbing revelations about covert CIA funding of US-based student organisations, and Senator Fulbright attempted, as chair of the Senate Foreign Relations Committee, to improve oversight of the spy agency (with little success). That same year, he gave lectures exploring the problems of US foreign policy and the dangers of close university–government links, and argued that a citizen's dissent could be a patriotic act of the highest order. These revelations and debates all had serious repercussions for notions of scholarly diplomacy.

It is perhaps unsurprising then, that in the Fulbright final report forms of 1966, questions touching on scholars' informal ambassadorship had been stripped right back to bare bones (compared to the 1963 version), asking scholars to: 'Please recount occasions on which you addressed or spoke to local audiences, participated in cultural or professional meetings, or wrote for local publications' and 'Please evaluate your experience in terms of its: (A) professional value; (B) personal or social value; and (C) contribution to international understanding'.[38] No longer was there any reference to misunderstandings or an expectation that the minutiae of all social contacts would be inventoried.[39]

That same year, historian Oscar Handlin, then on the BFS, released a public statement on 'Academic Freedom in International Educational Exchange' explaining the board's selection policies. According to the BFS's annual report for that year, 'The guiding assumption of the Board is that there is no conflict between the exchange program's goal of serving U.S. foreign policy objectives and a commitment to the traditional concepts of academic freedom'.[40] This was, surely, in response to mounting concerns about this aspect of the program. But it was unlikely to wash with those who were becoming increasingly vocal about the foreign policy/academic freedom dilemma. As Leo Marx would point out the following year, in the minds of many scholars there *was* a conflict between the two.

John Hope Franklin was ideally placed to appreciate the complex position in which Fulbright scholars found themselves, and which would only become harder to negotiate through the 1960s and 1970s as campuses became more and more politically explosive. He had accepted the Distinguished Visitor award to Australia despite deep misgivings about the country's racist history and ongoing White Australia policy. Franklin played a key role in the US educational exchange landscape, but had been burnt by experience with the State Department, when he felt he had been used as a token educated black man.[41] At the same time, he appreciated the real benefits and impacts of educational exchange, and in his memoirs detailed some of the extraordinary experiences he had during his Australian Fulbright visit in 1960 (covered in chapter 9).[42]

Not all scholars were aware of the complexity of their ambassadorial position – at least before departure. A postgraduate plant ecologist studying in Melbourne in 1966 reported that his exchange period had brought about the 'revelation that quite reasonable people, even citizens of one of the United States' closest allies, may disapprove of quite a lot of American foreign policy'. This was something he admitted 'humbly and simply' he had not understood earlier, and which had reshaped his 'understanding of international relations'.[43] Another American in Australia reported decades later: 'I felt a bit uncomfortable in my (perceived) role as spokesman for anything happening in the U.S. at that time (e.g., the Monica Lewinsky scandal)'.[44]

Meanwhile, a different kind of revelation awaited those American scholars who, unlike the plant ecologist, were already inclined to be critical of their own government's policies. Despite the BFS's attempts to make a clearer distinction between foreign policy and educational exchange, and Senator Fulbright's calls for Americans to overcome their ingrained 'fear of dissent', American scholars in this period could find that taking a critical stance was not always well received by their Australian hosts. A senior scholar in life sciences, for example, reported that 'both Australians and Europeans have told me that they are embarrassed by Americans who attempt comradeship by unduly criticizing the United States'. A postgraduate in soil science advised any future scholar to Australia that: 'He should not feel that he should be so open-minded that he can deprecate his own country in casual discussions; Australians seem suspicious of anyone who is not reasonably proud of his heritage. But don't overdo it!' – a delicate balance to achieve. Another scholar, studying comparative literature at Adelaide University, explored this social challenge in more detail, carefully demonstrating that criticism by a visiting scholar of your host country could be resented by locals while conversely criticism of your home country by your hosts could equally arouse unwelcome defensiveness in yourself.[45] Both were challenging.

Scholars, then, had to tread carefully, adjusting their critical faculties to a variety of social situations and audiences. Scholars were not alone. Administrators, too, expressed confusion about how to interpret the mutual understanding goal, at a time when campus and youth culture more generally was changing dramatically. At a seminar sponsored by the IIE on the Fulbright-Hays Student Exchange Program, held in September 1967 in Wingspread, Wisconsin, university, government, philanthropic and student representatives thrashed out questions about the premises, existing policies and the future of the program. One session was devoted to 'The Student Overseas as Ambassador and Interpreter of his Culture'. The big question of the day was: should a 'hippie' be 'selected out' on the grounds that he might 'misrepresent America while abroad?' The participants failed to reach a consensus on 'where to draw the line between an out-and-out hippie and today's American student who af[fects], for instance, long hair'. They did manage to agree, however, that a crew cut would not be a prerequisite for a Fulbright-Hays grant!

They also discussed the changing image of the Fulbrighter, who no longer seemed to fit the old template of the 'all-American boy', 'patterned after the Rhodes Scholar' who would 'go all over the place … feeling that he left the world better than he found it, return to campus and re-enter with as little trouble as possible'.[46] There was a sense that the old, familiar scholar 'types' had been superseded, in these troubled times when everything was up for questioning. What, we might ask, about women scholars as ambassadors? Of them, nothing at all was said, even though women had been part of the program since day one. The women's movement had not yet arrived in Fulbright program consciousness. But it was on its way.

In the mid-1970s there was an intense period of review of all aspects of the Fulbright Program, with a series of conferences held in the United States, Malaysia and Australia. With US government funding to the program reduced through the late 1960s and early 1970s, and in the face of a dramatic increase in the number of other student exchange programs, Fulbright Program administrators in the United States and partner countries came together to figure out how existing funds should best be allocated, and to reconsider how the program should position itself in relation to other schemes. They asked what was (or could be) unique about the program? One of the outcomes of these discussions was a stronger determination to clarify exactly what the 'mutual understanding' goal meant for scholars. This was echoed in the AAEF's own program review in 1982, when Executive Officer Bruce Farrer argued that they should 'be more active in directing the Program in ways that would benefit mutual understanding'. Farrer had in the mid-1970s replaced the AAEF Executive Officer Ian Willcock when questions were raised about Willcock's inappropriate use of an AAEF credit card. Willcock and Assistant Executive Officer Easton were formally reprimanded and in December 1973 they resigned, although Willcock stayed on for another six months until Bruce Farrer in mid-1974 became the new executive officer, a position he held for the next ten years. Farrer now acknowledged the (now familiar) problem: how to 'define those ways and produce an operational definition of "mutual understanding"'.[47]

The problem was not only what 'mutual understanding' might mean, but also how scholars and administrators might recognise it. There was 'mutual understanding' at a personal level, and then there was mutual understanding at the inter-governmental and institutional level. Whether they were – or even could be – the same, or were in conflict, and what form they took were not made explicit by the BFS. The term could be defined in a number of ways, and was left to scholars themselves to work out. Finally, there was a problem in assessing what kind of impact mutual understanding might have. In the 1970s some Australian alumni (often scientists) wanted 'every Australian academic' (particularly those in humanities) to have the chance to go to the United

States in order to overcome their prejudiced view of the country.[48] Sometimes, particularly in subsequent decades, it resulted in reaffirming belief in a scholar's own culture. One Australian scholar from the 1980s praised the Fulbright Program for opening up the United States to criticism: 'I believe that any program that cuts through the insular hide of US "exceptionalism" is to be pursued with vigor; it's the only way to go.'[49] Another pointed out how 'The exchange absolutely fosters mutual understanding between US and Australia. It shows that the way things are done in the US is not the only way of doing things. It makes one realize that different is not inferior, and sometimes different is superior.'[50] Most recently another said 'I certainly left much more critical of the US, having seen some things that AUS does much better'.[51]

One of the first tasks of the visiting scholar – whether student, lecturer or researcher – was to work out *how things are done*, and then to figure out how to fit into the existing scheme, or perhaps, to challenge it from almost-within as far as possible without offending. LeRoy Johnson's articulate account is a springboard for exploring some of the ways in which scholars have sought to engage with the expectations of being a Fulbright scholar and the 'mutual understanding' goal at its heart.[52] Johnson's 1965 report was insightful not only about the status of his own field of research, but also about the life of the academic and the social and cultural challenges of being an American in Australia. Some of the comments he made about his exchange find echoes in other Americans' reports throughout the decades. This is one of the most fascinating threads in Fulbright Program history: how scholars have experienced, perceived, made sense of, adjusted to, the quite significant differences between Australian and US academic cultures.

An aspect of the exchange experience that Johnson explored in his report was the 'social difficulty' of being somewhere in the middle (age-wise) between postgraduate students and senior staff in Adelaide. Perhaps, this being a small university compared to his own, the problem was exacerbated. But it does also raise the question of the social world of academia. To what extent did and do students and their supervising/teaching staff interact socially and how important was the issue of age in maximising the exchange experience? There was, early on, discussion around the 'ideal age' for Fulbright scholars, which, it seemed, varied according to nationality. 'Australians were especially vocal' about the matter of whom was best to fund and there was 'surprising consensus on the career-stage at which Australians would most benefit from a travel grant' when alumni were surveyed in the mid-1970s.[53] Few thought awards should be made either to undertake PhDs or as a reward for previous distinguished service, but most concurred that the postdoctoral or early career researcher 'in the ascendancy' of their career was the appropriate candidate. They did not consider at that time the gender implications of these age delimitations.

Perhaps more difficult for Johnson than his in-between age was the fact of being American. As the Rose report observed, Australians, 'unlike the Japanese and almost all the others' in the east Asia-Pacific region, were as exercised about who was coming from the United States as they were about who was to go.[54] 'My position with regard to other students and to the staff was a bit equivocal … though I have by no means felt excluded', Johnson wrote. 'In general, there is, however, a tendency for many university people here, both staff and students, to regard American education as inferior to either Australian or English education, so I had to work against this at first.' The challenge was to find a way to talk about America and being an American in a way that was not socially alienating. After discussing some practical difficulties in daily life Johnson analysed the social challenge in some detail. 'More serious adjustments must be made socially, I think, and they are all the more difficult because the differences are so subtle. Without intending to over-generalize', he said, 'the grantee should be prepared to meet a more reserved people than those to whom he may be accustomed, though by no means a straight-laced or stuffy people. Australians are apt to be less effusive and to hold themselves in reserve more'. His views on this were very direct: 'In the national image, this is generally termed stoicism, but I think that is glamorizing what is essentially emotional repression.'

Here we see Johnson drawing on his experiences to attempt to define an Australian 'character'. At the same time, he was very aware of how others might be assessing *his* character and his American-ness. This mutual gaze could be discomfiting, and it also raised the problem of how one should talk about the world(s) one inhabited (the one left behind and the one newly entered), and, equally, how to counter those perceptions or criticisms that seemed unfair or ill-formed. 'The grantee will also meet a good deal of defensiveness, especially at first, when he himself is hyper-conscious of the impression he is registering. It will be very difficult to criticize institutions and customs without incurring a good deal of resentment as a "bloody" outsider', Johnson observed, 'and this may prove to be a difficult position for anyone who is accustomed to criticizing his own country freely from within whenever he sees a wrong or an injustice. On the other hand', he said, it was even more difficult when the people you met were 'very quick to criticize the United States, sometimes with great justice and insight and sometimes not'. It was with this that most of the Americans Johnson knew 'had the greatest difficulty'. As he said, 'It is quite often difficult not to react against it and to be driven into a posture of defense which is not at all a natural one'. This unnatural 'posture of defense' is one that many scholars have found themselves taking reluctantly – and something already explored in the previous chapter.[55]

We have seen how, in the early twenty-first century, the award offer, while acknowledging scholars' right as private citizens to disagree with their government's foreign policy, required that scholars should act as 'goodwill ambassadors', and also try to protect the apolitical nature of the program by avoiding domestic political activity in the host country. Most telling is the final sentence of this clause, acknowledging that 'no ironclad rule can be laid down'. This approach emerged after six decades of program policy-makers, administrators and scholars grappling with the myriad complications that come with a search for transnational 'mutual understanding'. Whereas in the early days, the ambassadorial role was hardly mentioned (if at all) in award offers but fully fleshed out in report form questions, the reverse is now true. Scholars are told up front, even before applying, that they are required to act as 'goodwill ambassadors', but their final report forms are mute on this score. Scholars are now given an open-ended invitation to write a narrative of their 'Fulbright journey'. There are no questions about clearing up misunderstandings. The focus has shifted to the personal transformations and career-related developments experienced by scholars during their exchange, a shift reflecting other social, economic and educational developments in the transnational relationship over recent decades.

Notes

1 1968 US Scholar report, A1838 583/1 Part 5, NAA.
2 Richard Pells, *Not Like Us: How Europeans Have Loved, Hated, and Transformed American Culture Since World War II* (New York, 1997), p. 110.
3 Letter from Leo Marx to Francis Young, 4 September 1967, reprinted in 'The Responsibility of Intellectuals by Leo Marx and J.W. Fulbright', *New York Review of Books*, 9 November 1967.
4 Noam Chomsky, 'A Special Supplement: The Responsibility of Intellectuals', *New York Review of Books*, 23 February 1967.
5 George Steiner and Noam Chomsky, 'The Responsibility of Intellectuals: An Exchange', *New York Review of Books*, 23 March 1967.
6 Letter from Fulbright to Leo Marx, 14 September 1967, reprinted in 'The Responsibility of Intellectuals'.
7 'Protest' by Leo Marx, follow-up to 'The Responsibility of Intellectuals', in *New York Review of Books*, 15 February 1968.
8 J. William Fulbright, *Arrogance of Power* (New York, 1967), pp. 29–30.
9 Richard Kostelanetz, 'In Darkest Fulbright', *The Nation*, 13 June 1966, p. 726.
10 Note the early comment by Douglas J. Cole (electrical engineer, 1954) in USEF, *The Fulbright Programme: The First Eight Years and the Future* (Canberra, 1958), p. 19.
11 These conditions appear in standard award documents supplied to the author by the Australian-American Fulbright Commission in 2012.
12 Public Law 584, 79th Congress, 60 Stat. 754, approved August 1, 1946. Amendment to the Surplus Property Act of 1944. Reprinted in Walter Johnson and Francis Colligan, *The Fulbright Program: A History* (Chicago, 1965), Appendix I, pp. 329–31.
13 Randall Bennett Woods, *Fulbright: A Biography* (Cambridge, 1995), pp. 130–1.
14 See Richard T. Arndt, *The First Resort of Kings: American Cultural Diplomacy in the Twentieth Century* (Washington, DC, 2005), pp. 233–5, and Liping Bu, 'Educational Exchange and Cultural Diplomacy in the Cold War', *Journal of American Studies*, vol. 33:3, part 1 (December 1999), pp. 409–12.
15 'Agreement [Fulbright Agreement] between the Government of Australia and the Government of the United States of America for the Use of Funds made available in accordance with the Agreement on Settlement for Lend-Lease, Reciprocal Aid, Surplus War Property and Claims of 7 June 1946 – Date and Place of Signing: 26 November 1949 – Date of entry into force for Australia: 26 November 1949 – ATS Number: [1949] ATS 14 – Language: English'. In A13307 18/1, NAA.
16 Public Law 87–256, 87th Congress, H.R. 8666, September 21, 1961. Reprinted in Johnson and Colligan, *Fulbright Program*, Appendix II, p. 332.
17 A1838 250/9/8/7 Part 1, NAA.
18 USEF board minutes, 28 February 1955.
19 USEF board minutes, 28 February 1956.

20 11 May 1951, Clipping from *ACB* no. 115, in 'United States of America – Relations with Australia – Requests for Information on Fulbright Agreement', A1838 250/9/8/3 PART 1, NAA.

21 Johnson and Colligan, *Fulbright Program*, pp. 55–8; Arndt, *First Resort of Kings*, pp. 257–60; Wilson P. Dizard Jr., *Inventing Public Diplomacy: The Story of the U.S. Information Agency* (Boulder, 2004), pp. 56–8.

22 Johnson and Colligan, *Fulbright Program*.

23 Reports are in A1838 250/9/8/4/2 Part 3, NAA and in A1838 250/9/8/4/2 PART 2, NAA. Only a small number of grantee reports have survived from the early 1950s and 1968. Most were destroyed by the Australian-American Educational Foundation Fulbright (AAEF, the successor to USEF) in 1970. AAEF board minutes, 5 June 1970. Archives of the AAFC, Canberra.

24 Scholar report, 1953, in A1838 250/9/8/4/2 PART 2, NAA.

25 Margaret Thornhill, Scholar report, 1954, in 'United States of America – Relations with Australia – United States Educational Foundation – General', NAA: A1838 250/9/8/4/2 PART 3.

26 Scholar reports of John Rose Faust, and Barbara Ann Stay in NAA: A1838 250/9/8/4/2 PART 3; of Georgia Travis in 250/9/8/4/2 PART 2; of Charles Hartshorne in 250/9/8/3 Part 3.

27 USEF board minutes, 26 October 1953.

28 USEF board minutes, 12 July 1954.

29 USEF board minutes, 20 February 1956.

30 20 September 1956, FSD USIS Canberra to USIA, Washington. Subj: Emphasis on Youth. RG 59. EDX-12 AUSTL (Educational and Cultural Exchange – Australia), Box 390, NARA (College Park).

31 20 September 1956, FSD USIS Canberra to USIA, Washington. Subj: Emphasis on Youth. RG 59. EDX-12 AUSTL (Educational and Cultural Exchange – Australia), Box 390, NARA (College Park).

32 Final report to Con. Board of Assoc. Research councils Committee on International Exchange of Persons, Washington, DC, July 23rd, 1956. In Papers of Ernest Llewellyn, NLA MS.

33 Final report to Con. Board of Assoc. Research councils Committee on International Exchange of Persons, Washington, DC, July 23rd, 1956. In Papers of Ernest Llewellyn, NLA MS.

34 USEF, *The Fulbright Programme*.

35 25 June 1965, Confidential Airgram from American Embassy Canberra to Department of State, subject 'Emphasis on Youth', signed LeVan Roberts, Public Affairs Officer and 'Youth Coordinator'. In NARA.

36 1964, 'Final Report by American Grantee Before Leaving Host Country', form issued by US Department of State, in 'Reports by Visiting American Fulbright Scholars', A463 1965/2313, NAA.

37 Johnson and Colligan, *Fulbright Program*, pp. 84–5.

38 See 'Reports by Visiting American Fulbright Scholars', 1963–68, in A463 (A463/50), 1965/2313, NAA.

39 AAEF minutes, 17 March 1965, noted that the Department of State had designed a new report form. AAEF board members discussed possibility of adding some of their own questions – what they were most interested in was having 'more comments from grantees on the local educational system and local academic policies and procedures'.

At the next meeting (17 May) they had received the new form and in August 1966 the board 'commented on the improved communications resulting from the adoption of the new report form'.

40 'Educational Exchanges: New Approaches to International Understanding', BFS Annual Report 1966–67, p. 14.

41 Ray Arsenault and John Hope Franklin, 'Pioneers of History: The Sage of Freedom: An Interview with John Hope Franklin', *The Public Historian*, vol. 29:2 (Spring 2007), p. 42.

42 John Hope Franklin, *Mirror to America: The Autobiography of John Hope Franklin* (New York, 2005), pp. 184–5.

43 'Reports by Visiting American Fulbright Scholars', A463 1965/2313, NAA (Canberra).

44 US scholar, ecology, 1997, Survey, La Trobe University 2011.

45 Scholar report in NAA 'Reports by Visiting American Fulbright Scholars' A463 1965/2313 (online).

46 G.P. Springer, A report on the Fulbright-Hays Student Exchange Program Seminar, Sept. 20–22, 1967, Wingspread, Wis. [New York], Institute of International Education (1968).

47 AAEF board minutes, 25 February 1982, item on Program review.

48 Peter Rose, *Academic Sojourners: A Report on the Senior Fulbright Programs in East Asia and the Pacific* (United States Bureau of Educational and Cultural Affairs, Office of Policy and Plans, 1976), pp. 105–6, attached to Background Paper for Review Meeting, AAEF Dec. 1976.

49 1980s scholar in US history, response to Survey, La Trobe University, 2011.

50 Three-time scholar, zoology (first scholarship in 1960s, last in 2000s), response to Survey, La Trobe University, 2011.

51 LeRoy Johnson, Scholar report, 1965, NAA: A463, 1965/2313.

52 2000s scholar in conservation biology, response to Survey, La Trobe University, 2011.

53 Rose, *Academic Sojourners*, p. 109.

54 Rose, *Academic Sojourners*, p. 108.

55 LeRoy Johnson, Scholar report 1965. NAA: A463 1965/2313.

8

'Just because one is a woman': Forging careers and changing the gender landscape

When the Australian Fulbright Agreement was finally signed into existence in 1949, social worker Norma Parker, like many other women, was poised ready to apply. That Australian women were alert to the opportunities the new program offered is not surprising. They had been receiving CCNY travel grants to the United States since the 1930s.[1] That so many succeeded in the early years of the program is the more interesting story. Parker was foundation president of the newly formed Australian Association of Social Workers. On hearing the news of the signing, she immediately wrote to the Department of External Affairs to enquire about possi-bilities.[2] In 1951 she was granted a Senior Fulbright award.[3] It was the first to be awarded in social work and, out of a total of thirty-three awards to Australians that year, one of only two awarded to a woman.[4] Nevertheless Parker was not the first Australian woman to receive a Fulbright award. That honour belongs to undergraduates Adele Millerd, in plant biochemistry, and historian Dorothy Munro (later Shineberg), who were – in a perfect balance of science and human-ities – in the first cohort of 1950.[5]

It is significant that, from the outset, women were among those included in the granting of awards, albeit in a small minority. An understanding of the history of the Fulbright scheme in Australia would be incomplete without recognition of this pre-viously unexamined dimension. Here was a marked difference from the more famous Rhodes scholarships, which did not accept women as formal applicants until 1977, nearly thirty years later.[6]

There is evidence that Senator Fulbright himself showed 'a great deal of collegiality, appreciation, and respect' in his professional dealings with women, and that strong, pol-itical, active women were prominent in his closest personal relations.[7] Yet the Fulbright scheme was not conceived with an explicit equal opportunity agenda, and 'affirmative action' was a concept whose time had not yet come. Was it just fortuitous that women could take advantage in these early years, or was it more deliberate? Perhaps the Fulbright Program's inclusion of women was part of the broader cooperation between government departments, notably the US Women's Bureau, and various women's professional organisations which, Richard T. Arndt notes, drew together to educate women 'as an American responsibility'.[8] From a concern to concentrate on women in former fascist countries, attention soon turned to new Cold War imperatives and women became 'both tools and targets for public diplomacy'.[9] Whatever the reason driving the program administrators, who were also sometimes women, the inclusion of women scholars was an important aspect. It provides a new perspective on the Fulbright program's history, its value and its limitations. It reveals what Fulbright himself saw as 'the political implications of exposing individuals to new ideas and challenging experiences'.[10] Those women applicants who now put themselves forward for Fulbright awards were in the vanguard of what became a transformation in the gender landscape of higher education.

Breaking down the barriers

The end of the first decade of the Fulbright Program coincided with the upsurge of enrolments on university campuses when the first of the post-war baby boom generation reached university entry age. In the fifty years since, the number of students in tertiary education has increased dramatically and, particularly in later years, the rate of increase for women has outstripped that for men. It took some time, however, for the gender ratio to change, and the proportion of women amongst students and staff, to rise. The Fulbright scheme was part, not the solitary driver, of this expansion, and belongs with the increased government involvement in education in the aftermath of the Second World War. In the United States that included the GI Bill, and in Australia, the post-war reconstruction training scheme for returned servicemen. These measures broke down barriers of class and ethnic elitism, but they expanded the numbers of men attending universities and not the equivalent numbers of women. This masculinised campus life, in the 1950s and decades beyond, made it difficult for the relatively small number of women to compete for and achieve academic positions.[11]

Population growth from the post-war immigration program as well as the baby boom increased demand for all levels and sectors of education. The Menzies L-CP coalition government's planned expansion of higher education was based on the 1957 Murray Report, which was mired in gendered conceptions that did not help women. It allowed that Australian women could be students and graduates, but 'all other key subject positions' – citizens, doctors, teachers, researchers, academics – were 'constructed as men'. This was not just an oversight. In the language of the Murray Report, Australian academics were 'heroic, rational, dispassionate (almost monastic) men of the enlightenment, devoted to the selfless and disciplined pursuit of knowledge for its own sake', and they were 'unlike businessmen, the public and politicians'.[12] It was this kind of thinking, when it infused higher education decision-making, that made it difficult for women to meet the criteria for selection.

Until the years immediately prior to signing the Australian Fulbright Agreement, it was against the law for Australian married women to be teachers, lecturers, public servants or work in local government.[13] Women who wanted these careers were obliged to choose between staying single or keeping their marital status a secret from their employer and colleagues. Even when the law was changed the entrenched expectation that a professional career path was open primarily to men remained as an obstacle for talented and ambitious women to overcome.[14] In a study on Australian women undertaken on behalf of the Social Sciences Research Council and published in 1962, Norman McKenzie examined Australian women's access to careers, pay equity, jury service, education, the professions and public service. He found it paradoxical that Australia was markedly egalitarian, yet the absence of women in the nation's political and professional life was undeniable.[15]

Visitors to the country noticed this paradox and frequently remarked on it. Mrs Graham Bell held a degree in psychology and was married to a Fulbright lecturer in psychology at the University of Western Australia, when she spoke to the media of her amazement at the social separation of Australian men and women. 'Frankly I wonder', she said, 'how they ever get together enough to get married'. Her comments on Australian couples were reported in the Melbourne press under the headline 'How DO We Manage to Get Married?' She reportedly said Australian couples, 'have no mutually interesting experiences to discuss, and are thoroughly boring to each other', while in contrast, 'On the whole, American men and women, especially husbands and wives, have more interests in common and do more together than Australians'.[16]

While the Fulbright Program could not change the laws and customs of partner countries, it could encourage comment and observations from participating academics. It could also provide opportunities for career advancement, through international networking and enhanced prestige, to meritorious women. In its own quiet way, the program of educational exchange thus helped to alter the gendered landscape of Australian academic work over many decades. The Fulbright Program set out to identify and foster academic and intellectual leaders from around the world, and thereby widen the pool of talent from which future leaders would be drawn. The program not only facilitated the emergence of the United States as a destination for future Australian educators, tending to replace British universities; it also created a cohort of women for whom academic careers and achievements across a range of disciplines were possible. In effect, the program was actively inviting women into the international pool of future leaders. An example was Nancy Viviani (Senior Scholar 1977) whose international relations research took her to Harvard where she was appointed a fellow and where she would return as visiting professor in 1982 and again in 1989. Although Nancy Viviani had a distinguished academic career, it was to be her work as a developer of policy for government – on the need for Asian studies and languages in Australian schools, and on the place of migrants and refugees in Australia – that was to be more significant. She also had an important role as social development chief in Bangkok for the United Nations Economic and Social Commission for Asia and the Pacific in the mid-1980s.[17]

As women came forward and took advantage of the promise of Fulbright travel grants, they challenged and subverted the limited education and career paths available to them, and increased the opportunities for other women in the future. One of these was Myra Roper, principal of Women's College, University of Melbourne, and recipient of first a Carnegie grant (1950) and then a Fulbright award (1962). Roper became an expert on China in the 1960s. She was by then on the educational staff of the Australian Broadcasting Commission and was given a partial Fulbright grant to observe educational radio and television in the United States. In 1963 she made a documentary on China for Australian television and had a small career in commercial television. In an article comparing Australia (unfavourably) with the United Kingdom and United States, in 1952, Roper asked why there were no women in Australian public life. In a decade not usually associated with feminism, Roper attracted press attention with her bold pronouncements (dubbed 'Roperisms') on topics such as careers for girls and married women, equality of opportunity, and the need for new university courses for women. Such publicly expressed sentiments were reinforced by visiting American women whose receipt of a Fulbright award and other achievements were made visible in the daily and weekly metropolitan press, either on the news pages, or in the society or women's pages. These media conversations kept alive the issues of women's access to paid work, careers and equal pay and were pronounced in the decades after the end of the war and before the renewed upsurge of the women's movement.

Nevertheless, the administrative procedures of selection, programming, funding and decision-making that we have already explored in previous chapters, were also performed in a context of male domination of university life that only slowly came to be challenged and still today remains secure. We can see these changes reflected in the experiences of women who took up awards.

In giving awards to women, the USEF and Fulbright award selection committees were not immune to the conscious or unconscious bias that permeated and created discriminatory practice, as Adele Millerd's painful memory (recounted in a previous chapter) of her awkward and unpleasant USEF interview, attests. The difficulty of assessing research proposals on the subject of women, or which brought new theoretical (feminist) perspectives to research, was also problematic, and sometimes too challenging, for all-male selection committees.[18] The number of successful women applicants was, therefore, always small, numbers which have remained remarkably constant. There were thirty-two women in the first five years of the Australian–US program, and thirty-three in the next five. In 1950 there were two awards to women; in 1951 this rose to five (one Senior Scholar, four postgraduates) and in 1952 to six, reaching a crescendo of ten in 1954, of whom two, including Nancy Millis, were Senior Scholars. Numbers dropped back in 1955–58 but reached ten again in 1959. In the twenty-first century the raw numbers were much the same: hovering between a low of six in 2005 and peaking at eleven in 2009.

Numbers were initially boosted by those on teacher exchanges. They made up half of the numbers between 1950 and 1955, and in some years (1955, for example) there were equal numbers of teachers on exchange, as postgraduates and as senior scholars. Teacher exchange numbers lessened in the next five years (to ten out of 33) and there were only seven in the 1960s. The last teacher exchange award was made in 1988. Although some teachers (usually from elite secondary schools) received awards for Educational Development, this was not as classroom teachers on exchange. One of these was Freda Whitlam (1954 postgraduate), headmistress of Canberra Girls Grammar and later Presbyterian Ladies College Croydon in Sydney but perhaps better known as the sister of Gough Whitlam, prime minister of Australia (1972–75).

The disciplinary balance between sciences and humanities (discussed in chapter 4) is hard to ascertain because the records are incomplete. We do know that many women who benefited from the scheme did so because its purpose was actively developing areas of study that had not been part of the British model of higher education then dominant in Australian universities. In its early years, the Fulbright Program's major contribution to Australia was to foster particular disciplines, notably those – social work, nursing, early childhood education, library science, social welfare, home economics – in which Australia did not yet offer formal tertiary courses. This was also where significant numbers of women were employed, such as Olive Battersby who spent the 1952–53 academic year as a Senior Scholar in library science at Oregon State College.[19] Another early recipient (in 1953) was Margaret Looker (later Guy), matron of the Royal Prince Alfred Hospital, Sydney, who spent her time at the University of Chicago studying nursing education. Fulbright's recruitment of candidates from institutions beyond the universities – in libraries, laboratories, hospitals, secondary schools, teachers' and technical colleges – worked to the advantage of women. By the 1960s the number of postgraduate awards was outstripping other categories, and was quite evenly spread across disciplines, though with more in humanities and social sciences overall.

In 1966 the first postdoctoral award was made – to Lesley Clarke, in the field of animal and plant sciences – followed by another (to Gwenda Lewis in statistics) the next year and one each (unknown fields) for each of the next two years. The number of postdoctoral fellowships awarded to women reduced to five across the 1970s. Postdoc numbers rose in the mid-1980s to two or even more per annum, only to decline again in the mid-1990s, to a total of ten across the period 2000–9. The fields in 2000–9 reflect other concerns such as environmental science, counter-terrorism, marine ecology, rather than teachers, librarians and social workers.

'Australia's most outstanding pioneer[s]'

In 1960, when Australian historian Jill Ker (later Conway) arrived at Harvard University to pursue postgraduate study on her Fulbright award, it was not yet apparent that an important new era was dawning in women's lives. Conway's highly-acclaimed memoirs of her academic and personal journey from an isolated Australian sheep-farm to the top echelons of US college administration, capture the academic trajectory that was being opened up to women individually and collectively, but which was also fraught. When presented with the chance for an award to travel to the United States and expand their education, ambitious women grabbed the opportunity. They then had further experiences which resulted in enriched (and sometimes unexpected) outcomes. Women academics, like Conway, who were chosen for Fulbright awards on their merits in their particular disciplines, then expanded the horizons of themselves and other women through their increased exposure to, and understanding of, the gender dynamics of the world they had entered. Those women who had awards in the first few decades found their academic careers did not follow the same trajectory as men's careers. Some felt they had not reached the heights they might have under different conditions. Norma Parker, who built up the social work departments at both Sydney University and the University of New South Wales, was never promoted nor appointed to a position as full professor. Dorothy Shineberg, a married woman (and mother) in the 1950s and 1960s, found it difficult to obtain a research-only position or to advance as far in the profession as her important contributions should have made possible.[20]

Those who received awards in later decades were more likely to reach the higher levels of university administration. The first woman to break the glass ceiling in Australia and become a vice-chancellor (Professor Di Yerbury) was appointed in 1987 by Macquarie University. While Yerbury was never a recipient of a Fulbright award, that same year, Margaret Gardner, from the sociology department at Griffith University in Queensland, was awarded one of the four Fulbright postdoctoral fellowships given to women that year. She went off to the University of California, Berkeley. Today there are nine women – still only 23 per cent of the total number of vice-chancellors of Australian universities – and among them is Margaret Gardner. In 2002, she chaired a Queensland government taskforce on post-compulsory education and the pathways between schools, vocational education and higher education sectors. Three years later Gardner became vice-chancellor of Royal Melbourne Institute of Technology, and in 2014 vice-chancellor of Monash University. Nancy Milliss (Senior Scholar 1954) became the first chancellor of La Trobe University in 1967.

Women who showed initiative in applying for Fulbright awards showed the same initiative in other endeavours. One notable grantee from the early years was Lorraine Stumm who had already pushed through the male domination of her chosen career of journalism. She had been a wartime correspondent and was the first journalist to arrive in Hiroshima after the atomic bomb was dropped in 1945.[21] In 1952 she wrote about her experiences on her Fulbright award, among a group of Australians studying at Stanford University in California (see Figure 8.1).[22] Through contact with people of many nationalities, not just Americans, Stumm felt she had gained a much better understanding of human nature, so necessary to her field where 'more than a superficial understanding of people is needed'. In assessing her experience she said: 'I feel that student exchange is the greatest public relations drive for international goodwill that has ever been attempted.'[23]

We find among the women who had Fulbright awards were many other firsts: Jennifer McKimm-Breschkin (postgraduate, 1975), in medicine, went to Pennsylvania State. When she came back she worked on the newly discovered rotaviruses, and was part of the team involved in the development of the world's first anti-influenza drug. Margaret Britz (postdoctoral award, 1981), also in medicine, went to MIT, became the Foundation Chair of Food Science at the University of Melbourne and was also the first principal advisor for science and engineering policy for the Victorian government, charged with implementing the state's innovation policy. Some other examples are

Figure 8.1 Four Australians at Stanford University, California: L to R Lorraine Stumm, Ian Reed, Neilma Gantner and Violet Young, 'Aussie "Gang" at American University', *The Australian Women's Weekly*, 27 February 1952

Jean Adamson and Phyllis Scott, trailblazers in early childhood education, who both won Fulbright awards in 1956, and four years later established the first journal in their field in Australia, the *Australian Preschool Quarterly*.[24] Margaret Manion was the first woman to be appointed to an established chair (the *Herald* Chair in Art History) at the University of Melbourne, and was the first woman to chair the university's Academic Board. Elizabeth Watts (short-term Senior Scholar 1974) was the founding editor (1973–82) of the journal *The Aboriginal Child at School*, which in 1996 changed its name to the *Australian Journal of Indigenous Education*. Sponsored by the Aboriginal and Torres Strait Islanders Studies Unit at the University of Queensland, the journal has been a leading source of information and debate and a significant shaping influence in the field.

Like Norma Parker, who is considered one of the founders of social work in Australia, 'Australia's most outstanding pioneer of professional social work',[25] many of the women who received Fulbright awards are credited with creating new academic fields. Norma Parker blazed a trail for other social workers to follow and brought out American social workers she thought could help build the profession in Australia, using the Fulbright scheme where possible, and working hard to embed social casework practice into the Australian training system.[26] In medicine, Tania Sorrell (postdoctoral fellow, 1975), who went to the University of California, is seen to have pioneered the establishment of infectious diseases as a discipline of internal medicine in Australia. Dorothy Shineberg is credited with founding the field of Pacific history, with her very influential studies of Melanesian trade (*They Came for Sandalwood*) and on Pacific Islander labour in New Caledonia (*The People Trade*), and upon her return to Australia from her Fulbright award, in founding a course of undergraduate study at the University of Melbourne. There she taught many future scholars of Asia-Pacific studies. Among them was Greg Dening, who became a highly acclaimed and very influential historian-anthropologist of the Pacific, whose innovative methods transformed the discipline, and who also later had a Fulbright award himself.[27]

After a promising start there is, however, a pattern of decline across the next two decades. In 1967 Professor Rhoda Dorsey, educated at Smith College and a teacher at a liberal arts college for women in Baltimore, was visiting the ANU when she was asked 'just how big was the role of women in American academic life?'. She replied she thought prospects for women in academia and feminism had actually gone backwards since the 1940s. She thought fewer women were going on to do a PhD and the impulse of the feminist movement had died down.[28] Certainly Australian women's proportion of the awards was higher in the 1950s (14 per cent) than in subsequent two decades (8 per cent in the 1960s, 7 per cent in the 1970s). There might be slightly more if the larger number of scholars whose sex we have been unable to establish (14 per cent from Australia and 11.5 per cent from the United States in the 1960s; 7 per cent from Australia, 2.5 per cent from the United States in the 1970s) are also found to be women. We can only speculate on the causes of this decline.

The ratio of Australian women to men improved in the 1980s, after the USIA provided a sharp response to the proposed 1984 Australian program. In their recommendations, USIA officers criticised 'the "relative lack of titled projects" and the inclusion of "highly specific requests in unrelated fields", giving the impression of "an 'old boys' support system"'.[29] The proportion of women eventually became more equitable (43 per cent) in the 1990s, due to targeted policy changes. The appointment – finally! – of the first women to the AAEF board – Jacqueline Hochmann (later Taylor), in 1985, followed by Susan Dorsch in 1987 – no doubt pushed things along. Hochmann was director of the Westpac Art Gallery and known to the US consulate for whom she did some work.[30] Dorsch, who was elected chair of the AAEF board in 1990, was used to being a trail-blazer. She was the first female professor in the Faculty of Medicine at the University of Sydney, and in 1986 was appointed Pro-Vice-chancellor of the university and in 1989 deputy vice-chancellor. She was joined by former minister for Education in the Hawke Labor government, Susan Ryan, who was appointed to the AAEF board in 1990. Ryan had an MA in literature from the ANU, personal experience of living in the United States in the early 1970s, and as the only woman member of the Hawke Cabinet, had engineered Australia's anti-discrimination legislation through the parliament. Together they concurred that the AAEF needed a new executive director, new ideas were needed, and in 1991, Charles Beltz, who had held the position since 1987, was replaced by John Lake.[31]

Women board members also began to make a difference to the number of women getting awards, and the number of awards going to the visual and performing arts. Dorsch recalls considerable support came from the US ambassador but that the impetus was actually the visit to Australia of the (woman) chair of the US BFS, which had included women members since the first appointments were made by President Truman.[32] Ryan does not recall any opposition from other board members or pushing any particular agenda but acknowledges that she would have had an increased awareness of the importance and the way to assess women's candidature.

The low numbers across the first four decades of the program can be explained partly by BFS/USEF policies. Women's access to Fulbright grants was contingent on the terms of the funding and the external constraints under which the program operated. As we've seen in previous chapters, the first Australian Fulbright awards were only travel grants and Australian candidates had to show evidence of financial support from other sources. Sometimes this meant holding another grant simultaneously (such as a Carnegie award) and this possibly made it more difficult for women who struggled to compete for these awards which were given on criteria which favoured men in leadership positions. Many women thus depended on an Australian Federation of University Women grant. Patricia Lee (postgraduate award, 1954) was among those. She was a young microbiologist in Queensland when she succeeded (encouraged by her mentor) in applying for a Fulbright award, becoming only one of ten women to succeed that year. She also, importantly, received a Federation of University Women grant, and it was this which was critical in enabling her to take up the Fulbright to pursue her postgraduate studies. The AFUW provided her with the all-important living allowance, and also visa arrangements which enabled her to leave and re-enter the United States so she could also travel to the United Kingdom to further her laboratory experience.[33] The ready availability of these additional awards, and the success of women's applications, assuredly determined the fluctuations in Fulbright awards taken up in any one year. When US government funding was cut in the 1960s and 1970s, the proportion of women coming to Australia plummeted (from a high of 19 per cent in the 1950s, to a little over 6 per cent in the 1970s). It also seems that the decision to reduce the number of postgraduate awards and increase the number of Senior Scholars also benefited men. As we have seen, women were more numerous as postgraduates.

Women also fared better when particular disciplines were awarded grants. Perhaps not surprisingly, Australian women's proportion of the awards was lower in older disciplines like law (where the ratio of women to men was 1:28 in the 1960s) and economics (1:16) than it was in newer emergent disciplines being actively nurtured by Fulbright. The active development of awards to law coming from the close relationship between Harvey Griswold, dean of law at Harvard, and Zelman Cowan, dean of law at the University of Melbourne, did not flow on to women. The only Australian woman to get a Fulbright in the discipline of law in the 1970s was Margaret Thornton (postgraduate, 1979). She went to Yale rather than Harvard, and came from UNSW, not Melbourne. She later became Professor of Law and Legal Studies at La Trobe University (1990–2006) then Professor of Law at the ANU. With her (perhaps not unexpected) expertise in discrimination and equal opportunity she has been chair of numerous national, state and university councils and committees, including the NSW Women's Advisory Council, and the NSW Committee on Discrimination in Employment and Occupation. Over the life of the program there have been more than fifty-five Australian women and only eleven American women, in law.

'Mutual understanding' as gendered experience

Although it is fair to say, therefore, that Fulbright support for women academics was not initially high, and on the Australian side of decision-making, may even have been inadvertent, it has nonetheless fostered careers among a group of women who used their award to promote the benefits to other women. Matron Margaret (Looker) Guy returned from her Fulbright study to explain to *Sydney Morning Herald* readers that 'There's More to Being a Nurse than Bed-Making'. She argued that 'unless we cater for the girls of higher intelligence in the nursing profession they will go into other careers giving better educational and monetary advantages'.[34] This was a pitch to upgrade nursing to tertiary training in order to attract ambitious girls seeking professional careers, of which there were undoubtedly growing numbers in the 1950s. Without them, nursing, 'left with girls of lower educational and intelligence standards', would be the loser. Nursing subsequently but only slowly became an area of tertiary study in Australia. Pushing their own career forward under the auspices of the Fulbright scheme was also a means for advancing fields for other women's careers.

Women were encouraged to go to the United States where women were a larger minority on university campuses. Many more American women had gained a PhD. The first PhDs were granted in Australia in 1948. Eleanora (Nora) Gyarfas, who that year had migrated to Australia from Hungary, was among those pioneers. She was not only the first woman to be awarded a PhD at the University of Sydney but was the first PhD altogether in chemistry from that University.[35] In 1955 she was a Fulbright senior scholar to the University of Illinois.

Another reason the United States was attractive as a destination to Australian women (many of whom might have been educated at single-sex secondary schools) is because there was a strong tradition of women's colleges there.[36] The first woman to go to the US with the Australian program – Dorothy Munro (later Shineberg) – went to Smith College, where she completed an MA in history. Another who went to one of the women's colleges (to Bryn Mawr) was Margaret Manion (postgraduate 1969) now renowned as one of Australia's pre-eminent art historians for her scholarship on medieval and Renaissance art. She was preceded by Virginia Spate (postgraduate, 1962) who also went to Bryn Mawr to do a PhD in art history. Both have had very distinguished international careers. Manion served two terms as foreign adviser to the International Center for Medieval Art, New York. Spate's book on Claude Monet was awarded the 1992 Mitchell Prize for the best book on art history published in English.

The importance of the US women's colleges to Australian women's future careers is most remarkably connected in the story of Jill Ker Conway (see Figure 8.2). She expected to be writing a history of trade in the Pacific but was so impressed with what she observed of American women's achievements when she arrived at Harvard, that within a year, Conway had switched topics and chosen US women as the subject of her history dissertation. Fifteen years later she was the first woman appointed as president of Smith College, whose distinctive character as an all-women college Conway then successfully fought to retain as the pressures to go co-educational mounted. Not only

Figure 8.2 Sarah Belchetz-Swenson, *Jill Ker Conway I*, 1985

did her own life change: so consequently would the lives of other women as Conway pursued the self-consciously feminist aspirations of women's education.

Conway's distinguished career as an educator and academic is exemplary of the 'mutual understanding' goal of the Australian-American Fulbright Program. Furthermore, in embracing and furthering the newly emergent field of women's history, Conway's experience captures the unexpected changes in higher education that followed as women used the availability of the Fulbright award scheme to pursue their individual goals for career advancement and to construct their political subjectivity and professional identity. Not many of the awards were given for specifically feminist projects but there is evidence that the connections made through the Fulbright Program also facilitated the growth of women's studies as a discipline in Australia. Anna Yeatman, who in 1971 was a postgraduate in political science from the University of Adelaide to the New School for Social Research in New York, was appointed Foundation Professor of Women's Studies, at the University of Waikato, New Zealand in 1991. Historian Miriam Dixon got her Fulbright Senior Scholar award (1978) after she had published her major work of women's history, *The Real Matilda: Women and Identity in Australia, 1788–1975*, widely regarded as one of the landmark texts of the field of women's history in Australia. Dixon is also credited with teaching the first course in women's history at an Australian university.[37] Over time Australia's post-war immigration program changed the diversity of the population and we see that too being reflected in Fulbright awards. Mary Kalantzis, the child of Greek immigrants, went on a Fulbright award to the University of New Hampshire in 1990 and later became dean of the College of Education, University of Illinois, where she established a reputation in the field of multiculturalism and gender.

Fulbright scholars were selected not only for their academic record, but for personal skills that would further friendly relations through people meeting people on a basis of equality, interacting with their academic communities and ordinary people in everyday life. A good example here is Ruth Fink (later Latukefu). She was completing a doctorate in anthropology at Columbia University in New York, in 1957, mentored by Margaret Mead among others. Fink was invited to a three-week Quaker-organised seminar in Vermont, with other foreign students from every continent, where difficult political issues were discussed. Fink remembers this as a transformational time, grappling with big world issues and taking on micro-leadership roles, with men and women as intellectual equals. They were encouraged to discuss the most thorny political issues, including McCarthyism in the United States and the situation in Palestine.[38]

This idea of equality was a theme that US women coming as Fulbright visitors brought with them to Australia. The records show that the small proportion of American women who came to Australia with Fulbrights had a disproportionately big impact. The early US Fulbright scholars were trailblazers and senior figures in their particular fields in the 1950s. The first American woman to travel to Australia on a Fulbright award was Harriet Creighton (1952), Professor of Botany at Wellesley College and the first woman to be appointed secretary of the Botanical Society of America. Another pioneer was Mary Murphy (1953), Professor of Economics and Business Administration at the Los Angeles State College of Applied Arts and Science (previously mentioned in chapter 2). She was the first woman in the United States to become a certified public accountant and was not followed by another woman for twenty years; the first woman to address the International Congress of Accountants in London; and took pride in being the first Fulbright lecturer in accounting to go to Australia (and possibly anywhere in the world). She believed her selection as the first ever US Fulbrighter in accounting was 'revolutionary' and praised Australian accountants for 'being willing to accept a woman in what was usually regarded as a man's sphere'.[39]

Murphy attracted a lot of press attention as she moved around the country to different capital cities, where she noted the discrimination against professional women, advocated equality for women and men, 'in job, home and national life', and optimistically expected Australian women would soon achieve equal pay. She was portrayed by journalists as someone with a foot in both men's and women's worlds. In one article Murphy was reported as saying that 'She had found business and professional women progressive in outlook and very much aware of new developments in their specific fields'.[40] She was a keen promoter of international certification for accountants, and encouraged leadership from countries like Australia, with 'highly developed accounting systems', to 'lead the world to a set of uniform accounting standards'.[41]

The *Argus* in Melbourne reported Murphy as saying that Australia was 'approaching the stage where women will automatically receive equal pay for equal work'. She claimed, controversially, that in the United States, equal pay for equal sexes was 'taken for granted in all the professions' and that although Australia was twenty years behind the United States, it wouldn't take another twenty to catch up. A month later she went further at a Soroptomists Society luncheon. This was an organisation of business and professional women dedicated to improving the lives of women and girls. Murphy told them that 'Equality for men and women, in job, home and national life is Australia's quickest road to peace, prosperity, and a satisfactory place in international affairs'. She also quoted a UN Human Rights report which revealed that 'Australian women were taking a smaller part in public and professional activities than the women of India', where, for example, the Health minister was a woman. Murphy pointed out that Australia had no women Supreme Court judges, Queen's counsels, or magistrates.[42]

Other women among the early Fulbright awards were painter and Mount Holyoke College Professor of Fine Art Dorothy Cogswell, who had been the first woman to obtain an MA in fine art at Yale. She visited Australia as a Senior Fulbright Scholar in 1957 and noted that Australians bought more art, and Australian newspapers placed more emphasis on art, than their American counterparts.[43] American anthropologist, Patricia Waterman, took 'trunks of modern sound recording and photographic equipment, tinned food, office equipment, a small reference library and a few articles of clothing' when she and her ethnomusicologist husband Richard Waterman camped in Arnhem Land with Yolgnu in Yirrkala.[44] She became an advocate for the people she lived with in Arnhem Land, attempting to shift attitudes in an era when Aboriginal culture was commonly derided by white people. She collected Aboriginal bark paintings and took them back to United States in the 1950s, a collection which subsequently became the backbone of the art museum at University of South Florida.

As a science educator Marjorie Gardner (US Senior Scholar, 1973) brought international standing when she came from the University of Maryland to Macquarie University in Sydney. She had already been a consultant-lecturer at various summer institutes in India (1965–69) and a UNESCO consultant in science education to the governments of Thailand (1972–82), Qatar (1980–81) and the People's Republic of China (1982–83). Gardner was recognised with a variety of honors from US and UK professional societies. Palaeontologist Patricia Vickers-Rich (US postdoctoral fellow, 1973), went to Monash University in Melbourne, and found the exchange experience so vital to her career that she migrated to Australia three years later to pursue her research on the origin and evolution of Australasian vertebrates and their environments over the previous 400 million years. She subsequently rose to prominence as vice-president, then president (1992–98) of the Australian Association of Palaeontologists.

These American women on Fulbright awards brought with them to Australia ideas and experiences that went beyond their immediate academic research. Their success as scholars challenged the status quo, and showed women carving out new expanded career opportunities. They also upended some old traditions. When US historian Donna Merwick migrated from Wisconsin to teach at the University of Melbourne in the late 1960s she found it 'stuffy and alienating'. Australian universities were heavily dependent on British academic models of scholarship and networks, and only slowly was this being undermined by a turn towards the United States.[45] Merwick was among those who drove this shift as she joined with a group of historians (including Greg Dening, whom she was to marry) who transformed the methods of studying history under what came to be called 'the Melbourne school'. Her Fulbright award took her back to the United States as a short-term Senior Scholar in 1971. Her latest book won the 2015 Hendricks Award from the New Netherland Institute.

'The American woman who accompanies her husband'

Also important were the wives of men who had Fulbright grants. Although not on awards themselves, American women who came to Australia as the partners of Fulbright scholars need to be considered in any analysis of the Fulbright Program's impact, especially in its first two decades.

They did 'a lot of talking (formally and informally)': they were in demand as public speakers to women's organisations and reports of these were found in the press. The *Sun-Herald* in Sydney, for example, reported that the wife of Dr T.R. Schellenberg, a Fulbright lecturer who helped to establish archival management systems in Australia, was 'also a University graduate' and was lecturing 'on women's place in America' to groups of Australian women.[46] Indeed they were so sought after as public speakers that Frederick P. McKenzie (Research Scholar 1952–53) in animal husbandry, at the New England University College, later University of New England, claimed that wives should also be screened by the Fulbright selection process and should get some instruction in what they might say. Perhaps they did, because their comments are consistent. Their topic was usually the place of women in America, their right and need to work, and have careers. As Fred McKenzie's own wife told the press, in America, just because one was a woman didn't mean putting life plans on hold in order to make a home; men were encouraging their wives to finish their studies, and many women then took up careers 'while their families were growing up'.[47]

Travelling as a 'wife' but being an academic with their own career was the aspect most often commented upon in the press and magazines. The *Sunday Herald* reported an interview with Dr John A. Moore (from Columbia University) who was in Sydney on a Fulbright award to study frogs: 'With him is his wife, also a scientist, and their 11-year old daughter, Sally.' Mrs K.W. Porter, whose husband was reportedly on a Fulbright award in Melbourne, had a PhD in sociology from the University of Oregon, Portland, and was a child psychologist.[48] Mr and Mrs D.O. Hetzman were a 'US couple both Scientists', with Mr Hetzman going to Sydney University to study bacteriology.[49] In Adelaide, 'An American husband-and-wife team … Fulbright scholar Mr F.H. Bauer and Mrs Bauer' were interviewed.[50]

Many wives were able to pursue their own research projects while they were in Australia. Martha Carpenter was 'a young American Astronomer', who had gained a PhD from Cornell in 1947, 'having wanted to be an astronomer ... ever since she was a small child'. Martha Carpenter accompanied her husband, professor of industrial and labour relations at Cornell University, NY, Dr Jesse Carpenter, who came as a Fulbright economics lecturer to Sydney University. She was now attached to the CSIRO in Sydney, 'the only woman in a research team of four radio-astronomers, which is trying to discover what our galaxy would look like if you cut it in half'. Martha Carpenter had been teaching astronomy at Cornell for seven years and she found that women made good astronomy students, 'maybe because no girl will study astronomy unless she really wants to'. She reported that in the United States the proportion of women astronomers was high, which seemed pointedly to contrast with the situation in Australia.[51]

These American women visiting Australia under the aegis of the Fulbright Program contributed to a public discussion about women's education and careers, especially for married women. They illustrated the possibility for new areas of study. Mrs Fred McKenzie was described by the Western Australian press in 1953 as an 'American woman holding an uncommon degree', a Bachelor of Science in Public Administration. Their presence demonstrated what US women had already gained.[52] By commenting on what they observed in Australia, they were fostering ideas of change. Florence Kluckhon a Harvard sociology lecturer who travelled and worked collaboratively with her distinguished anthropologist husband, visited the country at this time. Though not on a Fulbright, Kluckhon lent her weight to the growing chorus of American voices on women's changing opportunities. She told the local press that women could, indeed should, have a life outside their homes, that women had been given a bad role: they were trained like men, they received the same schooling as men, but unlike men, they were then expected to drop it all when they married, 'thus setting up frustrations'.[53] This was a decade before Betty Friedan identified such 'frustrations' as 'the problem that has no name' in her pathbreaking book *The Feminine Mystique* which is frequently held to be the moment marking the beginnings of the revitalised women's movement in the 1960s.

The American wives who had degrees and often worked outside the home, represented marriage as a partnership of equals, with women's right to work and equal pay as part of the expanding horizons the United States promised. In these early decades the Fulbright scheme was sufficiently important to make it on to the news pages, as well as the society or women's pages, of the daily and weekly metropolitan press. Unfortunately there is not the same press coverage for later decades when media coverage played a much less important role in Fulbright Program publicity. Perhaps also the US cultural diplomacy focus on women fulfilling 'America's responsibility' had shifted by the 1970s.[54]

It is not possible to cover exhaustively the hundreds of women among the thousands of scholars who have travelled between Australia and the United States under the Fulbright Program. Inevitably these are only a small proportion of them and there is a tendency to concentrate on and illuminate achievements, such as that of Marilyn

Renfree (postdoctoral award, 1972). With her expertise in zoology, she subsequently received the Gottschalk Medal awarded by the Australian Academy of Science, and in 1997 became one of only six women ever to receive the Mueller Medal, awarded since 1904 by the Australian and New Zealand Association for the Advancement of Science; in 2000 Renfree was awarded the Gold Conservation Medal of the Zoological Society of San Diego. She was made an Officer of the Order of Australia in 2013.[55] Some other trailblazing Australian women have received national recognition of their achievements. In 2007 Margaret Gardner was made an Officer of the Order of Australia in recognition of her service to tertiary education, particularly in the areas of university governance and gender equity, and to industrial relations in Queensland. Margaret Manion was made an Officer of the Order of Australia for her contribution to the arts and education in 1988. She received the Centenary Medal in 2001. Others, like Virginia Spate who was made a Chevalier de l'Ordre des Arts et des Lettres by the French Republic, have won international recognition.

There were also women who broke the rules.[56] Further study might expose more complex life stories. Nevertheless those we have covered show that the opportunity for study and to build collegial networks that international travel on the Fulbright scheme offered, gave women a means to access educational and social opportunities that were often closed to them at home, as Whitney Walton found in her study of French women on cultural exchange.[57] Their Fulbright awards in turn opened up new career paths, fostered women's creativity, and helped create new disciplines, including those studying the lives of women. They encouraged and inspired other women also to apply for grants. Sometimes their daughters followed in their footsteps, for example Lotte Latukefu followed her mother Ruth Fink Latukefu's example by winning her own Fulbright award (postgraduate 1992) to study opera. Their experiences show how 'mutual understanding' could also be transformative, in leading to new gender subjectivities and diversifying the pool of leadership.

Notes

1   Caroline Jordan and Diane Kirkby, 'Women Modernists Gendering Leadership in Australian Art in the 1930s and 1940s', *Australian and New Zealand Journal of Art* (2018), vol.18:2.
2   Norma Parker's correspondence with External Affairs officers, including her thank-you note to Secretary Burton, is in 'United States of American – Relations with Australia – Requests for Information on The Fulbright Agreement', A1838 250/9/8/3 PART 1, NAA.
3   'Sydney Woman to Study in Chicago Under Scholarship', *Sunday Herald* (Sydney), 2 September 1951, p. 21.
4   Source is our database collated from records of Fulbright awards held by AAEF.
5   Adele Millerd and Alice Garner (Interviewer), Adele Millerd interviewed by Alice Garner in the Fulbright scholars oral history project, National Library of Australia Oral History Collection, 2011. Available online at: https://trove.nla.gov.au/work/ 160040646?q&versionId=174483047.

6 'Although the Rhodes scholarships were first awarded in 1903, women became eligible only in 1977 (a small number of Rhodes Visiting Fellowships were awarded to advanced women academics beginning in 1968).' The Rhodes Project at http://rhodesproject.com/background/ (accessed 30 August 2017).

7 Molly Battie, 'Fulbright Women in the Global Intellectual Elite', in Alessandro Brogi, Giles Scott-Smith and David J. Snyder, eds, *The Legacy of J. William Fulbright: Policy, Power, and Ideology*, (Kentucky, 2019) [p. 3].

8 Richard T. Arndt, *First Resort of Kings: American Cultural Diplomacy in the Twentieth Century* (Dulles, 2005), p. 118. Unfortunately there has been no study of the gender implications of the Fulbright Program although work is in progress, see e.g. Battie, 'Fulbright Women'.

9 Arndt, *First Resort of Kings*, p. 118; Battie, 'Fulbright Women' [p. 2].

10 Quoted in Randall Bennett Woods, *Fulbright: A Biography* (Cambridge, 1995).

11 Point also made by Alison MacKinnon, *Women, Love and Learning: The Double Bind* (Bern, 2010).

12 Catherine Manathunga, 'The Role of Universities in Nation-Building in 1950s Australia and Aotearoa /New Zealand', *History of Education Review*, vol. 45:1 (2016), pp. 2–15.

13 Marjorie Theobald and Donna Dwyer, 'An Episode in Feminist Politics: The Married Women (Lecturers and Teachers) Act, 1932–47', *Labour History*, vol. 76 (May 1999), pp. 59–77.

14 Explored in stories by professional women in Patricia Grimshaw and Lynne Strahan, eds, *The Half-Open Door* (Sydney, 1982).

15 Norman McKenzie, *Women In Australia* (Melbourne, 1962), p. 145.

16 'How DO We Manage to Get Married?', *Argus* (Melbourne), 11 August 1955.

17 Interview with Alice Garner, NLA.

18 Interview with Hugh Collins, conducted by Alice Garner, Melbourne, 2011–12, in NLA 'Fulbright Scholars' oral history collection.

19 USEF, *The Fulbright Programme: The First Eight Years and the Future* (Canberra, 1958).

20 Sharon Harrison, 'Dorothy Lois Shineberg (1927-2004)', in *Encyclopedia of Women & Leadership in Twentieth-century Australia*, online at http://www.womenaustralia.info/leaders/biogs/WLE0741b.htm (accessed 2 July 2018).

21 Lorraine Stumm, *I Saw Too Much: A Woman Correspondent at War* (Coopernook, NSW, 2000); Jeannine Baker, *Australian Women War Reporters: Boer War to Vietnam* (Sydney, 2015), pp. 6, 100–3, 107–13, 155–62, has no mention of the Fulbright award.

22 Lorraine Stumm, 'Aussie Gang at American University', *Australian Women's Weekly*, 27 February 1952, p. 17.

23 Lorraine Stumm in USEF, *The Fulbright Programme*, p. 54.

24 'Kindergarten and Pre-school Education' entry in *The Encyclopaedia of Women & Leadership in Twentieth-Century Australia*, online at www.womenaustralia.info/leaders/biogs/WLE0335b.htm (accessed 30 August 2017).

25 John Lawrence, 'A Tribute to Norma Parker', *Australian Social Work*, vol. 57:3 (2004), p. 303. Lawrence was a colleague of Parker's and won his Fulbright award in 1982. Other women social workers who followed her lead in receiving a Fulbright grant were Margaret Norton (1954), Diane Ward (1956), Sarah, aka Sadie, Philcox (senior scholar, 1959) and Val Douglas (1964).

26 For more on the Fulbright–social work story, see Alice Garner and Jane Miller, 'How the Fulbright Program Helped Establish Australian Social Work', *The Fulbrighter*,

vol. 25:1 (January 2015), at: www.fulbright.com.au/newsletter-jan2015 (accessed 15 March 2015); see: www.womenaustralia.info/awal/tag/norma-parker/ (accessed 2 December 2014).

27 Shineberg entry in *Encyclopaedia of Women & Leadership in Twentieth-Century Australia* at: www.womenaustralia.info/leaders/biogs/WLE0741b.htm; Dening's Fulbright experience is discussed in Sally Ninham, *A Cohort of Pioneers: Australian Postgraduate Students and American Postgraduate Degrees 1949–1964* (Melbourne, 2011), p. 148.

28 'The University Pace Differs', *Canberra Times*, 13 July 1967.

29 AAEF board minutes, 10 November 1983.

30 Information conveyed in conversation with Diane Kirkby, September 2017.

31 Interview with Susan Dorsch by Diane Kirkby, Sydney, September 2017; Susan Ryan, *Catching the Waves* (Sydney, 1999); also interview with Diane Kirkby, Sydney, November 2017.

32 Susan Levine, *Degrees of Equality:The American Association of University Women and the Challenge of Twentieth-Century Feminism* (Philadelphia, 1995); see aslo Battie, 'Fulbright Women', [p. 3].

33 Interview conducted by Diane Kirkby with Patricia Lee Taylor, Melbourne, January 2017.

34 *Sydney Morning Herald*, 14 September 1954, p. 11.

35 http://sydney.edu.au/arms/archives/history/senate_exhibitions/students_women_ history_university.shtml (accessed 12 May 2018).

36 MacKinnon, *Women, Love and Learning*.

37 Helen Doyle, 'Dixson, Miriam', in Graeme Davison, John Hirst and Stuart Macintyre, eds, *The Oxford Companion to Australian History* (Oxford, 2001); Susan Foley and Chips Sowerwine, 'Miriam Dixon', *The Encyclopaedia of Women and Leadership in Australia*, www.womenaustralia.info/leaders/biogs/WLE0265b.htm (accessed 3 July 2017).

38 Ruth Fink Latukefu and Alice Garner, Ruth Fink Latukefu interviewed by Alice Garner in Fulbright scholars oral history project [sound recording], National Library of Australia, 2010. http://nla.gov.au/nla.oh-vn4935868.

39 'Equal Pay for Sexes in Sight', *Argus* (Melbourne), 30 June 1953, p. 4. On her claim to being the first American Fulbrighter in accountancy, 'I Have Enjoyed Every Moment in Australia', *Advertiser* (Adelaide), 2 October 1953, p. 15.

40 *Mercury* (Hobart), 10 August 1953.

41 Andrew Sharp and Dale Flesher, 'Mary Elizabeth Murphy's Contributions to the Development of International Accounting', *The CPA Journal*, vol. 81:3 (March 2011).

42 'Equality as "Quickest Way to Prosperity"', *Argus* (Melbourne), 15 July 1953, p. 6.

43 'People Who Live in Glass Houses Don't Buy Paintings', *Sun-Herald* Women's Section, 8 September 1957.

44 'Arnhem Land Expedition', *Advertiser* (Adelaide), 29 May 1952, p. 2.

45 Ninham, *A Cohort of Pioneers*, pp. 191–7.

46 *Sun-Herald* (Sydney), 5 September 1954.

47 Frederick P McKenzie, US Scholar report, 1952–3, in NAA: A1838 250/9/8/3 Part 4. Mrs McKenzie was profiled in 'American Visitor has Uncommon Degree', West Australian, 17 January 1953, p. 12.

48 *Sunday Herald* (Sydney), 17 May 1953; *West Australian* (Perth), 22 May 1954.

49 'US Couple Both Scientists', *Sydney Morning Herald*, 7 June 1951.

50 'U.S. Pair at ESU Luncheon', *Advertiser* (Adelaide), 7 May 1953.
51 'Interstellar Dust Dims the Stars' Lights', *Sydney Morning Herald* Women's Section, 16 December 1954; *Canberra Times*, 14 October 1954.
52 This was the goal of cultural diplomacy according to Arndt, *First Resort of Kings*, p. 118.
53 'Family Not Broken When Women Work', in *West Australian* (Perth), 9 August 1952.
54 Arndt, *First Resort of Kings*, p. 118, doesn't take the story further.
55 'Marilyn Renfree', https://findanexpert.unimelb.edu.au/display/person12974 (accessed 4 August 2016).
56 Being explored by the authors in research conducted under ARC-funded project, LP150100904.
57 Whitney Walton, *Internationalism, National Identities, and Study Abroad: France and the United States, 1890–1970* (Stanford, 2010).

9

From 'White Australia' to 'the race question in America': Confronting racial diversity

In 2009, the controversial *Melbourne* tabloid columnist Andrew Bolt wrote an article criticising white-skinned people who identified as Aboriginal for the purpose of taking up indigenous awards and scholarships. One of those he targeted was a newly named Fulbrighter. Mark McMillan was a legal scholar who had just been awarded the 2009 Fulbright Indigenous scholarship (discussed in chapter ten). The irony would not be lost on McMillan, who was heading to Arizona State University to research the thorny matter of the legal determination of Aboriginal identity. His Fulbright web profile, created before Bolt's article, outlined his project and noted that 'Indigenous identity is a vexing issue in the theory of Australian law'. Courts and bureaucrats 'have been hesitant in making final determinations as to who is and isn't Aboriginal'. 'The logical conclusion,' McMillan argued, 'is that non-Indigenous decision makers are making decisions they are not comfortable making, about an issue that is so intrinsic to those individuals concerned, which is human identity.'[1]

McMillan and several others Bolt had named, came together to sue the journalist for defamation in the Federal Court. They won, but then had to endure a very unpleasant period of extensive and controversial national media coverage. The case raised difficult questions around identity in selection procedures for the Australian-American Fulbright Commission (AAFC) in Canberra. Previously they had trusted that applicants for the Indigenous award were telling the 'truth' about their indigeneity.[2] From now on, for legal reasons, they would have to demand documentary 'proof' of Aboriginality. For some potential applicants this requirement was offensive and led them to decide against applying, narrowing even further the pool of applicants. The award had struggled since its inception to get sufficient numbers,[3] reflecting the very tiny percentage of indigenous people engaged in Australian higher education, and the entrenched systemic barriers they confronted.[4]

This was not the first time that Fulbright administrators and directors had had to grapple with race-related matters – far from it. From the program's very earliest days, questions of race were fundamentally entwined in Fulbright programming decisions. Race consciousness and identification were often significant in scholar experiences. When young Queensland scientist Patricia Lee won her Fulbright award in 1954, the metropolitan press chose to report it as 'Chinese Girl Wins Award' although her family had lived in Australia for generations.[5] Racial identity questions were also tied in with the post-war mass migration scheme from Europe that was changing Australia. Fulbright scholars were active and outspoken on changing ideas about assimilation, the White Australia policy and its eventual dismantling, as well as civil rights struggles in the US, and African and Asian-Pacific independence movements.

Australia and the United States offered (and continue to offer) rich possibilities for comparison, with their shared colonial dispossession of Indigenous peoples, histories of segregationist practice and race-based legislation and protest against these, as well as experiences of mass migration, both spontaneous and planned. Although the histories of Indigenous, civil rights and migrant activism each have their own, complex trajectories – local, national and transnational – in this chapter we explore some ways they interconnected through, were shaped by and helped shape, the Australian Fulbright Program. It is apparent there was a recognisable impact on Australia of US scholars who visited and studied Australia, and also from those Australian scholars who returned from the United States with new knowledge and awareness. The 'rights consciousness' which emerged in the post-war United States and sparked the mass civil rights campaign, coincided exactly with the origins and trajectory of the scholar exchange program and was, inevitably, deeply interwoven with its unfolding history.[6]

Assimilation in 'White Australia'

The Fulbright Program began in a period when maintenance of a 'White Australia' was official policy actively pursued by departments of the Australian government. This meant immigration exclusion of peoples from Asia, Africa, the Middle East, islands of the Pacific, and other parts of the world, if they did not meet the criterion of being 'white' applied by officials and bureaucrats. It meant categorisation by race of the entire population, and the active pursuit of assimilation and integration to a homogenous culture required of Indigenous Australians and those immigrants from other countries who now lived in Australia. Over the sixty years of the Fulbright Program covered by this book, this policy gradually gave way to an official multiculturalism that replaced the White Australia policy and opened up immigration to new groups. We see this reflected in the exchange of scholars, both in the fluctuating research interests of different fields, and the consciousness and activities of scholars who went on exchange. We also see how the Fulbright Program played a small role in bringing these changes.

First, starting in the early 1950s, Fulbright programming procedures required the bi-national board to determine high-priority research and teaching areas for visiting Americans, based primarily on advice from Australian universities. Over the next two decades, programming documents reveal the Foundation's particular pre-occupation with assimilation and integration policies, both in relation to Aboriginal communities in Australia, and also to the effects of the new mass migration policies. In April 1953, for example, the number *one* priority area in the draft list of projects (or research areas) was 'Migrant Assimilation'. The previous year, in a document on requests for American 'junior' (i.e. postdoctoral) research scholars, the USEF had highlighted the issue of 'Race Relations', explaining that:

> The present large-scale selective immigration, into a population which is very homogeneous in extraction, offers opportunities for the study of the development of change of values, beliefs and attitudes about other ethnic or national groups ... The present situation in Australia is analogous to past phases in the history of the United States.

That this area of research should have been bumped up the following year to the number one research priority indicates the sustained, indeed growing, interest and concern in this early period in Australia's post-war mass migration scheme.

The second factor was the scholars who came to an Anglophile Australia over this period, who were often shocked by open anti-migrant hostility. In 1952, John Hough, a professor of classics and ancient history visiting the University of Sydney gave a talk to the AAA, and according to a newspaper article entitled 'We "Appal" an American', reported that 'he met Australians everywhere who made critical remarks about migrants'.[7] He went on to say: 'I don't stand up for everything America has done with migrants, but we assimilated ours the hard way'. He did not explain what he meant by this, but perhaps he thought the United States had managed more successfully to include migrants in its national story, to consider them integral to the perpetuation of a capitalist 'American Dream'. The following year, when Georgia Travis, a US scholar in social work, was asked to report on any difficulties she may have had with aspects of 'life or customs in the host country', she wrote of her problems 'with purchasing food because of the difference in names of foods. Because shop girls could not understand my needs I often felt "rejected"'. She recounted how she recently observed 'a new Australian' who was trying to buy a particular kind of bread in a crowded bakery. 'He pointed in vain, and the shopgirl said in a loud voice for all to hear, "Them blinky foreigners, they're all the same. If you want a poppy plait, why don't you say poppy plait?"' Travis said, 'If it hadn't been for my American accent I would have explained why he couldn't have figured out which loaf should be designated a poppy plait'.[8] Anti-migrant suspicion was, of course, not confined to 'shopgirls'. The Fulbright board members demonstrated their own discomfort with the changing Australian socio-cultural landscape, with their 1954 resolution that recent immigrants to Australia should be included in the program only if they showed 'sufficient evidence of assimilation'.[9] Board minutes did not record what they thought would constitute 'sufficient evidence', or how selection committees would determine this.

Recent migrants, 'new Australians', were at least eligible to apply for awards, even if their status as 'Australians' caused uncertainty among early administrators. Many post-war migrants from Europe had university degrees – from abroad and from Australian institutions – and a kind of Western cultural capital that was mostly not available (or denied) to Aboriginal Australians. It would not be until the late 1970s that Indigenous Australians, identifying themselves as Aboriginal, would start to come forward. The first to do that, we believe, was the poet and rights activist Kath Walker, later known as Oodgeroo Noonuccal, in 1978.[10] She was followed in 1984 by Kim Ackerman, curator of Indigenous cultures, Tasmania.

Indigenous Australians were, however, always an important part of the story of the program, because many visiting Americans were interested in researching their societies and cultures. It was one field of study that made Australia attractive as a destination for American Fulbright scholars. And departing Australians, many of them confronted by segregation and race conflict while in the United States – especially in the first three decades of the program – found themselves reflecting on white–Aboriginal relations when they came home.

Even before the Australian-American Fulbright Agreement was signed, in July 1949, a an American graduate student in anthropology and sociology wrote to the Commonwealth Office of Education in Sydney to ask whether a 'sincere and hardworking graduate student' might benefit from a travel grant to make a 'positive contribution', perhaps through a study of 'conservatism and change in different aspects of the culture of the Australian aborigines'. The letter-writer's name does not appear in the scholar records so we can assume that he was unsuccessful, perhaps because of his apparent lack of commitment to the topic he proposed, for his other suggestion was 'some type of study of the health system of Australia'.[11]

In program proposals from the early 1950s, USEF staff and academics actively sought applications from US scholars with experience in anthropological and social scientific research on Indigenous societies, and on so-called 'assimilation problems', which, as we have seen, related equally to a growing interest in the effects and management of large-scale migration. In 1952, the University of Western Australia requested an American scholar with field research experience, 'specializing in assimilation problems':

> The State of Western Australia is the largest in the Australian Commonwealth but its white population, compared with other States, is extremely small, amounting in all to less than half of million. This small white population is responsible for the care of approximately 25,000 persons who are classed as natives, so that it may be seen that there is an abundant supply of material for study and research in this field.[12]

A year later, the same proposal was repeated with this comment: 'Added importance is given to the request when it is realized that the aboriginal [*sic*] population is declining in numbers and that in a few years the anthropologists may find, as all too often happens, that his entry into the field is too late.'[13] The loss of the research field, it seems, was more worrying to the writer than the predicted loss of a people or culture (no matter how ill-founded the prediction). This, then, is the third aspect of the Fulbright program's racial history.

The language in Fulbright program records of the 1950s and 1960s does not stand up well to scrutiny. People who could themselves have been asked to contribute their understanding of a changing world were instead being cast as the 'material for study' and were often represented as passive objects for research. Aboriginal people were subjected to classificatory systems of skin colour and blood ratios, and considered to be a dying race. A physiologist planning his 1954 trip to Queensland requested the use of a Land Rover for field transport, explaining that his research involved measuring temperatures 'on aboriginals who have been reported ... to show unique features in their energy balance'. He was designing a battery-operated 'portable radiometer for measuring skin temperature', and explained that he had been advised 'that it will be necessary to penetrate to rather remote regions if uncivilized, i.e. clothingless, individuals are to be located'.[14] Ten years later, an American senior scholar in life sciences included 'aboriginals' in a list of fauna he proposed to describe 'properly' to his people back home.[15] In later years, Oodgeroo Noonuccal pointed out that she had hope for 'the young people of today, especially the university students, the educated, and the enlightened young people [who] are not listening to the anthropologists ... they're going to the blacks and saying "hey, what's this all about" ... before, 20 years ago, you only listened to your anthropologists, your archeologists, you didn't go to an Aboriginal to ask'.[16] The early records of the Australian Fulbright Program support this view; it was not until the 1990s that Aboriginal people's opinions began to be sought by administrators of the scheme, and then it came from the action of Aboriginal groups on campuses (see chapter ten).

Other scholars had (or developed, through their exchange experience) a more sophisticated appreciation of the complexity of Aboriginal societies, and, as it turns out, a significant number of Fulbrighters from both sides of the Pacific have contributed meaningfully to the process of improving understanding over the decades. For example, anthropologist Patricia Waterman and her ethnomusicologist husband Richard Waterman, won joint Fulbright awards to Australia in 1952. They had been inspired to come to Australia by anthropologist Charles Mountford who had visited the United States in the mid-1940s as a lecturer employed by the Commonwealth Department of Information.[17] They spent nine months in Arnhem Land, camping at Yirrkala. There they learnt Yolngu languages, recorded 500 songs (now in the AIATSIS library and also held at the Yirrkala Arts Centre) and noted (among other things) linguistic evidence of a history of Aboriginal contact with Malays, and Spanish and Portuguese speakers. The Watermans, in talking to the Australian press, stressed that this was by no means a 'dying race', that the people they came to know had a vigorous cultural life.[18] The Watermans' stories of Arnhem Land gained a great deal of press attention, including an interview upon their return home with Studs Terkel.

Several years later, Australian political scientist Charles Rowley went to the United States and Canada on a CCNY Commonwealth travel grant. He had been in New Guinea during the war and was now teaching at the Australian School of Pacific Administration, which trained patrol officers for service in Papua New Guinea (still an Australian-controlled 'territory'). His intention was to study Native American administration and social welfare. In his report he made a strong argument against assimilation policies, as well as noting how little the Australian government spent on Indigenous welfare and education compared to the United States. Upon his return, Rowley wrote an article titled 'Aborigines and Other Australians'.[19] This piece strongly influenced a young Australian physics post-graduate student and Quaker, Barrie Pittock. During a hitchhiking trip several years earlier through New South Wales, Pittock had been shocked by the discrimination he witnessed against Aboriginal people in communities he passed through. In 1963, Pittock applied for a Fulbright travel grant to take him to the National Center for Atmospheric Research in Boulder, Colorado. He selected that particular institution so that, alongside his physics research, he could also learn about Native American societies and their approaches to self-government in the region. He was especially inspired by D'Arcy McNickle, an Indigenous sociologist who lived in Boulder and was co-author of *Indians and Other Americans* – a title played upon in Charles Rowley's later article.

Rowley took up a position directing a major research study funded by the Social Sciences Research Council and the Myer Foundation into contemporary Australian Aboriginal society.[20] He published the project findings in three volumes, with the first appearing in 1970. With this publication, Rowley 'provided the first systematic account of dispossession and discrimination' and a 'point of entry for social scientists other than anthropologists into the field of Indigenous studies'. In 1971, Rowley, who was by now a professor at the University of Papua New Guinea, won a Senior Fulbright award to the University of California-Santa Barbara, where he worked on one of the subsequent volumes. Barrie Pittock, upon returning to Australia, maintained a strong involvement in Aboriginal affairs, writing comparative pieces about Native American and Aboriginal interests, and playing a memorable part in the Aboriginal Advancement League during its tumultuous transition to a black-run organisation. Pittock's comparative work, connecting Australian and American Indigenous communities and experiences, influenced land rights discussions back home. Decades later, Indigenous scholar Samia Goudie used her Fulbright award to work in the area of trauma recovery with Indigenous communities. She focused on the use of 'representation, Media and narrative' to support recovery from intergenerational and historical trauma and developed ongoing relationships with American Indian communities in the United States.[21]

These Australian Fulbright scholars were part of an intertwining of interests, experiences, publications and activism around US Indigenous communities and struggles, which was apparent in the trajectories of other scholars. The Australian colonial role in Papua New Guinea provoked a good deal of reflection on the nature and effects of colonialism on Indigenous people, in a time when many former colonies were seeking and gaining independence. The effects of colonialism in creating Indigenous disadvantage were often hidden from the circumscribed urban lives of

Australian students and academics. Quite often those who spent time in PNG, whether on missions, or aid or government projects, developed a more acute appreciation of Australian Aboriginal experience and struggles as a result. The question of colonialism and its impacts was an area where historical differences between the United States and Australia led to fruitful scholarly debate.

'Integration and racial problems in the United States'

Whether the focus was on migration, colonialism, integration and assimilation, or Indigenous affairs, there was a strong preoccupation with race relations flowing through the early Fulbright records. This was particularly evident in the early 1950s, in American scholars' final reports to the Foundation and BFS/State Department at the end of their Australian sojourns. Asked to note the questions they were most often asked by local people they met, their responses reveal how curious Australians were about the race relations in the United States, alongside other domestic and political concerns. H. Arlin Turner (literature, 1952) said: 'Many are interested in the race question in America, as in a way parallel to the race question in the whole Pacific area.' Mary Brush Jones (economics, 1952) was asked regularly about (among other things) 'the status of women; the Negro problem … immigration and the effect it has had'. John Rose Faust (political science, 1953–54) reported he was asked: 'Is the negro problem in the United States being solved?' And Mary E. Murphy (accounting, 1953) 'endeavored to offset … misinformation as to race relations in the U.S., specifically, the Negro situation in American communities'. According to one American history lecturer in Australia in April 1953, of all Australian students' preoccupations, 'The negro question was the one which bulked largest in students' minds, and the one in which their curiosity was greatest'.[22]

One Fulbrighter suggested to the board of directors that, given what he saw as 'widespread misconception in Australia about the nature and extent of the negro problem in the US', the Foundation might promote 'better understanding' if some 'qualified negro students could be encouraged to apply for Fulbright grants' to Australia. In response, the board 'considered the possibility of having negro grantees at the senior level as well as in the student category, and agreed that in general a research scholar or lecturer of outstanding quality would be more likely to achieve the desired purposes'.[23] The 'desired purposes' seem to have been to convince Australians that there were genuine opportunities for educational or professional advancement for African-Americans in the United States despite what news reports seemed to suggest. But they also fit neatly with State Department efforts at this time to counter the very damaging effects of their race relations on perceptions abroad of US society.

When Foundation board member and Director of Technical Education in NSW, Arthur Denning, went to the United States on a State Department Leader grant in September 1957, he took the opportunity to follow up on this suggestion when he met with government officials and CCNY people. A State Department deputy assistant secretary in Washington, DC reported a visit from Denning during which he had argued that 'Australians got a distorted picture of integration and racial problems in the United States Press and that a lecture tour by someone of high caliber would admirably help clarify Australian opinion in these matters'.[24] The State Department's response was positive, which is hardly surprising when we consider that Denning's visit coincided exactly with several weeks of intense international interest in and condemnation of the stand-off at Little Rock, Arkansas (Senator Fulbright's home state), where nine African-American children had tried to enrol at the newly desegregated high school and been prevented by the Arkansas National Guard, called out by Governor Orval Faubus. Television cameras captured it all.

When Denning returned to Australia, his report 'aroused considerable interest and was discussed at length' by the board, who also noted that American grantees' final reports 'made frequent reference to the need for a better understanding by Australians of the colour problem in the US'. The board decided, given the State Department support for the proposal, to offer an award 'to a mature and highly qualified lecturer, preferably in the scientific field'.[25] Why a scientist? Was it that scientists were more highly respected in Australia than humanists? Or perhaps they thought a scientist would be less likely to court controversy than a humanities scholar?

An answer of sorts can be found in a letter Denning wrote to John W. Gardner, president of CCNY, asking for suggestions for a 'distinguished colored American' to come to Australia for three months. He asked Gardner: 'Should we have a scientist or medico, who is unlikely to be expected to talk on segregation or an eloquent scholar in the humanities or social sciences?' CCNY's Stephen Stackpole replied with a list of four possible 'Colored Americans' and noted it would be 'unrealistic to believe that a scientist would be less likely than another to talk or be asked about American life generally or the color problem in particular'. At the top of Stackpole's list was acclaimed historian of slavery and head of the multi-racial Brooklyn College, Professor John Hope Franklin, whom he considered 'the best bet'. The others he suggested were two judges, William Henry Hastie of the US Court of Appeals in Philadelphia and Edward R. Dudley, of the Domestic Relations Court of New York (and former ambassador to Liberia), and two sociologists: Professor St Clair Drake of Roosevelt College in Chicago, and Howard University's Edward Franklin Frazier.[26] When the board discussed the proposal at its next meeting in April 1958, it came up with its own shortlist, featuring Franklin, the two sociologists, and a new addition: Hildrus A. Poindexter, Chief Public Health Officer for the US Embassy in Surinam. For some reason the judges were left off the list.

Finally, in March 1960, the board members recorded their pleasure at the BFS's approval of Professor John Hope Franklin as a Fulbright 'Distinguished Visitor'. Not only was Franklin the first black American to come to Australia under the program, but the first in this new award category, which was essentially a renamed and revamped Short-Term Senior Scholar award (whose first recipient had been Edward Ryerson, president of Inland Steel, in 1958).[27] Efforts to lure high-profile Americans like Walter Lipmann, Dean Acheson, George Kennan and Sidney Hook (a very telling wish list in the Cold War context) had come to nought in the period when Franklin's name was being considered. But they would not be disappointed in their first Distinguished Visitor ('DV'). The timing of his visit, beginning on 11 June 1960, could not have been better. For in 1960, some seventeen African nations won independence from their former colonial masters, ten of which were announced in the months when Franklin was touring Australia. Race, colonialism and self-determination were on the front page of daily newspapers and on everyone's lips.

Franklin had some misgivings about going to Australia, given its racial policies, which, in ironic understatement, he said 'left much to be desired'.[28] He also understood that his invitation sat within the web of State Department efforts to counter international criticism of US domestic racial policies – a campaign whose history Mary Dudziak has traced in her *Cold War Civil Rights*.[29] But Franklin decided to go despite these concerns, in the interest of countering bias against African-Americans. The historian was amazed at his reception in Australia. 'Huge overflow crowds greeted me everywhere, at airports as well as the lectures' he reported. 'I was received by the Commonwealth Governor General and the Minister of Education in New South Wales. There seemed to be almost nation-wide interest in my visit'. He was bemused by the US ambassador's description of his visit as 'the most important thing that had happened to Australian-American relations within the past decade'.[30] He gave over fifty formal lectures around the nation, many of them touching on African-American history, slavery and segregation, and these were covered extensively by the press. He appeared on television and radio programs, including ABC Radio's *Guest of Honour*, ABC-TV's *Spotlight* (alongside Australian Fulbright alumnus Sir Zelman Cowen) and Channel 7's *Meet the Press*. He made friends with Australian academics, dean of law Zelman Cowen and Adelaide historian Douglas Pike, with whom he continued a warm correspondence after his return home.[31]

In a chapter in his autobiography devoted to the Australian trip, Franklin recalled that 'Having spent all of my life in some measure aware of my appearance as a black man, it was revelatory to be met with Australia's courteous disinterest'.[32] Children didn't stare at him in the street. Australians, moreover, 'seemed to have no preconceived notions about me as a scholar, or, as the Europeans had, about the status of blacks in the United States. They also did not seem to draw any analogies between blacks in the United States and Aborigines in Australia'.[33] This was 1960, and on that last score, things would change quickly over the next decade.[34] Franklin wrote that he was particularly honoured by a visit from a delegation of 'the first Australians', the first he had ever met, 'and I was interested to discover the similarities and contrasts, if such comparisons were at all in order, with Native Americans'. He found members of the group to be 'intelligent and articulate. They complained that they did not enjoy equal opportunities and that Aborigines as a people could ascend much higher in Australian society and culture if only they had a chance'.[35] The questions that Franklin raised were ones that preoccupied a striking number of Fulbrighters in years to come. Nevertheless it would be a long time – some eighteen years – before the first Australian Aboriginal Fulbrighter would be selected, and have the opportunity to explore connections along these lines.

In its annual report for 1960, the Foundation wrote of Franklin's visit that 'it is no exaggeration to say that his has been the greatest single contribution to the Fulbright exchange since the inception of the program'. The US ambassador wrote to him: 'The impact of your visit has been profound among both the universities and the general public and I can say with confidence that it has been the most outstanding individual effort on behalf of the program during its ten years of existence in this country'. At the most recent BFS meeting in 1961, Franklin was reported to have 'noted a great interest in American history ... and concluded that the interest in all things American was as great as in any European country he had visited'. He also felt 'he had "left five years of my life in Australia" at the conclusion of this, the "most exciting experience he had had"'.[36] For the Foundation, this was a public relations coup, of a kind they had not yet experienced, as well as an endorsement of the value in their newly created Distinguished Visitor program; it raised the profile of the exchange program in Australian eyes, right across the country, while generating a greater curiosity about and awareness of 'all things American'. For the US ambassador and State Department, Franklin's visit appeared to be the ideal antidote to widespread negative publicity surrounding the racial conflict in the United States.

Franklin's story reveals a great thirst for understanding, demonstrated by both the US scholar reports that led to his selection and the intense public attention he received. Also it uncovers the behind-the-scenes efforts to use the Fulbright Program to promote a more benign image of US race relations, something which posed a serious dilemma for individual scholars. Franklin reflected on this dilemma at some length. In his autobiography he explained that he only agreed to Fulbright lecturing assignments on the condition that he would not be obliged to whitewash the racial situation in the United States. 'I did not want to be used merely to paper over or mislead the world regarding the state of race relations in the United States. On the other hand', he wrote, 'if the government wished to use me as an example of what was possible, I had no objection so long as I could speak as I wished and my involvement was genuinely in the interest of improving the racial climate in America'. To that end, he said 'I quickly set myself the rule that so long as there was no effort to dictate what I would say, I was amenable to any overture, and I am pleased to say that no one ever asked of me anything that would compromise my professional or scholarly integrity'.[37]

His refusal to endorse his government's record is evident in a press report on one of his public talks in Melbourne, in which the journalist quoted Franklin's criticism of the incumbent President Eisenhower's 'insensitivity' to the racial question in the United States.[38] Freedom to speak independently, which was consistent with the vision of scholarly integrity the Fulbright Program promoted, was not the happy experience of all scholars. Sondra Silverman found when she was a student in Canberra in the early 1960s that her disruptive activities got her into trouble with the USEF board. Her behaviour was deemed inappropriate for a Fulbright student and a request for an extension of her award was initially denied. Her colleagues at the ANU defended her and she managed to stay on, but it was a close call.[39] Her political activities brought her to the attention of ASIO, which kept a file, including talking to the Canberra Jaycee Club about Cuba, gathering petition signatures against Apartheid in South Africa, playing and commenting on 'Negro protest movement songs' at a meeting of the Council for Civil Liberties, and later, demonstrating at the visit to Canberra of Henry Cabot

Lodge, who had been US ambassador to Vietnam in 1963–64.[40] The ASIO agent who compiled this record wondered if, because of her dark colouring, she had 'coloured blood', although why this mattered was not revealed. In later life she commended the Fulbright board and the ANU for being able to differentiate between academic and political activities, something ASIO was clearly not able to do.[41]

Nearly fifty years later, Franklin revealed that it was in 1960 that he 'became highly aware of the fact that my government was trying to use me'. It seems, though, that it was not the Australian Fulbright-sponsored trip that brought this home, but a subsequent, last-minute invitation from State Department to join an all-white US delegation to the independence ceremony in Nigeria in October. From that point on, he was more wary, but this didn't stop him accepting President Kennedy's invitation to join the BFS in 1962, for which body he travelled widely around Africa and Asia in particular. He remarked that 'people tended to want to test the sincerity of the United States in international affairs by looking at and studying what they were doing to their own darker people'.[42] Race was at the heart of how the United States was to be judged.

Scholar activism for reform

Franklin's story is an important one for the way it brings together a number of threads of great importance in the history of the Fulbright program and the challenge of racial diversity. When Franklin's impending arrival in Melbourne was announced in the *Age* on 22 June 1960, there was another article on the same page, under the heading 'Group Pleads to Admit Asians', reporting the launch the day before of the Immigration Reform Group's history-making pamphlet.[43] 'Control or Colour Bar' argued against Australia's racial immigration policy and is frequently taken as the turning point when White Australia began its long slow death.[44]

They were inspired by a speech given at Melbourne University by an American Fulbright postgraduate scholar, Arthur Stein, who would later become Professor of Political Science at the University of Rhode Island. Stein also criticised the Australian race-based migration policy, warning that if the government did not alter it voluntarily, it would soon be forced to, under UN pressure. He observed that 'there seemed to be very little realisation in Australia that the Afro-Asian bloc of the U.N. would shortly hold 45 out of 100 votes. This bloc was likely to hold together on colonial and similar issues'.[45] Several key members of the Immigration Reform Group had research interests in Asian Studies. They would go on to win Fulbright awards in the 1970s, and also played important roles in the development of their field in Australia, including Ken Rivett (1971 postgraduate in economics) and Jamie Mackie (1977 senior scholar in political science, to Brookings Institution).

In this way the Fulbright story in Australia has been implicated in changes of policy direction surrounding race, migration, and indigenous self-determination. The administrative records provide the warp, the scholar experiences the weft. Travelling in the other direction and following some Australian Fulbrighters to the United States, we find connections made there would come to have a powerful impact back home in several domains. Where John Hope Franklin was a Distinguished Visitor on a whirl-wind tour of Australian capital cities, visiting university lecture theatres, radio and television studios, most scholars had a very different experience. They usually settled in one place, usually for a year, sometimes longer, where they would throw themselves into intensive study, research and/or teaching, and take part in the normal daily living experiences of their neighbourhood. Australian scholars were sent to institutions in all corners of the United States, and quite a few found themselves in the Southern states, where segregation was legislated and often violent.

Elaine Barry, a literature student from the University of Queensland who later became an associate professor of American studies at Monash, travelled on a Fulbright grant to the University of South Carolina in the autumn of 1959. When she arrived in Richmond, Virginia, on a Greyhound bus, and alighted in the middle of the night to wait for a connecting bus to Columbia, she saw a sign in the bus station saying 'White cafeteria' and another saying 'Colored Cafeteria'. She says: 'You know, I was so naïve I didn't *get* it for a while ...', until she noticed only black people were going into the Colored Cafeteria, 'and that was when it *hit* me like a bombshell, and this was the country I was going into'. Once in South Carolina, she found that 'as long as you stayed off the race question, they were gracious, charming, hospitable people, but you couldn't possibly talk race'. The campus was still segregated. Towards the end of her eighteen-month stay, Elaine Barry remembered the student union president announcing pub-licly that 'The first Negro [he pronounced it "Nigra"] that comes into this university, I'll shoot him dead'. Barry understood this threat was a serious one. She also remembers, early on in her time in Columbia, getting on a bus with her (white) roommate. People up the front stood up to offer her a seat. 'No, no, that's fine', Barry replied, and headed towards the back. 'To her credit', Barry recalled, her roommate followed, but said, when they were sitting down, 'Do you realise what you've done? See that sign?' Barry had, of course, taken a seat in the 'coloured' section of the bus.

She remembers coming to understand that 'part of the Fulbright plan, maybe particularly in a place like South Carolina, was wanting to win hearts and minds of foreigners, and so there were more foreigners doing graduate work in the English department than there were Americans'. Barry made friends with students of many nationalities, and was still in touch with some of them fifty-odd years later.[46] This is a very common theme in scholar stories from across the six decades of the program – that not only did they learn a great deal about American society and people, and the importance of regional and state differences (and prejudices), but they also lived along-side and learnt from other international students. Many postgraduate scholars stayed in International House type accommodation, and engaged in stimulating conversations with roommates about colonialism and resistance, academic freedom, religious beliefs and a host of issues that opened their minds to other ways of seeing and thinking.

Anthropologist Ruth Fink, whom we met earlier, had an unforgettable experience when, while writing up a dissertation at Columbia University on her research into the Wajarri Aboriginal community in Western Australia, she was invited to join a Quaker-run Summer Seminar in Vermont, to which about forty other foreign students, from twenty-five different countries, were invited to discuss the most pressing and difficult issues of the day. The overarching topic the participants were to explore was: 'The Elements of Peaceful Cooperation in a World of Diversity: An examination of cultures, beliefs and objectives and a search for methods of relating them constructively for university human welfare.' As a child of German Jewish refugees to Australia, who had been researching and writing about the 'acculturation' of fringe-dwelling Aboriginal communities in NSW, Fink had plenty to contribute to these discussions.[47]

The detailed information brochure sent to participants explained that the seminar, which was to take place over four weeks in a group of school buildings in the 'rolling and wooded hills' of Woodstock, South Vermont, would be a 'conscious experiment in international living and negotiation'. Its organisers, a professor of philosophy and religion from Antioch College, Morris Keeton, a professor of economics from Swarthmore, Joe Conard, and an American Friends (Quaker) staff member, Grace Perkinson, sought to enable an 'intimate fellowship of students from many lands', and provide 'a valuable means of placing their American experiences in a broader international perspective'.[48]

Fink remembers this as an extraordinary and intense experience, and certainly the highlight of her time in the United States. She wrote a report on the seminar, full of praise for the organisers who created 'an environment of critical self-examination', and for her fellow students who 'showed courage in their convictions and who were nevertheless willing to learn, and not rigidly bound by pre-conceptions'. She noted that this was 'not an easy group to handle, all of us were individualistic, frank in our remarks', but the Quakers (or American Friends) who facilitated discussions 'made no attempt to curb us' and allowed complete freedom of expression.

In this environment Fink felt entirely at ease. Above all, she was free to express her 'individual personality' in a way she had not been in the academic world of New York City, which she had found rushed, 'impersonal, bureaucratic and disinterested [*sic*] in individuals'. At the Woodstock seminar, students from countries that were at loggerheads with each other were able to discuss their national and personal differences in a civilised and constructive way. They also talked about other politically sensitive issues of special relevance to contemporary (or recent) American developments, including McCarthyism and atomic warfare. At the final session of the seminar, each student revealed a 'really significant change' in their 'thinking and feeling', and Fink went away 'much more optimistic about the possibilities for a sane and peaceful future' than she had felt beforehand.[49]

Although the seminar was organised by the Quakers, and was not officially Fulbright-sponsored, in many ways it sought, and realised particularly effectively, the same goals as Senator Fulbright's scheme. Scholars were confronted with philosophies and political views very different from their own, they were required to talk them through in a civilised manner, and to seek common ground. If participants did not always agree, they could at least say they had reached a better understanding of each other's point of view. This is exactly what Senator Fulbright would describe in 1966 as a desirable outcome of the scholarly exchange program. 'No part of our foreign policy does more to make international relations human relations and to encourage attitudes of personal empathy, the rare and wonderful ability to perceive the world as others see it', he wrote. 'Thus conceived, educational exchange is not a propaganda program designed to "improve the image" of the United States as some government officials seem to conceive it, but a program for the cultivation of perceptions and perspectives that transcend national boundaries.'[50]

Eight years later, he developed this argument: 'I do not think such exchange is certain to produce affection between peoples, nor indeed is that one of its essential purposes; it is enough', he said, 'if it contributes to the feeling of a common humanity, to an emotional awareness that other countries are populated not by doctrines we fear but by individuals – people with the same capacity for pleasure and pain, for cruelty and kindness, as the people we were brought up with in our own country.'[51]

It is one thing to gain a better understanding of people from other nations. It is another to decide what to do with this knowledge, particularly in this very troubled period of the late 1950s through 1960s, when change was so desperately needed on the race relations front in Australia and the United States. And here we come to the problem of political engagement and what was/was not (officially) allowable under the Fulbright scheme.

When South Australian teacher and children's author Colin Thiele went to the United States on a Fulbright Educational Development award in 1958, a series of lectures on aspects of American society, economics and education was organised for him and his fellow teachers from other lands. One of the speakers was Howard University History Professor Rayford W. Logan, who in 1944 had edited a book called *What the Negro Wants*. The book had argued that 'if the United States is going to assume a position of moral leadership in world affairs, it behooves her to clean her own house first. We must not be blind to the fact that this housecleaning is not an easy job, for the dust and dirt have been accumulating for a long time.'[52] For Australian Fulbrighters visiting the United States in the late 1950s, when the civil rights movement was growing in strength and resolve, some asked themselves whether, perhaps, they should help their hosts with this housecleaning? Colin Thiele did not take this step – or if he did, he didn't record it in his travel diaries. But one scholar who was driven to act on his newfound understanding was economics student Bill Ford (see Figure 9.1).

Ford, the son of a coal lumper, grew up on the docks in Sydney, and went to work in heavy industry before returning to school and then enrolling at university. With a degree in political science, he left in 1958 for the University of Illinois on a Fulbright travel grant and an S.C. Johnson Fellowship, to study at the Institute for Labor and Industrial Relations. Living in an international house he shared a room with an Indian student, Ravinda Nanda, who introduced him to Indian food. When Ford moved on to graduate school at UCLA, he made friends with an African-American student in his sociology class, Bob Singleton. He became involved in John Kennedy's presidential campaign, and 'learnt so much about American politics from that'. In fact, he worked in a black neighbourhood in Southwest LA, 'you know, not far from where the riots were in Watts' and remembers it as 'an incredible period'. At that time, Bob Singleton and his wife Helen joined the Freedom Ride to Mississippi, where they were arrested and jailed for forty days. So Bill Ford bought a plane ticket to Jackson, Mississippi, in time to attend the Singletons' arraignment.[53] This is how he told the story:

Figure 9.1 Bill Ford (centre) with friends at the International House, University of Illinois, during his Fulbright award, c. 1959

so I went down into the black community when I got off the plane, and walked around the black community just asking if anyone had seen Bob or Helen Singleton? People just looked at me – what? That's what Bob said you know, 'How come the Ku Klux Klan didn't get you?' you know, it was amazing, and I found them. And they were under very strong instructions to show no emotion, to either … the black people to the whites, the whites to – and Helen sees me, and she comes running over and grabs me and hugs me and kisses me.

With his voice shaking, Bill Ford concluded his story, 'and the next day I go to the arraignment'. He walked into the courtroom and sat down with a history student he knew from UCLA 'on the Black side of the aisle' to show his support, a very brave act at the time, and one that the Singletons recall with amazement. He and his companion were the only people not on arraignment in the courtroom, and when everyone else had been dealt with and moved along, the judge, puzzled, called an adjournment to look for their (non-existent) files. At that point they slipped out. Not long after, Ford headed home to Australia. Many years later Bob Singleton wrote of Bill Ford 'as the bravest white person I have ever met'. He did not want Ford to think he was thought of 'as simply a white person' but it was unheard of for a white person to do as Ford did, willingly walk into a Southern courtroom 'and sit on the Black side'. Singleton wrote, 'We Freedom Riders had numbers and solidarity. You stood alone'.[54]

Back in Sydney, Ford began teaching economics to 'grey flannel [wearing] cadets, who had no interest in *macro* economics, you know, they were all gonna go and make a fortune in some company'. But black American civil rights struggles were all over the papers and television screens. In May 1963, University of Sydney students protesting against the fire-hosing of peaceful protestors in Birmingham, Alabama, found themselves chastised by observers for ignoring the dire racial situation in their own backyard.[55] Bill Ford, thinking back to the Singletons in Mississippi, envisaged the adoption of US-style civil disobedi-ence tactics as a way of raising awareness of racist policies under which Aborigines lived and laboured. He talked to Charles Perkins, Sydney University's first Indigenous student, and leader of the newly formed Student Action for Aborigines (SAFA). Ford then helped students prepare for a mixed black and white student bus trip, designed to expose racism and inequalities in rural New South Wales, advising on non-violent protest tactics.[56]

Speaking alongside Ford at the preparatory meetings was US postgraduate Fulbrighter, Sondra Silverman (now Farganis), who had come from Brooklyn to research civil liberties in Australia during the two world wars.[57] Though neither Ford nor Silverman joined the Australian bus tour, historian and Freedom Ride participant Ann Curthoys has acknowledged their galvanising role in the early stages of planning. Silverman had learnt about non-violent and interracial protests as a member of the Congress of Racial Equality (CORE) in New York.[58] Ford also acted as a Sydney-based spokesperson, fielding press inquiries while the bus was on the road.[59]

The Freedom Ride in the summer of 1965 generated extensive press coverage of Aborigines' desperate living conditions and of segregationist practices in rural New South Wales, and gave fresh impetus to the movement for a referendum to alter the Australian Constitution, to ensure that Aboriginal people would be counted in the census, and to enable the Commonwealth (that is federal) government to legislate spe-cifically for Aboriginal people. The referendum had an overwhelming 'Yes' result in favour of the constitutional change, in 1967.[60]

This is a case – and it is certainly not the only one – where we can trace quite expli-citly the contribution of the individual exchange experience, to significant, broader social and political changes, which were and are, in the largest sense, about increasing 'mutual understanding'. Both Bill Ford and Sondra Silverman got deeply involved in domestic politics in their host country. They were both driven to act against racist pol-icies in their host countries in ways that did not fit award expectations but which had meaningful impacts on the lives of others.[61]

An example of a Fulbright scholar who only subsequently became prominent in support of Indigenous issues was Sir Ronald Wilson. On his Fulbright award, Wilson completed a Master of Laws degree at the University of Pennsylvania in 1957. He later became the first West Australian appointed to the High Court (1979–89) and was Human Rights Commissioner, 1990–97.[62] The years of the Hawke-Keating ALP gov-ernment (1984–92) and the 1992 Mabo judgement in the High Court on traditional ownership, ushered in an era of reconciliation with Aboriginal people. Wilson had been the sole dissenting judge on the Mabo decision that overturned *terra nullius*, a legal doctrine that had underpinned dispossession of Aboriginal lands.[63] But later, working with prominent Aboriginal elder Mick Dodson, in 1997 Wilson helped produce the ground-breaking report into the Stolen Generations, *Bringing Them Home*.

Mutual understanding, particularly where it touched on the vexed area of race relations, led in numerous cases to political activism, and this is a tricky zone for any international exchange program. Fulbright scholars are expected to learn as much as they can about their host country. This has led not only to a sense of connection, but to a strong desire to change things. Involvement in domestic politics in the host country is, discouraged by the program policy-makers. What were grant holders were to do when they came up against the limits to 'mutual understanding'? This was a question that only they could, in the end, determine.

Aboriginal identity and activism have grown in significance over the seventy years of the Australian Fulbright program's existence. The program has played a small role in developing opportunities for Australia's Indigenous scholars, such as poet Oodgeroo Noonuccal (1978), curator Kim Akerman (1984), photographer/curator Peter Yanada McKenzie (1994) and historian Sue Stanton (1995), to establish valuable trans-national networks in areas of great importance. By 2009 when Mark McMillan won his award to explore the complex subject of Aboriginal identity, the US had its first African-American President. Racial and ethnic diversity had become more apparent in Australian candidates selected for awards.

The role of Fulbright exchange in perpetuating or exposing racism in both countries, in facilitating awareness or 'mutual understanding' of racial issues, in fostering self-determination and cultural knowledge, deserves a deeper scholarly scrutiny than this brief treatment has allowed. We have only been able to point to the most visible occasions and recognize certain patterns.

The 'race question in America' runs deep and pervasively. As a leading liberal, William Fulbright himself was a Southerner with an Achilles heel when it came to civil rights of African-Americans. It was not until the last years of his life that he began seriously to question his own racial blind spot that had facilitated his electoral success in Arkansas and no doubt enabled him to retain his Senate seat.[64]

Achieving 'mutual understanding' could be a long journey.

Notes

1 From Mark McMillan's Fulbright web profile, at http://fulbright.com.au/scholars/australian-scholars/previous-australian-scholars?id=303 (accessed 17 February 2014).
2 When the new scholarship was approved, Professor Susan Dorsch, then chair of the board, 'did not think it appropriate to specifically request ATSIC to verify a candidate[']s eligibility'. AAFC board minutes, 23 November 1992.
3 'Report on the 1993/94 Australian program', in AAFC board minutes, 23 November 1993. The first awardee, in 1994, was artist Peter McKenzie. In the minutes of 20 May 1997, the board again recorded its concern 'about the poor response to the Aboriginal and Torres Strait Islander awards' despite going to 'considerable lengths to bring the award to the notice of appropriate individuals and groups'.
4 'Despite initiatives over recent years to redress their under-representation, Aboriginal and Torres Strait Islander students' participation in higher education remains

significantly below the population parity rate'. Judith Wilks and Katie Wilson, 'A Profile of the Aboriginal and Torres Strait Islander Higher Education Student Population', *Australian Universities' Review*, vol. 57:2 (2015), pp. 17–30.

5 'Chinese Girl Wins Award', *Brisbane Courier* [1954]; Interview with Diane Kirkby, Melbourne, January 2017.

6 On 'rights consciousness' see James Patterson, *Grand Expectations: The U.S.1945–74* (New York, 1997).

7 'We "Appal" an American', *Argus* (Melbourne), 22 November 1952.

8 1953 US Scholar report, Georgia Travis, in 'United States of America – Relations with Australia – United States Educational Foundation – General', A1838, 250/9/8/4/2 PART 2, NAA.

9 USEF minutes, 26 April 1957.

10 Sue Abbey, 'Noonuccal, Oodgeroo (1920–1993)', *Australian Dictionary of Biography*, National Centre of Biography, Australian National University, http://adb.anu.edu.au/biography/noonuccal-oodgeroo-18057/text29634, published online 2017 (accessed 31 July 2017). Note it doesn't mention the Fulbright award.

11 11 July 1949, Letter from Stanley Applebaum of New York to Commonwealth Office of Education, Sydney Branch, in A1361 4/7/5 PART 1, NAA. [43–4] re poss of Fulbright to Aust.

12 Program proposal for Academic Year 1952, in 'Supplement no. 2 to Annual Program Proposal… USEF in Australia Jan 1 1951 – Dec 31 1951', in CU Records [our emphasis].

13 1953 Program proposal, in CU collection MC 468 Box 114.

14 Oodgeroo Noonuccal, in her 1981 interview with Bruce Dickson, 'The Legacy of a True National Treasure of Australia', on Dropbearito.com (Cultural Crossroads: Australia / America), p. 2 of 4, accessed 3 September 2017.

15 'United States of America -Relations with Australia – United States Educational Foundation – General' at A 1838 250/9/8/4/2 PART 3 [NAA online]. In agenda for 12 July 1954 board meeting, p. 6.

16 [Earl A. Bell Scholar report, 1964]. His exact words: 'Of course, Koala bears, kangaroos, rabbits and aboriginals need to be described properly.'

17 Phillip Jones, 'Charles Pearcy Mountford', *Australian Dictionary of Biography*, vol. 15 (Melbourne, 2000).

18 'Aborigines Can Add Much To Civilisation', *Advertiser* (Adelaide), 6 March 1953, p. 3.

19 1958–59 Carnegie Corporation NewYork III. IIIa. Box 292 Folder 2 Charles Rowley.

20 Samia Goudie was interviewed by Alice Garner for the NLA Fulbright Scholars Oral history (not open to public access). Her final report outlines some of her work with American Indian communities in the Trauma recovery field. Report supplied by Samie Goudie to authors.

21 Stuart Macintyre, *The Poor Relation: A History of Social Sciences in Australia* (Melbourne, 2010), pp. 151–64.

22 28 April 1953, FSD Am.Consul Syd to DOS, IIA: Submission of Australia Country Prospectus, pp. 29–31 Quotes from American history lecturer Bruce Miller.

23 United States Educational Foundation [USEF] board minutes, 29 October 1956.

24 3 October 1957, 'Official-Informal Unclassified' communication from Howard P. Jones, Deputy Assistant Secretary, to William J. Sebald, American Ambassador, Canberra. In RG 59. 1955–59 Central Decimal File, 511.433/9 – 1757/, NARA.

25 USEF Board minutes, 20 February 1958.

26 20 March 1958, Stephen Stackpole, Carnegie Corporation of New York, to Arthur Denning. In CCNY Records Series III. Grants Sub-series III.a; Box 131 folder 19 Arthur Denning. Columbia University Library.

27 Ryerson was retrospectively described as a 'Distinguished Lecturer'.

28 John Hope Franklin, *Mirror to America: The Autobiography of John Hope Franklin* (New York, 2005), p. 187.

29 Mary Dudziak, *Cold War Civil Rights: Race and the Image of Democracy* (Princeton, 2000).

30 'An Australian Experience 1960', in letter from John Hope Franklin to Trusten Russell, Conference Board of Associated Research Councils, October 11 1961, John Hope Franklin Papers, Rubenstein Library, Duke University.

31 Correspondence files, Franklin papers.

32 Franklin, *Mirror to America*, p. 188.

33 Franklin, *Mirror to America*, p. 186. Other sources on Franklin's tour include Australian newspaper press coverage, and a report to the BFS quoted in USEF Annual Report 1960, NAA 'United States – Educational Foundation – Policy' A1838 583/1 PART 6.

34 For a compact history see Richard Broome, *Aboriginal Australians* (Sydney, 2001).

35 Franklin, *Mirror to America*, p. 188.

36 USEF Annual Report 1960, NAA 'United States – Educational Foundation – Policy' A1838 583/1 PART 6.

37 Franklin, *Mirror to America*, pp. 184–5.

38 *The Age* (Melbourne), 24 June 1960, p. 6.

39 USEF board minutes, 18 July and 12 September 1962, 19 March 1963.

40 Sondra Silverman, ASIO file, NAA. Cited with permission of Sondra Farganis (née Silverman).

41 Sondra Farganis response to survey, Survey, La Trobe University, 2011.

42 Ray Arsenault and John Hope Franklin, 'The Sage of Freedom: An Interview with John Hope Franklin', *The Public Historian*, vol. 29:2 (2007), pp. 40, 42–3.

43 'Negro Coming as Fulbright Scholar', *The Age* (Melbourne), 22 June 1960; 'Group Pleads to Admit Asians', *The Age* (Melbourne), 22 June 1960.

44 Gwenda Tavan, *The Long Slow Death of White Australia* (Melbourne, 2005).

45 Elaine Barry and Alice Garner. Elaine Barry interviewed by Alice Garner in Fulbright scholars oral history project, NLA, 2010.

46 Ruth Fink Latukefu and Alice Garner, Ruth Fink Latukefu interviewed by Alice Garner in Fulbright scholars oral history project, NLA, 2010.

47 'Change Urged in Migration Policy', *The Age* (Melbourne), 18 June 1960, p. 9.

48 American Friends Service Committee Information Sheet: International Seminar, South Woodstock, Vermont, July 11 – August 8, 1958. From Archives of the American Friends Service Committee.

49 American Friends Service Committee International Seminars. Participant's Comments. 12 August 1958. Ruth A. Fink. From Archives of the American Friends Service Committee, Pennsylvania, USA.

50 Fulbright, *The Arrogance of Power* (New York, 1966), pp. 176–7.

51 Senator Fulbright's speech in response to Kissinger's tribute to Fulbright on his retirement from the Senate, reproduced in the BFS annual report, December 1974.

52 Rayford W. Logan, *What the Negro Wants* (Chapel Hill, 1944), p. 63.

53 G.W. Ford and Alice Garner, Bill Ford interviewed by Alice Garner in Fulbright scholars oral history project, NLA 2010. Unpublished three-page account by Professor Robert Singleton, Economics, Loyola Marymount University, of his Freedom Ride involvement. Copy given to authors by Bill Ford.
54 Email from Bob Singleton to Bill Ford, Wednesday 19 November 2003, in possession of the authors.
55 Ann Curthoys, *Freedom Ride: A Freedom Rider Remembers* (Sydney, 2002), pp. 1–4.
56 Peter Read, *Charles Perkins: A Biography* (Ringwood, 2001), pp. 103, 106, also a photo of Ford and Perkins.
57 Sondra Silverman (now Farganis) was, at the time, a postgraduate student at the ANU in Political Science, see Sondra Joyce Silverman, 'Civil Liberties in Australia – World War I and II: Censorship and Internment' (PhD, ANU, 1967).
58 Sondra Farganis interview with Diane Kirkby, NYC, June 2017.
59 The most comprehensive account of the Australian Freedom Ride is Curthoys', *Freedom Ride*, for Bill Ford's role in fielding questions and responding to vitriolic and supportive mail, pp. 17, 30, 32–3, 45–7.
60 The vote in favour was 90.77 per cent. Australian National Archives fact sheet, www.naa.gov.au/about-us/publications/fact-sheets/fs150.aspx (accessed 24 September 2010).
61 Bill Ford, Fulbright Scholars Oral History, NLA.
62 Antonio Buti, *A Matter of Conscience: Sir Ronald Wilson* (Crawley, WA, 2007).
63 The Mabo story, the subsequent Native Title legislation and the public reaction is recounted in Broome, *Aboriginal Australians*, pp. 233–43.
64 Many have tried to make sense of William Fulbright's anti-Civil rights voting record. See Woods, *Fulbright: A Biography*, pp. 230, 331–2 and 479. See also Daniel Yergin, 'Fulbright's last frustration', *New York Times*, 24 November 1974, p.262.

10

'In the climate of continuing financial restraint': Finding a sustainable future in the neo-liberal university

The election of Ronald Reagan as US president in 1980 heralded the arrival of a new era for the Fulbright Program. Policies profoundly opposed to government intervention were to transform the relationship of public institutions and programs to their sources of funding and the political support of their programs.[1] Free market economics promising increased wealth brought major cutbacks in government spending across the board. Public universities and departments involved in education and foreign affairs were not spared, and the ripple effects quickly reached the Fulbright Program.

The scheme's administrators and supporters in the United States and partner nations had already been fighting to maintain funding to the scheme since neo-liberalism emerged as a political force in the late 1970s. Under President Jimmy Carter a 'draconian shift' occurred in US monetary policy: 'The long-standing commitment in the US liberal democratic state to the principles of the New Deal ... was abandoned in favour of a policy designed to quell inflation no matter what the consequences.'[2] The assumption that 'mutual understanding' was worth expenditure of taxpayers' money came under renewed scrutiny. Those working behind the scenes had their work cut out for them over the ensuing decades of streamlining and number-crunching. That the scheme survived at all is a testament to the energy and commitment of many people – scholars, public servants, alumni and administrators – working quietly to protect Fulbright's big idea.

Neo-liberalism was theoretically an economic project, a 'design for the reorganization of international capitalism', but it was the political project – 'to restore the power of economic elites' – that dominated the next four decades.[3] In that period Australia had a Liberal-National Party (L-NP) coalition government under Prime Minister Malcolm Fraser (1975–83) who aligned with the economic policies of Margaret Thatcher's British government (elected in 1979). Thirteen years of ALP government followed, first under Prime Minister Bob Hawke, who had once been the recipient of a US Leader scholarship, and then under his former treasurer, Paul Keating. While Australia also underwent deregulation and transformation, having this Labor government afforded some protection against the consequences of a doctrine that 'has meant in short the financialization of everything'.[4]

During a Program Review discussion in December 1976, the bi-national AAEF board agreed that 'Although there appears to be no adequate way of quantifying the benefit to mutual understanding produced by the Fulbright scheme, the anecdotal evidence testifying to the worth of the Scheme was overwhelming'. This, for the board, was 'persuasive'. Unfortunately, it appeared that a 'lack of quantitative measures' of these benefits of mutual understanding was 'a factor in neither of the two governments being disposed to increase their cash allocation to offset the effects of inflation'. Looking back over the previous decade, they recorded that while the Foundation's cash income had increased marginally, inflation effects meant that the real income had seen a 'substantial decline'.[5]

In 1981, the bi-national board discussed how to get the most out of a reduced budget in this leaner, meaner era. Cutting the number of awards would be necessary, but the chair, vice-chancellor of Newcastle University, Professor Don George, argued that an exchange program 'did not have to be big to be good'. Another review meeting was planned, 'to draw out ways in which the benefit derived from the funds that are received, might be maximized' in the Australian program.[6]

Funding worries were accompanied by changed programming requirements, delivered to the Commission by a newly formed US agency, known as the US Information and Communications Agency (USICA).[7] These caused consternation for the executive officer, Bruce Farrer, who believed that the draft of a new procedures manual, supposed to replace the 1964 guidelines, 'appeared to offend against the spirit and intent of the binational agreement and to cut across the degree of autonomy which the AAEF has always been assumed to have by virtue of the agreement'.[8] Adding to the stress of this time was the Australian government's 1983/84 budget allocation for the program, which remained at the 1982/83 figure of $240,000. This was well below the US allocation of US$375,000 for the 1983 financial year, in a program that was intended to be cost-shared in equal amounts.

Dealing with uncertainty had ramifications in the AAEF office, with more frequent changes of executive officers than had previously been experienced. In late 1984 Ian Hossack was appointed to replace Bruce Farrer who had given notice the previous year. During a brief transitional period, the AAEF had its first woman executive officer, when Noeline Milson was acting executive officer for two weeks in January 1985. Ian Hossack was at the helm until March 1987, when he was replaced by Charles Beltz. The position had been renamed 'executive director' in November 1986.[9] This terminology change most likely reflected the fact that the Fulbright Foundation was a non-profit organisation, whereas the term executive officer was usually used to designate the leader of a *for*-profit organisation. While the reasons for the name change were not discussed in the board minutes, it is telling in a period when government and (new) non-government sources of funding for the program would become a hot topic and reminds us of earlier nomenclature battles.

Change was here to stay. In late October 1987, stock markets crashed around the world. The Australian All Ordinaries Index fell 25 per cent in one day, and nearly 42 per cent by the end of the month, while in the United States, the Dow Jones dropped 21.63 per cent. Headlines screamed 'crisis'. At 8.50 a.m. on that drizzly 20 October, a day that would come to be known as 'Black Tuesday' in Australia, and 'Black Monday' in the United States, the AAEF board met in Canberra. There is no mention in the minutes of the catastrophic situation in the global markets, even though news must surely have reached the directors by lunchtime. But they did discuss in detail a major new Fulbright development – one that would bring the program into much closer alignment with the corporate world so powerfully hit by neo-liberalism and now the stock market crash.

The demise of the public university

1987 was a landmark year in Australian higher education history. That year John Dawkins, minister for Education, Employment and Training in Hawke's Labor government, released a discussion paper that, when implemented as policy, would transform the tertiary sector. It heralded another big expansion, just as the Murray Report had done exactly thirty years earlier, but the principles of funding conceived 'in the climate of continuing financial restraint' were fundamentally different, 'requir[ing] close attention to the efficient use of resources'.[10] A new era of mass education and reduced government expenditure had begun. There were implications in these changes for the Australian Fulbright Program. Most notably, after some fifteen years of free tertiary education, the introduction of the Higher Education Contribution Scheme (HECS), by which students repaid the cost of their education, along with the imposition of full, up-front fees for international students, threatened to reduce the American program significantly if waivers could not be arranged. There were also implications for administering the scheme.

In the same year as Dawkins' White Paper, 1987, the AAEF board held a retreat during which it re-assessed the Fulbright Program from every angle. One important policy change arising from this retreat was that the American program would no longer be shaped around university recommendations. Instead, the American competition for awards would now resemble the Australian one and be 'open' to all fields. There would still be some suggestive prioritisation of research areas, but these would apply equally to Australian candidates, and would be determined not in response to university proposals but by the board, whose members intended to 'take a greater initiating role' in shaping the program. The board framed this new policy as 'opening the way for American applicants across the whole spectrum of academic, professional and artistic endeavours to apply with a chance of success'. It considered that this 'would be warmly received by the USIA and the Council for International Exchange of Scholars (CIES) in Washington who had been concerned about the shape of this particular program'.[11]

Indeed, one of the USIA concerns, to which the board was responding with this new policy, had been that procedures in earlier years of having universities 'suggest' names for US awards had enabled the program to be run somewhat like 'an "old boys" support system'.[12] The board now had two women directors: Jacqueline Hochmann (appointed February 1985) and Susan Dorsch (from January 1987), joined by Susan Ryan in 1990. As we saw in the previous chapter, it was under their watch that important changes in selection policies were implemented. There had been some improvement in the 1980s in the proportion of women receiving awards (22 per cent of awards compared to a shameful 9 per cent in the 1970s). The 1990s would see a jump to 38 per cent, evidence of the influence that having a better gender balance on the board of directors could make to gender parity in scholarships.[13]

In the wake of the Dawkins reforms, other changes followed in 1988-90. The following priorities guided selections of both American and Australian scholars: (1) International Trade Issues; (2) Pacific Basin (or Rim) Issues; (3) Developments in Higher Education Policies; and (4) the Impact of New Technologies and Reseach & Development (R&D).[14] This was a highly concentrated focus, significant in its regional emphasis and for its third priority, which was clearly a direct response to the radical changes in Australian higher education then underway.[15]

A sting in the tail?

At the 'Black Monday' October 1987 AAEF board meeting, David Buckingham, the Commonwealth Department of Education's representative on the Fulbright board, announced to his colleagues that the Australian government had agreed to a 50 per cent increase in its annual contribution to the exchange program. This news was very welcome, as the Fulbright funding situation had reached a state of crisis, or, at the very least, embarrassment on the Australian side. Since the early 1980s, the Australian contribution to the exchange program, though maintained at the same dollar amount, had dropped well below the United States' contribution in real terms, so that by 1987, it sat at 28.1 per cent compared to 58.4 per cent of total bi-national program funding in 1976. This was a neat reversal of the situation in the late 1960s and early 1970s, when US congressional budget cuts had meant there was a disparity for some years, during which the Australians contributed more to the program than their partners. The Gorton L-NP government in 1968 had kept up its contribution at this time, predicting (correctly, as it turned out) that should circumstances change, they might one day have to rely on the Americans to do the same for them.

The increasingly stark funding imbalance of the mid-1980s had led to concerted lobbying of government by Fulbright administrators and board members, so the October 1987 funding decision was gratifying. There was an important catch, though. The Foundation would be required to match the additional funds, to the tune of $AUD 120,000 a year, for the next three years. This would entail a significant cultural shift for the Foundation's staff and board members, one that reflected the increasing marketisation of the higher education sector over this period.[16]

Until this point, 'private' or non-governmental contribution to the exchange program in Australia had been minimal. Academic volunteers contributed in a range of important ways, such as sitting on selection committees or hosting scholars. Funding did not rely on non-government cash sources such as philanthropic or corporate donations. The situation was different in the United States, where universities and philanthropic or privately funded educational organisations had been involved from the beginning, in either administering or contributing financially to Fulbright awards. For example, for the first six months of the program's life, the Carnegie Corporation and Rockefeller Foundation had funded the IIE and Conference Board of Associated Research Councils to administer the awards until congressional funding for the exchange could be secured.[17] Also, many US universities offered scholarships, fellowships and fee waivers to foreign Fulbright scholars who were only eligible for travel grants in their own (non-US) currency under the Fulbright scheme. In contrast, as explained previously, in partner countries like Australia, Americans who won Fulbright awards received a maintenance allowance as well as travel costs as part of their award, making up for the lack of private sources of funding in Australian universities.

Indeed, at the US end, proponents of the Fulbright Program, from its earliest days, had touted it as a particularly successful example of 'private'–public cooperation. The program could not survive without non-government contributions, given Congress was not in the habit of funding education, but this private–public claim also worked on an ideological level. In the Cold War climate, significant private support was seen as evidence of the health of US-style free enterprise and civic responsibility, versus a Soviet-style command economy and ideological stranglehold on education. Ideally, this robust private interest in educational exchange should protect the program from partisan political pressures. In practice, not a few philanthropic foundations were closely linked to highly politicised anti-Communist funding exercises, some of them covert.[18]

So while the culture of philanthropic and corporate support for educational exchange was much more powerfully rooted in the US discourse around Fulbright (and education in general), in Australia the scheme was seen as essentially government-initiated and funded, and there was no established tradition of seeking funding for awards from non-government sources – until 1987.

There is no evidence in the archives of a concerted push from the American end for the Australian government's new funds-matching requirement. Indeed, Australia was the first ever Fulbright partner country to require this of its bi-national Foundation, and it appears that American program administrators may have been surprised by the decision. However, this significant shift in funding policy does reflect the broader political and economic picture in which Reagan (and the UK Thatcher) governments played a key role in reshaping higher education along business models.

The mid-1980s was a period when the United States, United Kingdom and Australia were all recalibrating their education policies according to prevailing deregulatory economic orthodoxies. In July 1987, the Hawke government created a new super ministry, bringing together Education, Employment and Training, with John Dawkins as minister. In the context of the 'Dawkins Revolution' that followed, the new Fulbright funding arrangements made perfect sense. Dawkins' mission was to push (among other things), the development of links between universities and business, and a user-pays principle in higher education funding, both for domestic students (in the form of the Higher Education Contribution Scheme) and for foreign students.[19]

So, in the late 1980s, not only did AAEF staff in Australia have to master the art of fundraising, they also had to deal with other aspects of the Dawkins reforms, including the introduction of full fees for overseas students in Australian universities, which affected their program directly. In a curious twist, Dawkins' predecessor as minister for Education, Senator Susan Ryan, who had campaigned unsuccessfully against the re-introduction of university fees, resigned from the Senate in December 1987, and joined the Fulbright board three years later, when the board was grappling with the effects of her successor's policies.

In order to raise the significant sums required by the new agreement, the Foundation realised it needed to secure tax deductibility status, but this proved a more difficult task than expected, and despite repeated applications and entreaties, the Commonwealth Tax Office only granted them tax deductibility in 2003.[20] In the meantime, the AAEF sought other ways of enabling sponsors to make tax-deductible donations to the program. Two years after the new government funds-matching requirement was announced, Executive Director Charles Beltz reported to the board on an arrangement made with the ANU. The university had agreed to operate a 'Fulbright Scholarship Fund' along similar lines to the Sir Gordon Menzies Scholarship Fund (created for the Harvard Club) and the Cambridge Commonwealth Fellowships Trust. The ANU would pass on to the Foundation any donations made to this Fulbright Scholarship Fund. In return, the Foundation agreed to have two ANU representatives sit on Fulbright selection committees. This was a pragmatic decision, but board members expressed some concern about relying on what was essentially a 'gentleman's agreement', for the ANU would retain legal control of the Scholarship Fund, even if the Foundation operated it 'in practice'.[21]

Early in 1992, board members noted that the newly created Australian Centre for American Studies at the University of Sydney had been given tax-exempt status, while the Foundation continued to rely on the ANU arrangement. Their continued appeals to the Tax Office were going nowhere, and the parliamentary secretary had advised the treasurer that there was 'little prospect of AAEF being listed separately in the gift provisions of the Income Tax Assessment Act'. So, deciding 'not to make further entreaties', they resolved to seek advice on 'how to word a letter to potential corporate donors about the possibility of Fulbright contributions being classified as tax deductible on the basis of being legitimate business expenses which enhanced the public image of the company'.[22] This was really an acknowledgement of what the new sponsorship policy, forced upon them by government, meant in practice: convincing possible funding partners of the publicity value of being associated with what would come to be known as the Fulbright 'brand'. The language of marketing is now deeply embedded into the program's functioning, in a way that would have been unthinkable to early administrators – just as it is in universities. It took another ten years before the Foundation could advise potential donors that it had tax-deductible status. It was a very long wait.[23]

There were other obstacles, too, to the initial fundraising efforts by the Foundation in 1987. Not only was the new funds-matching policy introduced at the very start of the financial crash, but it coincided with the lead-up to the Australian bicentennial celebrations of 1988. This meant that every company and its dog was being asked for money. Added to this, some board members were unaccustomed to the actual act of fundraising. Chair of the board L. Roy Webb, vice-chancellor of Griffith University, an economist specialising in microeconomic reform and international education, 'indicated that he did not feel very comfortable in the role of fundraiser which really required special skills and a significant allocation of time which was very difficult to accommodate in the heavy schedule of commitments in his official position in his university'. Fellow director Professor Susan Dorsch (see Figure 10.1), an immunologist and (at the time) pro-vice-chancellor of Sydney University, similarly 'expressed strong reservations on her part about a role in fundraising'. She went further, declaring that she 'did not see that as a valid responsibility for Board members whose primary task was to guide and direct the Fulbright Program'.[24]

In March 1988, the board minutes record a planned amendment to the Foundation by-laws, to allow an Australian business representative to take the place of the Department of Foreign Affairs and Trade official who had been a director since the 1964 agreement came into force. Thus, the Australian members would now be: two academics, one Department of Education official, and one businessperson. Though little was made of this in the minutes, it was in fact a very telling shift. While an American businessman had sat on the Australian board since 1950, Australian directors had always been senior academics, public servants in Education or Foreign Affairs, or (in the first years at least) judges. Admitting an Australian representative

Figure 10.1 Professor Susan Dorsch, Chair of the Australian Fulbright board meeting President George Bush Sr, 1992

of the corporate world at this time into the closely guarded Fulbright decision-making territory symbolised an opening up to business and non-government interests that reflected the broader, and quite revolutionary, changes to the educational world occurring in Australia at this time.

The first Australian business representative to be appointed to the board was Brian Finn, the Sydney-based managing director of IBM Australia. The fact that he led the Australian arm of a US company indicated the kind of business networks the Foundation hoped and expected to tap into. In the ensuing few months, the board held discussions about how the Foundation might improve its fundraising efforts. When Richard A. Ware, chair of the US BFS, visited the Foundation in November 1988 – the same month that Brian Finn joined the board – he suggested that they consider forming 'an ancillary body to the Board specifically for fundraising'. The board decided to await the creation of the Alumni Association, which was then on the cards, for it believed the fundraising body could benefit from alumni involvement.[25] Things moved slowly in the Fulbright world. A fundraising advisory committee was eventually formed, but not for another twelve years, in August 2000.[26]

One of the challenges for the Foundation was raising the program's profile beyond the academic world. It was 'not widely known in the private sector', and the board believed that for fundraising to be successful a 'good deal of "awareness-raising"' was required.[27] It also took some time to determine what was and wasn't possible in this new money-seeking caper. In May 1990, the US ambassador expressed some concern about his role in relation to AAEF fundraising efforts. He had attended the previous meeting of the board at which he had expressed interest in the activities of the Foundation and a 'willingness to assist'. Since then the Ambassador had expressed a certain 'wariness' at the proposal put to him during that board meeting. They had asked him to host a few functions for business leaders. The Ambassador had approached Washington for clarification about his expected role in public relations or fundraising activities.[28] Three months later, the board received a welcome clarification of the ambassador's possible role in fundraising activities. 'Whilst he could not host fundraising functions or actively seek donations, he could act as a guest of honour at such functions. He had repeated his willingness to act in this latter capacity for the Foundation.'[29]

In these discussions around the creation of an Advisory Board for fundraising, in 2000, there was some debate over whether this body should instead be called a 'Board of Trustees', but this latter title 'implied greater control and responsibility' than they wished to confer, so they stuck with 'Advisory Board'.[30] This is reminiscent of the debates over wording at the very start of the program's Australian life, when Department of External Affairs officers had difficulty stomaching the notion of a 'Board of Directors' rather than an 'Advisory Committee'.

The board had to grapple with other big questions raised by the new funding arrangements, particularly regarding what kinds of companies or organisations should be approached (or not); what guidelines should be put in place to ensure the program's continued scholarly integrity; and how alumni might contribute to this process. Establishing guidelines and monitoring award sponsorship thus became a very significant responsibility of the board, and one its members could not afford to get wrong.

Building a culture of philanthropy

The board's first real dilemma concerned processes for selection, and the extent to which the donor would be involved. One of the first non-government sponsors of an award was Mrs Ruth Whitford, the widow of a Tasmanian Fulbright scholar from the 1950s, Dr Richard L. Whitford. In March 1990, Mrs Whitford offered a 'Memorial Endowment' of $100,000, proposing that the Foundation invest the sum and its interest be used to fund graduate scholarships 'in perpetuity', in the form of supplements to Fulbright awards. Upon her death, the remainder of her estate would be added to the initial donation. Mrs Whitford proposed some specific eligibility requirements, giving preference to Tasmanian educators, namely:

> giving first preference to qualified Tasmanians in the field of educational administration, second preference, if no Tasmanian was elected, for Fulbright applicants in educational administration from other states, and third prefer-ence to Tasmanian secondary teachers, preferably from schools involved in the School Mates scheme, applying for teacher exchange at the secondary level.[31]

Not only did Mrs Whitford give clear indications of her selection criteria, but she expressed a strong wish that the first scholarship be granted to her nominee, Mr Robert Eccleston, 'so long as Mr Eccleston had "minimum qualifications" for a Fulbrighter'. This caused the board some anxiety, for its members 'did not wish to set a precedent by side-stepping normal Fulbright Program selection procedures which were based on open competition'. The board also expressed concern that eligible candidates for the scholarship might not be found each year and thought that 'further consider-ation should be given to possible alternate forms that the scholarship might take'. Just over a year later, the board came to a final agreement with Mrs Whitford, and Robert Eccleston was selected for the first award.[32]

Other early corporate sponsors included David O. Anderson, Robert Holmes à Court, Fulbright alumnus Harold Clough, the Salomon Bros, *Time Australia*, and an Alumni Association-initiated award named for early Fulbrighter and influential edu-cator W.G. Walker. The problem the board had foreseen in discussing the Whitford scholarship – of a possible shortage of eligible applicants given restricted selection cri-teria – came to pass with the first David O. Anderson award, which in August 1992 had received a very small number of applicants.[33] Unlike the other 'standard' Fulbright awards, which had no real restrictions as to research field or focus, the sponsored awards were generally in a named field and sometimes state-specific. Thus the pool of applicants was inevitably smaller. Given that the Fulbright Program prided itself on a rigorous nationwide selection process with academic record given first priority, this development posed something of an ethical challenge to selectors and board members. They had little choice but to make it work, however.

It was in this context of seeking opportunities for sponsored awards that a pro-posal for a targeted scholarship for Aboriginal and Torres Strait Islander people was introduced (as discussed in Chapter 9), probably on the initiative of Executive Director John Lake. The AAEF board discussed the proposal at some length and in general, as we know, supported it. Nevertheless the board did express concern that 'the pool of eligible candidates may not be sufficient to enable an award to be made each year, that the Foundation might draw criticism if an expectation grew that this was an annual award and no award was made in particular year due to an inadequate pool of eligible applicants'.[34] This problem would apply for any of the sponsored awards, and indicates the discomfort some board members felt with the new territory the AAEF was moving into.

Just as for the Whitford award, there were some vexing questions surrounding application and selection procedures for the ATSIC award.[35] Attracting strong applicants was crucial. Working with a sponsoring partner threw up some new challenges for the Foundation. Hitherto AAEF had total control over the 'messaging' of the scheme. In May 1993 ATSIC had prepared a poster advertising the Postgraduate Student Award for Aboriginal and Torres Strait Islander People. The Executive Director John Lake questioned the appropriateness of the poster. He was seriously concerned. He advised the board that 'the poster had been funded by ATSIC and had been approved for production by Senior officers of the Commission'.[36] The dilemma was the extent to which the AAEF could maintain real control of the management of an award that was funded primarily (or even solely) by an outside body with its own goals and ways of doing things.

Now that the ATSIC award was an actuality, another issue arose. A representative of the Koori people had approached the AAEF representative at the University of Melbourne, Jean Hagger, seeking involvement in the selection process. This, Lake said, 'was not possible and the Executive Director would make the position clear'.[37] Board members read the letter and endorsed his response. When the first applications for the new award were assessed in 1993 the board then noted with disappointment 'the small number of applications for [both] the Aboriginal and Torres Strait islander and the Journalism awards'. They agreed that in future, Aboriginal and Torres Strait Islander people would be asked to help promote the ATSIC award.[38] Subsequently, the numbers increased dramatically.

'You are a Fulbright scholar': cultivating the alumni

Funding challenges meant the development of alumni networks came to be seen as urgent through the 1990s and 2000s. This was in fact not a new realisation, for the board had encouraged the formation of alumni groups as early as 1956, and a group called the 'Fulbrighters' had formed in Melbourne in 1959, holding annual dinners for several years.[39] In 1974 the BFS annual report noted that efforts had been made in the United States to create a database of American alumni of the Australian program, with the hope of engaging them in discussion about the program.[40] But that seems to have been more about keeping in touch with others who had similar interests and experiences, a social networking opportunity rather than a fundraising exercise. It appears that the early alumni association(s) must have lapsed, because in 1986, when responding to a USIA cable suggesting alternative sources of funding for Commissions worldwide, the board noted that 'there is no such tradition here'. Still, the board agreed that 'as a Fulbright Alumni Association is developed in Australia, alumni support for the Foundation should be encouraged'.[41]

After 1987, it was apparent to all those who had to take on the money-raising work that those with the greatest personal interest in the program's fortunes were likely to be the people who had benefited from it in the past, many of whom were in positions of considerable power and influence, in both Town and Gown worlds. At this point the administrators realised there were great gaps in the archives. In the early 1970s, boxes and boxes of scholar files had been destroyed for the sake of freeing up office space (a historian's nightmare). Fortunately, board minutes, which often included lists of scholars' names, had been preserved. Some alumni, including nuclear physicist Dale Hebbard and geochemist Bill Compston, began to scour what records remained, to compile as complete a record as they could of all recipients of Fulbright awards since 1950, both Australian and American. This was published as the Directory of Fulbright scholars in 1990, an invaluable resource for our history project.

The Alumni Association has now been active for several years, with state chapters running their own networking and social events, welcoming incoming scholars, advising those about to depart for the United States, and sometimes supporting follow-up projects that have developed out of Fulbright partnerships. There are still many Fulbright alumni, though – indeed the majority – who choose not to join the association. There is still a reluctance amongst many Australians to identify themselves as alumni of a particular institution or program. This is an interesting cultural difference between the two countries, which, though it has lessened somewhat (and it is possible that the Fulbright Program has contributed to that lessening), continues to be significant, and is one of the obstacles to the Australian Commission's efforts to build the Fulbright 'brand' locally. The term 'brand' is one that some (usually younger) alumni embrace – it was mentioned quite often in survey responses for this project, for example – but one that others would likely reject as superficial, for its particularly corporate resonance. Many of those interviewed for this project were not members of alumni associations, and yet they were keen to talk about their Fulbright experience, often in great detail. They simply did not choose to define themselves as Fulbright alumni above other aspects of their lives.

In the United States there is a much stronger culture of promoting one's personal connection to educational institutions. In Australia, where reliance on government to fund education dies hard, the culture of alumni philanthropy has been much harder to build.[42] While university graduates might feel a sense of connection to the institution where they studied, this has not, until recently, necessarily translated into a willingness to donate money. Contrast this with US universities, where it seems every building, courtyard, laboratory, library reading room or museum, is named after a donor who attended the university. As the funding cuts have bitten, we are seeing more of this in Australia, but it still feels to many like a cultural import rather than a homegrown phenomenon.[43]

Executive Director John Lake, who was appointed in August 1991 and served until 1998, believed strongly that for the Foundation's fundraising efforts to bear fruit, it was necessary to build the national profile of the exchange program. Up until this point, the Foundation staff had been working away in nondescript office spaces, moving every few years to cut costs. Since the early 1950s, they had worked out of rooms at the US Embassy, Canberra University College, a private house, and then Churchill House. In the early 1990s, when office rental rates increased again, Lake came to the conclusion that a focus for fundraising should be the building of a 'Fulbright House', which would accommodate the program staff, meeting and events rooms for scholars and alumni, and spaces which might be hired out to tenants to bring in much-needed income. Board members were not immediately sold on this idea, expressing concern 'about taking on debt' and that 'real estate ventures would distract the Foundation from its main function of promoting educational exchange'. They also felt they 'lacked expertise in real estate investment'.[44] On the other hand, they understood that more alumni donations might be generated by such a project and could see how Fulbright House might benefit the Alumni Association and Fulbrighters in general. If a university were to grant some land for them to build on, the proposal was worth considering.[45] A year later, the board's directors expressed reservations 'about Fulbright House diverting the Foundation from its fundamental purpose'. A lot of energy was being channelled into this project, at the expense of the core business of managing scholarships. At the same time, they acknowledged 'that some years ago the Australian Government had imposed the condition that the increase in its grant should be matched by private fundraising and fundraising had been part of the Executive Director's employment brief'.[46] They felt they had little choice but to continue down the path laid out before them.

There is no doubt that the Australian higher education system was taking on elements of US-style user-pays principles, and the Dawkins revolution of the late 1980s threw up yet another (related) challenge to the Fulbright Program administrators. Overseas Student Charges, first flagged in 1980 under the Fraser government, came into effect in January 1989. The Foundation had to start seeking waivers from universities in 1988 – the same year it was first grappling with the new fund-matching requirements. It had to appeal to each university to cover the fee, and initially, twenty-three out of twenty-five universities agreed to this.[47]

An important development at this time for the Australian program was a move towards parity between Australian and US awards. That is, Australians would now receive a stipend where before they had only qualified for travel money and insurance. This was partly because opportunities for Australian students and scholars in the United States were not as bountiful as they had once been. This was probably due to a combination of financial belt-tightening by US institutions, and the explosion of international education, meaning much greater competition for existing scholarships and fellowships from students and scholars around the world.

The cutbacks took their toll on the number of Australians able to travel to the United States. From a high of 568 in the decade of the 1960s (cf. 501 in 1950s, and 515 in 1970s) numbers dropped dramatically (to 385) in the 1980s, and even further to less than half the original numbers (240) in the 1990s, and were only 216 between 2000 and 2009. The commitment to the US–Australian relationship was, however, still the element of the Fulbright scheme which made it unique, and in the 1990s there was fresh resolve on the part of the board to emphasise this when making selections for awards. Fewer awards would be made but each would be of higher value which would help to maintain the prestige of the program. Efforts were also made to encourage visual and performing artists by insisting that state selection committees have at least one member from the arts. To attract younger applicants who were outstanding performers and considered to have great potential in their fields the name of the Senior Professional Award was changed to the Professional Award. The 1990s also saw the establishment of a system of awarding funds to assist a university to run a symposium to be called the Fulbright Symposium. The first year the scheme attracted a field of twenty applicants and saw the ANU awarded $10,000 for a symposium on the topic of 'Managing international economic relations in the Pacific region in the 1990s' which was held in 1991. The theme reflected the economic preoccupations of the previous decade. What followed did likewise.

The new century brought attacks on the World Trade Center and the Pentagon that deepened even further Australia's diplomatic and military alliance with the United States. The subject of the 2004 Fulbright Symposium – 'Civil-Military Cooperation and the War on Terror' – indicates the new more militarised directions scholarship was to take in the twenty-first century. The symposium was hosted by the University of Queensland with guest speakers General Peter Cosgrove, Head of the Defence Force; Mick Keelty, Australian Federal Police Commissioner; Major General Michael G. Smith AO (retired), Director of Austcare; Graham Tupper, Executive Director of the Australian Council for Overseas Aid and Thomas Bruneau, Director of the Center for Civil-Military Relations, US Navy Postgraduate College, California.[48]

For that first decade of the next century Mark Darby was now the executive director. His appointment was announced in February 1999. Darby had a lot of experience in working with NGO managements and an academic career as a lecturer in leisure and tourism studies at University of Technology Sydney in the 1990s. He had also worked on engaging a younger cohort in international development programs in the Youth Ambassador scheme. He saw his first task as modernising the AAEF office. He recalled it was upstairs, 'up a fire escape, no air conditioning … You couldn't take anyone into the Fulbright office, it was embarrassing', with its 1950s furniture and archaic filing system. This was a reflection of deeper problems needing attention. 'The Not-For Profit infrastructure was not there, it was academics who had never run a Not For Profit.' Darby saw a need to make changes. 'This was a Board that spent nothing on marketing, who [metaphorically] bought a new kettle from the Goodwill, used plastic plates … You couldn't raise corporate donations that way', Darby believed. So 'the Board took away one scholarship and put funds into corporate fundraising, hosting Fulbright dinners'. The US Embassy had given the Australian Fulbright Program funds of $500,000–600,000 to buy a building, and the AAEF had been sitting on it for three years, but with a new executive director 'the Chair of the Board said our core business was scholarships not real estate, [instead] we will build an office that suits us'.

Darby saw the problem as one of instilling the understanding of the Fulbright vision in the award recipients. 'We pressed the Prime Minister [at that time John Howard] to write a personal letter to recipients, gave them a certificate ... also had the US Ambassador hosting an end of year gathering'. Darby's goal 'was about positioning the program ...[things] had been ad hoc, but we decided to do things every year, as part of the program, to engage people, establish a Fulbright tradition ... to provide support networks in America to bring them together, to feed off each other, to meet the Ambassador, to meet alumni, to know something about the history of the Fulbright Program'. It was under Darby's watch that the Foundation was rebadged the 'Australian-American Fulbright Commission' (AAFC) in 2000. This was a deliberate revival of the name and history of the program's founder, positioned in 21st century terms as a 'brand' that would help rebuild the profile of the scheme. As Darby says, he wanted to convey to those receiving their awards that it was something special: 'you owe it to them and to yourselves to be the best you can, if you treat this as just another research grant then you are missing the point, this will change your career ... you are not here by default ... you've earnt it, you are no longer a postgraduate student, you are a Fulbright scholar, you need to think about this and what it means'.[49]

Figure 10.2 Dennis Altman signing a copy of his book *The Homosexualization of America: The Americanization of the Homosexual* in A Different Light Bookstore, Los Angeles, CA, c. 1982

Those who were administering the program now recognised that keeping the Fulbright Program alive and relevant into the future meant adapting to the massive onslaught on the public sector from short-sighted neo-liberal policies. The Fulbright Program would 'grimly retain its integrity, its transparent bi-nationalism and its structural protections at home and abroad'.[50] But we must ask, at what cost?

Notes

1 David Harvey, *A Brief History of Neoliberalism* (Oxford, 2005), pp. 19–22.
2 Harvey traces its ideological origins to 1947 and its implementation in US monetary policy to 1979, *Neoliberalism*, p. 23.
3 Harvey, *Neoliberalism*, p. 19.
4 Frank Bongiorno, *The Eighties: The Decade That Transformed Australia* (Melbourne, 2015); Harvey, *Neoliberalism*, p. 33.
5 AAEF board minutes, 3 December 1976 Special meeting (Program Review).
6 AAEF board minutes, 12 February 1981.
7 In 1978, 'USIA was combined with the Bureau of Educational Cultural Affairs of the Department of State into a new agency called the United States International Communications Agency (USICA). Use of the name United States Information Agency (USIA) was reinstituted in August 1982. The agency was abolished effective October 1, 1999. The non-broadcasting functions were folded into the Department of State and the International Broadcasting Bureau (IBB) began operations as an independent agency reporting to the Broadcasting Board of Governors (BBG)'. From Overview of archives on U.S. Information Agency (RG 306), National Archives website, www.archives.gov/research/foreign-policy/related-records/rg-306.html (accessed 3 September 2017).
8 AAEF board minutes, 28 October 1982.
9 AAEF board minutes, 6 November 1986.
10 John Dawkins, Higher Education: A Policy Discussion Paper, Canberra, AGPS, 1987, p. 1; for a full study of these reforms see Stuart Macintyre, Andre Brett ad Gwilym Croucher, *No End of a Lesson: Australia's Unified National System of Higher Education* (Melbourne, 2017).
11 AAEF board minutes, 2 March 1987, item 8.3: 1988 Program Proposal.
12 AAEF board minutes, 10 November 1983, item 6.2 1984 Program.
13 The percentages of women scholars are based on our database of Australian and American scholars, by decade and by gender. These figures may not be exact given that records of some scholars, particularly from before the 1970s, have been lost and only their first initial provided, so their gender could not be determined, however we believe the figures to be accurate enough to draw conclusions about fluctuations in gender parity over the decades.
14 'Australian-American Educational Foundation (Fulbright Commission): Report 1988–1989' (Canberra, 1990), p. 6.
15 'Major Changes to Program', *The Fulbrighter*, vol 1:1 (July 1987), p. 2.
16 Margaret Thornton, ed., *Through a Glass Darkly: The Social Sciences Look at the Neoliberal University* (Canberra, 2014).

17 Walter Johnson and Francis Colligan, *The Fulbright Program: A History* (Chicago, 1965), p. 38.
18 Kenneth Osgood, 'The Unconventional Cold War' (review essay), in *Journal of Cold War Studies* Vol 4:2 (Spring 2002), pp. 85–107.
19 Simon Marginson, *Educating Australia: Government, Economy, and Citizen Since 1960* (Cambridge, 1997), p. 160.
20 AAEF board minutes, 28 May 2003.
21 AAEF board minutes, 7 March 1990.
22 AAEF board minutes, 23 February 1992.
23 AAEF board minutes, 23 May 2003.
24 AAEF board minutes, 8 August 1988.
25 AAEF board minutes, 28 November 1988.
26 AAEF board minutes, 20 May 1997; AAEF, 22 August 2000.
27 AAEF board minutes, 10 March 1989.
28 AAEF board minutes, 21 May 1990.
29 AAEF board minutes, 21 August 1990.
30 AAEF board minutes, 22 August 2000.
31 AAEF board minutes, 7 March 1990.
32 AAEF board minutes, 21 May 1990.
33 AAEF board minutes, 20 August 1992.
34 AAEF, 20 August 1992, item 12; interview with Susan Dorsch by Diane Kirkby, Sydney September 2017.
35 AAEF board minutes, 23 November 1992 Item 17. Fulbright Award For Aboriginal And Torres Strait Islanders.
36 AAEF board minutes, 25 May 1993, Item 20. Other Business. Postgraduate Student Award for Aboriginal and Torres Strait Islander People Poster.
37 AAEF board minutes, 24 August 1993, Item 5. DIRECTOR'S REPORT.
38 AAEF, 23 November 1993, Item 13. Report on 1993/94 Australian Program and the Coral Sea Scholarship.
39 USEF board minutes, 30 April 1956; 15 July 1959; 12 September 1961.
40 BFS annual report, December 1974.
41 AAEF board minutes, 6 November 1986.
42 On the importance of Fulbright alumni in fundraising see Molly Battie, 'Fulbright Women in the Global Intellectual Elite' in Alessandro Brogi, Giles Scott- Smith and David J. Snyder, eds, *The Legacy of J. William Fulbright: Policy, Power, and Ideology* (Kentucky, 2019), [p. 3].
43 Sue Cunningham, 'The Rise in University Philanthropy in Australia', *Higher Ed.Ition*, 16 December 2016, www.universitiesaustralia.edu.au/Media-and-Events/HIGHER-ED-ITION/Articles/2016–2017/The-rise-of-university-philanthropy-in-Australia (accessed 3 September 2017).
44 AAEF board minutes, 24 February 1992, p. 3.
45 AAEF, 24 February 1992: 'Members considered the possibility that more Alumni donations would be generated by such a project as it was envisaged that Fulbright House would directly benefit the Alumni Association (and Fulbrighters in general) by the provision of meeting rooms, office space and possibly some overnight accommodation.'
46 AAEF board minutes, 23 February 1993.

47 AAEF board minutes, 28 November 1988, 27 November 1989 and 27 November 1989.

48 *The Fulbrighter Australia*, vol. 17:1 (March 2004), p. 2.

49 Mark Darby, interview with Alice Garner, Washington DC, 2011. In possession of the authors. The renaming of the AAEF to the Australian-American Fulbright Commission was approved by the board on 22 August 2000.

50 Arndt, *First Resort of Kings*, p. 226.

Conclusion

At the end of the first decade of the twenty-first century the Fulbright Program celebrated sixty years in Australia. There had been changes, especially in the funding arrangements, but there were also several continuities.

Despite the recommendations of the 1976 Rose report that scholarships were preferably left open, they had in fact become far more targeted and there were many fewer available. The number of scholars going on exchange was significantly lower than in earlier decades. Postgraduates stayed for shorter periods to conduct specific research rather than enrol in lengthy PhDs. Indigenous scholars now had a specific award and the gender ratio of successful applicants had improved, so that between 1990 and 2009 women made up approximately 43 per cent of the total. It was even harder for humanities and social science scholars to compete against scientists and medical researchers. The AAFC board had increased in size, but was still disproportionately male, although it had increased the membership of women to three since the first woman was appointed in 1985. While two women had acted temporarily as executive directors at times of transition between appointments, Dr Tangerine Holt was the first woman to be formally appointed as executive director of the Commission, in 2011.

Talk of commissioning an official history had come to nought back in 1990.[1] The history finally written – this book – was not commissioned but was the outcome of an independent approach by Fulbright alumna Diane Kirkby to Executive Director Mark Darby to seek Australian Research Council funding for a Linkage Project of scholarly investigation.

This study has located the Australian-American Fulbright Program in a context of the transpacific diplomatic and military relationship between the two countries that was rarely direct and never specifically referred to in Fulbright publications. Nevertheless the ANZUS alliance and its enduring importance has been a necessary backdrop to this account. It gave greater weight to the meaning of the campus unrest of the 1960s and 1970s, and to the level of government funding for Fulbright awards. There were also periods of conflict and distrust in that alliance when national foreign policy objectives diverged – such as when there was an ALP government in Canberra and a Republican administration in Washington – that strained the relationship.[2] That diplomatic history has its own historical literature. The Fulbright–ANZUS dynamic arguably warrants its own systematic analysis. More conspicuous for academics going on exchange was the power of unpopular government policies to undermine the good-will between them and their peers, and indeed to endanger the program itself. For while they knew their government's reason for being involved in educational exchange was to promote an agenda of 'international understanding', their own priority as academics was to pursue scholarly interests. Personal and professional goals were of 'uppermost importance' and many saw it as 'unseemly' for them to engage in the kind of extra-curricular activities that would eat into their research time.[3]

The history of Fulbright award recipients as 'Academic Ambassadors' grappling with the conflicts that may have thus been created, especially for those individuals 'not always … in agreement' with national foreign policies, has been the substance of this account. For much of the period covered, Australia and America's mutual interest in fighting the Cold War domestically and regionally encouraged government investment in universities and strengthened the academic exchange program. The awkward balan-cing act we have observed between national foreign policy priorities and government funding of tertiary institutions and scholars, warrants further scrutiny of its meaning for the public university. Such questions are implicit in a government-funded program that sees academics as ambassadors, placed at the forefront of national foreign policy. Remaining independent of overt government influence was a challenge for the BFS in Washington and the Australian board administering the Fulbright Program locally. The seeds of potential interference and the possibility of resistance were sown at the outset and re-emerged constantly, as we have shown here. Sometimes interference was on political grounds, at other times it was by means of economic manipulation, which may indeed be the more insidious.

'Mutual understanding' as the central goal of the program, was a nebulous con-cept that was never actually defined and is difficult for the historian to document. Although the phrase was most commonly used as a rhetorical guiding principle, it was left to scholars to interpret and apply to their own experiences. Used benignly it has been a crucial ideal, albeit at times hard for those involved in the negotiation, setting-up and management of the program, on both sides of the Pacific, to realise or demonstrate in practice. Fulbright's initial idea, according to his biographer, was that future leaders of the various countries involved in the exchange would be able to talk to one another with a more sophisticated understanding of each other's society and culture: he imagined that US diplomacy would be more meaningful and respectful if public servants and policy administrators had first-hand knowledge of at least one other culture.[4]

Clearly not everyone involved saw this goal for the administration of the program in quite this way. It was not necessarily benign, nor could it always be sustained as the program evolved. Awards were given to categories of researchers – distinguished professors, Senior Scholars and scientists – more often than Fulbright's vision would have encouraged. Academic exchange worked best for those with something to con-tribute and much to learn, not from sending those who were more likely to be 'too big, too status-conscious, and often over-the-hill'.[5] At times national priorities in research agendas dominated selections and the interpretation of 'mutual' became more instrumental at best, more controlling of academic freedom at worst.

Indeed Fulbright's own statements illustrate these concerns. He grew much more outspokenly critical of his own government's tendency to confuse intellectual exchange with political manipulation. There were plenty of USIS officers, for example, who saw their role as seeking to influence Australians to embrace a US-style approach to trade unions, business management and trade (among other things). Some might ask therefore whether there is evidence that sixty-plus years of Fulbright exchanges have simply resulted in American domination of Australia, and that facilitating academic exchange with the United States has not served Australia's own interests. Then we must also ask: was that in fact the goal of the program? Perhaps it was for those who sought to control its direction. Fulbright himself talked about 'mutual understanding', not 'conversion' or enforcing change along American lines. 'He did not argue that it was America's destiny to force its culture on others.'[6] He didn't have to. US cultural hegemony was presumed and the idea that America's national interests were inseparable from the world's was built into the structure and mechanics of exchange. Undoubtedly there has been real and genuine change in academic culture in Australia.

It's a complex story, not a simple cause-and-effect outcome, but one thing is clear: over the period we have studied, Australia reoriented itself towards the United States diplomatically, militarily and culturally. The Fulbright Program cannot be held entirely responsible for causing this reorientation, but it was undoubtedly a player in US cultural diplomacy. Its effect was felt in the higher education sector, in breaking down resistance, demonstrating alternatives, boosting careers and fostering new relationships between intellectual elites. Americans coming to Australia brought fresh insights to old methods. Many returning Australians brought back ideas of how to bring change to their disciplines as well as their institutions, especially teaching methods. With the prestige of a Fulbright award added to their CV, enriched by what they had learnt from their time away and the international contacts they had made, these potential leaders now advanced their careers up the academic hierarchy to become actual leaders. They figure prominently among vice-chancellors and faculty deans.

As a consequence there has been an 'Americanisation' of Australian universities that was recognised and discussed in a report on the Fulbright Program undertaken in the 1970s.[7] All of those interviewed at that time saw the 'character of Australian academic life' changing to an American from a British orientation, some with enthusiasm ('the best thing that has happened'), others with dismay at the loss of a more focused, discipline-based undergraduate education that produced 'seemingly more professionally' competent graduates.[8] Critics were more likely to be in humanities, while scientists welcomed the introduction of course-based doctoral programs. Most who had observed the United States themselves were eager to bring back new ideas, especially of teaching techniques and faculty–student interaction.[9] These changes – of broader curricula and more innovative teaching methods – accelerated in subsequent decades as Australia's public universities found ways to expand their enrolments to cope with declining government funding. The increasing government control and surveillance that flowed after the Dawkins reforms of the 1980s has not however been as pronounced in the US system.

In sum, the Fulbright Program was an integral part of the process of redefining 'Australia' geographically in the Asia-Pacific, from being 'a province of the English-speaking world, whose capital was once in Britain' to one whose capital 'is now in the USA.[10] Yet the most creative and enduring aspects of academic exchange are not entirely controllable: they spring from the curiosity of researchers open to new experiences, encountering the unpredictable and being prepared to act on their new knowledge. Many scholars reported changing their fields once they had spent some time in the United States, like 'the mathematician who shifted to math education ... the endocrinologist who went into community medicine, [or] ... the engineer who shifted his entire orientation to a concern with servo-mechanics and automation.[11] The change that living away triggered could be totally unexpected, as the experience of Dennis Altman demonstrated. Altman had a postgraduate award in 1964 to undertake Southeast Asian studies at Cornell University. He spent 'two not very happy years as a graduate student at Cornell' – suffering homesickness, 'unprepared for the foreign-ness of the United States' and 'discomforted by the bitter cold of snow and wet in an upstate New York winter'. Yet his experiences of life in America 'would fundamen-tally affect my future life'. He discontinued his studies in Southeast Asian studies and embraced US politics, drawn into it by the issues of the Vietnam War. This started his life-long relationship with the United States that he describes as 'second only to the relationships with my immediate family for its length and intensity' as he crisscrossed the United States and became involved with an emerging gay rights movement.

Altman's activism increased on his return to Australia in 1969. In Sydney he was a founding member of the gay rights organisation. He published his first book in 1971, a landmark work for the gay rights movement. But this was not the career he had expected. He had become 'by accident, a "spokesperson" for the modern gay movement'. This, he said, 'was only possible because of my time in the United States in the late 1960s'. Like many Fulbright alumni, he has also had a distinguished academic career. In 1985 Dennis Altman was appointed to a position at La Trobe University where he became professor of politics, and one of Australia's most prominent public intellectuals. Twenty years later (in 2005) he held the Gough Whitlam and Malcolm Fraser Chair in Australian Studies at Harvard. In 2008 he joined in seeking ARC funds to undertake this Fulbright history research. 'Had I in fact gone to the London School of Economics', as he had originally intended, 'I may well have become a better ... pol-itical scientist', he reflected in his memoirs, 'but almost certainly I would not have become a gay activist'.[12] The Fulbright concept of 'mutual understanding' was not limited in its scope. There were instances when the Fulbright vision that America's 'mission was to make the world safe for diversity' was demonstrably achievable.[13]

The surprising strength of the Fulbright Program has been the loyalty to its ideals that it has generated among its alumni. While Australians are less inclined to enthuse verbally or express this through action, when asked to comment they have responded positively more often than negatively, and many willingly serve voluntarily on state selection committees. No doubt true dissenters do not participate. Government cutbacks pushing the program to rely on private sector funding, threaten to undermine this support and, ironically, to pose a new challenge to the integrity and continuing independence of the program. It may also be giving more control back to the United States. There it was Fulbright alumni (notably women) who came to the support of the program to help preserve its financial future.[14]

A compromised integrity has always been the biggest threat to the success of the program, if we are to measure success in terms of a serious and independent academic endeavour traversing the Pacific that nurtures a genuine, critical mutual regard. Since its first conception in a bubble of post-war internationalism that quickly gave way to Cold War imperatives of domestic and global politics, the Fulbright Program has claimed its identity as autonomous and academic. Australian program administrators and scholars have fought over the decades to maintain this identity, and now take strength from their pride in the program's legacy. The future, however, looks no less challenging. How the Fulbright Program moves forward will continue to be affected by geopolitical forces in the Asia-Pacific region and what Australians and Americans – the people and the governments they elect – seek from their knowledge of each other.

Notes

1 AAEF board minutes, 21 May 1990.
2 James Curran, *Unholy Fury: Whitlam and Nixon At War* (Melbourne, 2015).
3 Peter Rose, *Academic Sojourners: A Report on the Senior Fulbright Programs in East Asia and the Pacific* (United States Bureau of Educational and Cultural Affairs, Office of Policy and Plans, 1976), p. 30, attached to Background Paper for Review Meeting, AAEF, December 1976.
4 Randall Bennett Woods, 'Fulbright Internationalism', *Annals of the American Academy of Political and Social Sciences*, vol. 491 (May 1987), p. 23.
5 Rose, *Academic Sojourners*, p. 108.
6 Woods, 'Fulbright Internationalism', p. 23.
7 Rose, *Academic Sojourners*, p. 102.
8 Rose, *Academic Sojourners*, pp. 102–3.
9 Rose, *Academic Sojourners*, pp. 102–3.
10 Coral Bell, *Dependent Ally: A Study in Australian Foreign Policy* (Sydney, 1988), p. 186.
11 Rose, *Academic Sojourners*, p. 109.
12 Dennis Altman, *Defying Gravity: A Political Life* (Sydney, 1997), p. 63.
13 Woods, 'Fulbright Internationalism', p. 23.
14 Molly Battie, 'Fulbright Women in the Global Intellectual Elite', in Alessandro Brogi, Giles Scott-Smith and David J. Snyder, eds, *The Legacy of J. William Fulbright: Policy, Power, and Ideology*, (Kentucky, 2019), [p. 10].

Bibliography

Primary sources

Survey of Australian and American Fulbright Alumni, 2011 [La Trobe University]. In possession of the authors.

Archives

Columbia University, Special Collections
Carnegie Corporation of New York Records. NY NYCR91- A6 Series III Grants. Box 128 Folder 1: Crawford R.M.

Duke University, David Rubenstein Rare Books and Manuscripts Library
John Hope Franklin Papers.

National Archives of Australia (NAA)
A10302 1960/204 United States Educational Foundation 1956–60.

A1067 A46/2/4/10 Social and Cultural Matters. Land-lease [*sic*] Cultural Fund. 'Fulbright Agreement' 1946–8.

A11099 1/65 Notetaker E J Bunting – Notes of meetings 18 December 1963 – 15 April 1964 [Notes on Cabinet meetings] 1963–64.

A13307 18/1 Agreement [Fulbright Agreement] between the Government of Australia and the Government of the United States of America for the Use of Funds made available in accordance with the Agreement on Settlement for Lend-Lease, Reciprocal Aid, Surplus War Property and Claims of 7 June 1946 – Date and Place of Signing: 26 November 1949 – Date of entry into force for Australia: 26 November 1949 – ATS Number: [1949] ATS 14 – Language: English.

A1361 20/4/12 Part 1 Scholarships, Bursaries, Fellowships – Foreign – Institute of International Education (New York) 1949–60.

A1361 4/7/5 Part 1 Re-establishment and rehabilitation in overseas countries – lend-lease settlement funds – available for culture (Fulbright bill) 1946–49.

A1361 4/7/5 Part 2 Re-establishment and rehabilitation in overseas countries – lend-lease settlement funds – available for culture (Fulbright bill) 1949–52.

A1838 250/9/8/1 United States of America – Relations with Australia – Cultural 1947–62.

A1838 250/9/8/2 Fulbright Agreement papers 1949–50.

A1838 250/9/8/2 Part 4 United States of America – Relations with Australia – Cultural Fund – Fulbright Agreement 1949–50.

A1838 250/9/8/3 Part 1 United States of America – Relations with Australia – Requests for information on Fulbright Agreement 1949–52.

A1838 250/9/8/3 Part 2 United States of America – Relations with Australia – Requests for information on Fulbright Agreement 1952–53.

A1838 250/9/8/3 Part 3 United States of America – Requests for information on Fulbright Agreement 1953.

A1838 250/9/8/4 Part 3 United States of America – Educational Foundation – Board of Directors and meeting of board – Relations with Australia 1952–53.

A1838 250/9/8/4/2 Part 2 United States of America – Relations with Australia – United States Educational Foundation – General 1953–54.

A1838 250/9/8/4/2 Part 3 United States of America – Relations with Australia – United States Educational Foundation – General 1954.

A1838 250/9/8/7 Part 1 United States of America – Educational Foundation Programmes 1950–51.

A1838 583/1 Part 1 Australian-American Educational Foundation – Policy 1963–64.

A1838 583/1 Part 2 Australian-American Educational Foundation – Policy 1964–65.

A1838 583/1 Part 6 United States – Educational Foundation– Policy 1955–61.

A250/9/8/3 Part 2 United States of America – Relations with Australia – Requests for Information on Fulbright Agreement 1952–53.

A3300 874 1948 [file – pink tab] [Foreign policy] – (US) – lend lease – Cultural fund – (under Fulbright Act) (general policy) 1948.

A432 1950/838 Subversive Activities – Proposed United States Legislation 1950–51.

A463 1963/611 United States Educational Foundation in Australia – Fulbright programme – Policy 1958–64.

A463 1964/5174 Part 2 Australian/American Educational Foundation – Policy 1965–66.

A463 1964/774 Part 1 Proposed Joint United States of America/Australia successor to Fulbright Scheme – Policy 1961–64.

A463 1964/774 Part 2 Proposed Joint United States of America/Australia successor to Fulbright Scheme 1964.

A463 1965/2313 Reports by Visiting American Fulbright Scholars 1965–68.

A6126 144 Norman Denholm Harper 1951–55.

A9790 8132 Lend Lease Educational and Cultural (Fulbright) Agreement 1946–48.

Cabinet Notebooks – Fact Sheet 128 at www.naa.gov.au/collection/fact-sheets/fs128.aspx.

National Archives and Records Administration, Washington, DC (NARA)

Operations-General: Restrictions on Operational Use of Certain Categories of Individuals' (4 September 1973) from US Digital National Security Archive (online).

Overview of archives on U.S. Information Agency (RG 306), National Archives website, at: www.archives.gov/research/foreign-policy/related-records/rg-306.html (accessed 3 September 2017).

Record Group 59: General Records of the Department of State, 1763–2002.

RG:59 13-A.2a FULBRIGHT PROGRAM in AUSTRALIA, Aust. Desk files.

September 1973 Operations-General directive titled 'Restrictions on Operational Use of Certain Categories of Individuals' prohibited the 'Operational use' of 'Fulbright grantees'. US *Digital National Security Archive* online. (Found at NARA Maryland).

Series: Central Decimal Files, 1910–63.

National Library of Australia

Colin Thiele Papers, 1939–92.

Douglas Berry Copland Papers, 1907–71.

Ernest Llewellyn Papers, 1911–2004.

Records of the Australian Association for Cultural Freedom, 1953–69.

Robin Gollan Papers, 1920–2005.
Sir John Latham Papers, 1856–1964.
Sir Percy Spender Papers, 1937–78.

University of Arkansas Special Collections
MC 468 Bureau of Educational and Cultural Affairs Historical Collection (CU), Records
     c.1938–84.
-Group III Fulbright Program, Box 114.
-Group XVI Post Reports, Box 316.

University of Melbourne Archives
1950/409 Fulbright Bill.
1960/622 Franklin, Prof. J.H.
1960/636, 1961/535 Fulbright Program.
Norman Denholm Harper Papers.
Raymond M. Crawford Papers.
UM312 Registrar's Correspondence.

**US Educational Foundation (USEF)/Australian-American Educational Foundation
(AAEF)/Australian-American Fulbright Commission (AAFC), Canberra**
AAEF 24 August 1993 Item 5. DIRECTOR'S REPORT.
AAEF 25 May 1993 Item 20. Other Business. Postgraduate Student Award for Aboriginal
     and Torres Strait.
AAEF 3 December 1976 Special meeting (Program Review).
AAEF Board Minutes 1965–67, 1970, 1981–89, 1990, 1992–93, 1997, 2000, 2003.
AAEF Information Booklet, 9th Edition, July 1984, Sect. 2.3, p. 5, cited in AAEF Board
     Minutes, 2 August 1984.
AAEF Record of the Sept 23 1967 Special Conference, in Australian-American Educational
     Foundation Background Papers for Review Meeting, 3 December 1976.
AAEF Report on 1993/94 Australian Program and the Coral Sea Scholarship.
Agreement between the Government of the United States of America and the Government
     of the Commonwealth of Australia on Settlement for Lend-Lease, Reciprocal Aid,
     Surplus War Property, and Claims, signed at Washington and New York on 7 June,
     1946, by James F. Byrnes, Secretary of State of the USA, and H. Evatt, Minister of
     External Affairs of the Commonwealth of Australia. 60 Stat. 1707; Treaties and Other
     International Act Series 1528.
Australian-American Educational Foundation (Fulbright Commission) Report 1988–1989
     (Canberra, 1990).
Government concerning Taxation Provisions of the Pending United States-Australian
     Fulbright Agreement.
The Fulbrighter Australia, newsletter of the AAEF/Fulbright Commission, 1950s–2009.
United States Educational Foundation, board minutes, 1950–51, 1953–62, 1964.
United States Educational Foundation, First USEF Annual Report [1951].
United States Educational Foundation, 'General Requirements and Conditions' September
     1958.
United States Educational Foundation, *The Fulbright Programme: The First Eight Years and
     the Future* (Canberra, 1958).

Board of Foreign Scholarships (BFS)

Annual Report of the Board of Foreign Scholarships Toward mutual understanding... a report on Academic Exchanges (Washington, DC: The Board, 1967–68).
Annual Report of the Board of Foreign Scholarships (Washington, DC: The Board, 1970).
Annual Report of the Board of Foreign Scholarships (Washington, DC: The Board, 1974).
The Fulbright Program in the Eighties: Summary of Conference Proceedings (Washington, DC: Board of Foreign Scholarships and the US International Communication Agency, 16–17 October 1980).

Government and miscellaneous publications

Allen W. Hatheway and Lothar M. Klingmuller, 'Willard Lacy', A Paper in the AEG Website *Biography* Series, 27 July 2005, http://gap.entclub.org/taxonomists/Brown/1954b.pdf.
Australian Diary no. 071, 1953, directed by Jack S. Allan. In the National Film and Sound Archive collection, title 67328.
Dawkins, John, Higher Education: A Policy Discussion Paper, Canberra, AGPS, 1987.
Fulbright, J. William, *The Arrogance of Power* (New York, 1967).
Johnson, Walter, *American Studies Abroad: Progress and Difficulties in Selected Countries. A Special Report from the United States Advisory Commission on International and Cultural Affairs*, July 1963.
Joughlin, Louis, 'The Selection of Fulbright Scholars', *American Association of University Professors Bulletin*, vol. 46:1 (1960), pp. 8–17.
King, Peter, 'Whither Whitlam?', *International Journal, Pacific Affairs*, vol. 29:3 (Summer 1974), pp. 422–40.
Latham, John, 'Education and War', Professor John Smyth Memorial Lecture (Melbourne, 1943).
Mack, Andrew, 'US Bases in Australia: The Debate Continues', *Australian Outlook*, vol. 42:2 (1988), pp. 77–85.
Murray, K. *Report of the Committee on Australian Universities* (Canberra: Government Printer, 1957).
Newton, obituary at www.obitcentral.com/obitsearch/obits/ks/ks-cowley20.htm (accessed 16 August 2012).
Odegaard, Charles, 'The Fulbright Exchange Program in Operation', *ACLS Newsletter*, December 1949, 13–14.
Playford, John, 'Political Scientists and the CIA', *Australian Left Review* (April–May 1968), pp. 14–28.
Rose, Peter I. *Academic Sojourners: A Report on the Senior Fulbright Programs in East Asia and the Pacific* (United States Bureau of Educational and Cultural Affairs, Office of Policy and Plans, 1976).
Springer, G. P. A Report on the Fulbright-Hays Student Exchange Program Seminar, Sept. 20–22, 1967, Wingspread, Wis. [New York], Institute of International Education, 1968.
'United States Relations with Australia: Policy Statement of the Department of State', classified Secret, Washington, 18 August 1948. In United States Department of State, *Foreign relations of the United States, 1948*, vol. 6: The Far East and Australasia, pp. 2 and 7. At http://digicoll.library.wisc.edu/cgi-bin/FRUS/FRUS-idx?type=div&did=FRUS. FRUS1948v06.i0006&isize=M (accessed 23 August 2012).

Interviews

Alice Garner (Interviewer) *Fulbright scholars oral history project*, 2009–12, National Library of Australia: Joanne Daly, Michael Good, Peter van Sommers, Adele Millerd, Deborah May, Nancy Viviani, Jeremy Hearder, Peter Newman, Peter Coaldrake, Ruth Fink Latukefu, Garth Nettheim, Arnold Zable, Bill Ford, Hugh Collins, Sherry Saggers, Dale Hebbard, Samia Goudie, Kaye Basford, Elaine Barry, Angus Trumble, William Riedel Murray Littlejohn, Keith Neighbour.

Alice Garner (Interviewer) Short interviews of Fulbright alumni, possession of the authors, La Trobe University: Basil Balme (WA), Bruce Crawford (TAS), Derek McDougall (VIC), Don Watts (WA), Hans Drielsma (TAS), Stephanie and Lyndsay Farrall (TAS), Geoffrey Soutar (WA), Leah Mercer (WA), Sabra Thorner (NYC).

Alice Garner (Interviewer) of Australian Fulbright Commission officers John Lake (WA), Mark Darby (Washington DC), and of board member Don Debats, La Trobe University.

Bruce Dickson (Interviewer), Oodgeroo Noonuccal, 1981 'The Legacy of a True National Treasure of Australia', on Dropbearito.com (Cultural Crossroads: Australia / America), p. 2 of 4, accessed 3 September 2017.

Diane Kirkby (Interviewer) of Australian Fulbright Commission Board Members Susan Dorsch (NSW) Susan Ryan (NSW) 2017 La Trobe University.

Laws

Public Law 584, 79th Congress, 60 Stat. 754, approved August 1, 1946. Amendment to the Surplus Property Act of 1944.

The Mutual Educational and Cultural Exchange Act of 1961, or Public Law 87–256 (75 Stat. 527), signed by President Kennedy on 21 September 1961.

United States Information and Educational Exchange Act of 1948', Public Law 402, H.R. 3342, January 27, 1948.

Memoirs of Fulbright scholars

Altman, Dennis, *Defying Gravity: A Political Life* (Sydney, 1997).

Conway, Jill Ker, *Road From Coorain* (London, 1998).

Conway, Jill Ker, *True North* (London, 1994).

Conway, Jill Ker, *A Woman's Education* (New York, 2001).

Coombs, H.C., *Trial Balance* (Melbourne, 1981).

Cowen, Zelman, *A Public Life: The Memoirs of Zelman Cowen* (Melbourne, 2006).

Franklin, John Hope *Mirror to America: The Autobiography of John Hope Franklin* (New York, 2005).

Heseltine, Harry, *In Due Season: Australian Literary Studies: A Personal Memoir* (Melbourne, 2009).

Websites

Alice Garner, Australia-American Fulbright program Timeline, at: http://www.tiki-toki.com/timeline/entry/293784/Australian-American-Fulbright-Program/#vars!date=1943-05-29_17:56:20!

Australian-American Association website: https://australianamerican.org/, accessed on 14 September 2017.

Encyclopedia of Women and Leadership in 20th-century Australia, at: http://www.womenaustralia.info/leaders/ (July 2018).

Secretariat of the Pacific Community website: www.spc.int/en/about-spc/history.html, accessed on 16 October 2012.

Students at the University of Sydney' Archives and Records Management Services, at: http://sydney.edu.au/arms/archives/history/senate_exhibitions/students_women_history_science.shtml.

Secondary sources

Abjorensen, Norman and James C. Docherty, eds, *Historical Dictionary of Australia*, 4th edn (London and Lanham, 2014).

Albinski, Henry S., *Politics and Foreign Policy in Australia: The Impact of Vietnam and Conscription* (Durham, NC, 1970).

Altbach, Philip G. and Ulrich Teichler, 'Internationalization and Exchanges in a Globalized University', *Journal of Studies in International Education*, vol. 5:1 (Spring 2001), pp. 5–25.

Anderson, Fay, *An Historian's Life: Max Crawford and the Politics of Academic Freedom* (Melbourne, 2005).

[Anon.] 'The Fiftieth Anniversary of the Fulbright Program', *International Educator*, vol. 5:4 (1996), pp. 13–24.

Arndt, Richard T., *The First Resort of Kings: American Cultural Diplomacy in the Twentieth Century* (Dulles, 2005).

Arndt, Richard T. and David L. Rubin, eds, *The Fulbright Difference, 1948–1992* (New Brunswick, 1993).

Arsenault, Ray and John Hope Franklin, 'Pioneers of History: The Sage of Freedom: An Interview with John Hope Franklin', *The Public Historian*, vol. 29:2 (2007), pp. 35–54.

Australian Dictionary of Biography, National Centre of Biography, Australian National University.

Baker, Jeannine, *Australian Women War Reporters: Boer War to Vietnam* (Sydney, 2015).

Barrett, Russell H., *Promises and Performances in Australian Politics, 1928–1959* (New York, 1959).

Battie, Molly, 'Fulbright Women in the Global Intellectual Elite', in Alessandro Brogi, Giles Scott-Smith and David J. Snyder, eds, *The Legacy of J. William Fulbright: Policy, Power, and Ideology*, (Kentucky, 2019).

Bayne, Peter, 'Evatt, Herbert Vere', in Michael Coper, Tony Blackshield and George Williams, eds, *Oxford Companion to the High Court of Australia*, 1st edn (Melbourne, 2001).

Bell, Coral, *Dependent Ally: A Study in Australian Foreign Policy* (Sydney, 1988).

Berman, William C., *William Fulbright and the Vietnam War: The Dissent of a Political Realist* (Kent, Ohio, 1988).

Bloomfield, Alan and Kim Nossal, 'End of an Era? Anti-Americanism in the Australian Labor Party', *Australian Journal of Politics and History*, vol. 56:4 (December 2010), pp. 592–611.

Bongiorno, Frank, *The Eighties: The Decade that Transformed Australia* (Melbourne, 2015).

Brasch, Nicholas, *Australia's Immigration Policy: 1788–2009* (Sydney, 2009).

Brogi, Alessandro, Giles Scott-Smith and David J. Snyder, eds, *The Legacy of J. William Fulbright: Policy, Power, and Ideology*, (Kentucky, 2019).

Broome, Richard, *Aboriginal Australians*, 3rd edn (Sydney, 2001).

Bu, Liping, 'Educational Exchange and Cultural Diplomacy in the Cold War', *Journal of American Studies*, vol. 33:3, part 1 (1999), pp. 393–415.

Bu, Liping, *Making the World Like Us: Education, Cultural Expansion, and the American Century* (New York, 2003).

Buti, Antonio, *A Matter of Conscience: Sir Ronald Wilson* (Crawley, WA, 2007).

Cain, Frank, *The Australian Security Intelligence Organisation: An Unofficial History* (Ilford, UK, 1994).

Camilleri, Joseph, *Australian-American Relations: The Web of Dependence* (Melbourne, 1980).

Campbell, Craig, 'Cold War, the Universities and Public Education: The Contexts of J. B. Conant's Mission to Australia and New Zealand, 1951', *History of Education Review*, vol. 39:1 (2010), pp. 23–39.

Capling, Ann, '"Allies But Not Friends": Anti-Americanism in Australia', in Richard A. Higgott and Ivona Malbasic, eds, *The Political Consequences of Anti-Americanism* (New York, 2008).

Capp, Fiona, *Writers Defiled: Security Surveillance of Australian Authors and Intellectuals, 1920–1960* (Melbourne, 1993).

Chomsky, Noam, Laura Nader, Immanuel Wallerstein, Richard Lewontin and Richard Ohmann, eds, *The Cold War and the University: Towards an Intellectual History of the Postwar Years* (New York, 1997).

Coleman, Peter, Selwyn Cornish and Peter Drake, *Arndt's Story: The Life of an Australian Economist* (Canberra, 2007).

Cowen, Zelman, *Sir John Latham and Other Papers* (Melbourne, 1965).

Cull, Nicholas, *The Cold War and the United States Information Agency: American Propaganda and Public Diplomacy, 1945–1989* (Cambridge, 2008).

Cunningham, Sue, 'The Rise in University Philanthropy in Australia', *Higher Ed.Ition*, 16 December 2016, at: www.universitiesaustralia.edu.au/Media-and-Events/HIGHER-ED-ITION/Articles/2016–2017/The-rise-of-university-philanthropy-in-Australia (accessed 3 September 2017).

Curran, James, 'Beyond the Euphoria: Lyndon Johnson in Australia and the Politics of the Cold War Alliance', *Journal of Cold War Studies*, vol. 17:1 (2015), pp. 64–96.

Curran, James, *Unholy Fury: Whitlam and Nixon at War* (Melbourne, 2015).

Curthoys, Ann, *Freedom Ride: A Freedom Rider Remembers* (Sydney, 2002).

Cutlip, Scott M., *The Unseen Power: Public Relations: A History* (Routledge, 2013).

Daum, Andreas, Lloyd Gardner and Wilfred Mausbach, eds, *America, the Vietnam War and the World* (Cambridge, 2003).

Davison, Graeme, John Hirst and Stuart Macintyre, eds, *The Oxford Companion to Australian History* (Melbourne, 2001).

Dawes, N., *A Two-Way Street: The Indo-American Fulbright Program 1950–1960* (Bombay, 1962).

Deery, Phillip, 'Decoding the Cold War: Venona, Espionage and "The Communist Threat"' in Peter Love and Paul Strangio, eds, *Arguing the Cold War* (Melbourne, 2001).

Deery, Phillip 'Scientific Freedom and Post-War Politics: Australia, 1945–55', *Historical Records of Australian Science*, vol. 13:1 (2000), pp. 1–18.

Dizard, Wilson P. Jr., *Inventing Public Diplomacy: The Story of the U.S. Information Agency* (Boulder, 2004).

Druett, Joan, *Fulbright in New Zealand* (Wellington, 1988).

Dudden, Arthur and R. Dynes, *The Fulbright Experience 1946–86* (New Brunswick, 1987).

Dudziak, Mary, *Cold War Civil Rights: Race and the Image of Democracy* (Princeton, 2000).

Ellis, Robert B. and David S. Waller, 'Marketing Education in Australia before 1965', *Australasian Marketing Journal*, vol. 19:2 (2011), pp. 115–21.

Ellis, Robert B. and David Waller, 'Marketing Education in Australia before 1965', in Robert Walker, ed., *American Studies Abroad* (Westport, 1975).

Encyclopaedia of Women & Leadership in Twentieth-Century Australia, at: www.womenaustralia.info/leaders/biogs/WLE0741b.htm.

Foley, Susan and Chips Sowerwine, 'Miriam Dixon', *The Encyclopaedia of Women & Leadership in Australia*, at: www.womenaustralia.info/leaders/biogs/WLE0265b.htm.

Foster, S.G. and M. Varghese, *The Making of the Australian National University, 1946–1996* (Sydney, 1996).

Garner, Alice, and Diane Kirkby, 'Behind the Scenes of the Australian-American Fulbright Program since 1949', Fulbright Symposium, *Soft Power, Smart Power* (Canberra, 2015).

Garner, Alice, 'Geoffrey Rossiter: Founding Executive Officer', *Fulbrighter*, October 2014.

Garner, Alice, and Diane Kirkby, '"Tactful Visitor, Scientific Observer, or 100 per cent Patriot": Ambassadorship in the Australia-U.S. Fulbright Program', in Alessandro Brogi, Giles Scott-Smith and David J. Snyder, eds, *The Legacy of J. William Fulbright: Policy, Power, and Ideology* (Kentucky, 2019).

Garner, Alice and Diane Kirkby, '"Never a Machine for Propaganda"? The Australian-American Fulbright Program and Australia's Cold War', *Australian Historical Studies*, vol. 44:1 (2013), pp. 117–33.

Garner, Alice and Jane Miller, 'How the Fulbright Program Helped Establish Australian Social Work', *The Fulbrighter*, vol. 25:1 (January 2015), at: www.fulbright.com.au/newsletter-jan2015.

Gienow-Hecht, Jessica, 'Shame on US? Academics, Cultural Transfer and the Cold War: A Critical Review', *Diplomatic History*, vol. 24:3 (Summer 2000), pp. 465–94.

Gray, Geoffrey, '"A great deal of mischief can be done": Peter Worsley, the Australian National University, the Cold War and Academic Freedom, 1952–1954', *Journal of the Royal Australian Historical Society*, vol. 101:1 (June 2015), pp. 25–44.

Grimshaw, Patricia and Lynne Strahan, eds, *The Half-Open Door* (Sydney, 1982).

Groennings, Sven, 'The Fulbright Program in the Global Knowledge Economy: The Nation's Neglected Comparative Advantage', *Journal of Studies in International Education*, vol. 1:1 (Spring 1997), pp. 95–105.

Guangqiu, Xu, 'The Ideological and Political Impact of US Fulbrighters on Chinese Students 1979–89', *Asian Affairs*, vol. 26:3 (Fall 1999), pp. 139–57.

Harper, Norman, ed., *Pacific Circle: Proceedings of the Second Biennial Conference of the Australian and New Zealand American Studies Association* (St. Lucia, Qld., 1968).

Harvey, David, *A Brief History of Neoliberalism* (Oxford, 2005).

Hasluck, Paul, *A Time for Building: Australian Administration in Papua and New Guinea, 1951–1963* (Melbourne, 1976).

Hasluck, Paul, *The Government and the People, 1939–1941* (Canberra, 1952).

Hasluck, Paul, *The Government and the People, 1942–1945* (Canberra, 1970).

Haynes, Johnson and Bernard Gwertzman, *Fulbright: The Dissenter* (London, 1969).

Hergenhan, Laurie, *No Casual Traveller: Hartley Grattan and Australia* (St. Lucia, Qld., 1995).

Higley, John, John Nieuwenhuysen with Stine Neerup, eds, *Nations of Immigrants: Australia and the USA Compared* (Cheltenham, UK and Northampton, MA, 2009).

Hollander, Paul, ed., *Understanding Anti-Americanism: Its Origins and Impact at Home and Abroad* (Chicago, 2004).

Hubberd, Christopher, *Australia and US Military Cooperation: Fighting Common Enemies* (Aldershot, UK, 2005).

Hudson, W.J., *Casey* (Melbourne, 1995).

Iriye, Akira, *Cultural Internationalism and World Order* (Baltimore, 1997).

Jahn, Beate, *Liberal Internationalism: Theory, History, Practice* (Basingstoke, UK, 2013).

Johnson, Walter and Francis Colligan, *The Fulbright Program: A History* (Chicago, 1965).

Jordan, Caroline and Diane Kirkby, 'Women Modernists Gendering Leadership in Australian Art in the 1930s and 1940s', *Australian and New Zealand Journal of Art* (2018), vol. 18:2.

Kramer, Paul A., 'Is the World Our Campus? International Students and U.S. Global Power in the Long Twentieth Century', *Diplomatic History*, vol. 33:5 (2009), pp. 775–806.

Lawrence, John, 'A Tribute to Norma Parker', *Australian Social Work*, vol. 57:3 (2004), p. 303.

Lebovic, Sam, 'From War Junk to Educational Exchange: The World War II Origins of the Fulbright Program and the Foundations of American Cultural Globalism, 1945–50', *Diplomatic History*, vol. 37:2 (April 2013), pp. 280–312.

Levine, Susan, *Degrees of Equality: The American Association of University Women and the Challenge of Twentieth-Century Feminism* (Philadelphia, 1995).

Lloyd, Clem, 'Not Peace but a Sword: The High Court under J.G. Latham', *Adelaide Law Review*, vol. 11:2 (1987), pp. 175–202.

Love, Peter and Paul Strangio, *Arguing the Cold War* (Melbourne, 2001).

Lowe, David, *Australian Between Empires: The Life of Percy Spender* (London, 2010).

Lowe, David, *The Colombo Plan and 'Soft' Regionalism in the Asia-Pacific: Australian and New Zealand Cultural Diplomacy in the 1950s and 1960s* (Geelong, 2010).

Lowe, David, *Menzies and the 'Great World Struggle': Australia's Cold War 1948–1954* (Sydney, 1999).

Lowe, David and Daniel Oakman, eds, *Australia and the Colombo Plan 1949–1957 (Documents on Australian Foreign Policy)* (Canberra, 2004).

Lucas, Scott, 'Campaigns of Truth: The Psychological Strategy Board and American Ideology, 1951–1953', *The International History Review*, vol. 18:2 (1996), pp. 279–302.

Macintyre, Stuart, *Australia's Boldest Experiment: War and Reconstruction in the 1940s* (Sydney, 2015).

Macintyre, Stuart, *The Poor Relation: A History of Social Sciences in Australia* (Melbourne, 2010).

Macintyre, Stuart, Andre Brett and Gwilym Croucher, *No End of a Lesson: Australia's Unified National System of Higher Education* (Melbourne, 2017).

MacKinnon, Alison, *Women, Love and Learning: The Double Bind* (Bern, 2010).

Maher, Laurence, 'Downunder McCarthyism: The Struggle against Australian Communism 1945–1960 Part One', *Anglo-American Law Review*, vol. 27:3 (1998), pp. 341–89.

Manathunga, Catherine, 'The Role of Universities in Nation-Building in 1950s Australia and Aotearoa/New Zealand', *History of Education Review*, vol. 45:1 (2016), pp. 2–15.

Marginson, Simon, *Educating Australia: Government, Economy, and Citizen Since 1960* (Cambridge, 1997).

McDonald, Geraldine, Pam Kennedy and Barb Bishop, *Coming and Going: Forty Years of the Fulbright Program in New Zealand* (Wellington, 1989).

McKenzie, Norman, *Women In Australia* (Melbourne, 1962).

McPhee, Peter, *'Pansy': A Life of Roy Douglas Wright* (Melbourne, 1999).

Meaney, Neville, 'Australia, the Great Powers and the Coming of the Cold War', *Australian Journal of Politics and History*, vol. 38:3 (1992), pp. 316–33.

Meikle, Jeffrey L., 'Leo Marx's "The Machine in the Garden"' (review), *Technology and Culture*, vol. 44:1 (2003), pp. 147–59.

Moorhouse, Frank, *Cold Light* (Sydney, 2011).

Murphy, John, *Evatt: A Life* (Sydney, 2016).

Murphy, John, *Harvest of Fear: A History of Australia's Vietnam War* (Sydney, 1993).

Ninham, Sally, *A Cohort of Pioneers: Australian Postgraduate Students and American Postgraduate Degrees, 1949–1964* (Melbourne, 2011).

Oakham, Daniel, *Facing Asia: A History of the Colombo Plan* (Canberra, 2004).

Oakham, Daniel, 'The Politics of Foreign Aid: Counter-Subversion and the Colombo Plan, 1950–1970', *Pacifica Review: Peace, Security and Global Change*, vol. 13:3 (2001), pp. 255–72.

Oakham, Daniel and David Lowe, eds, *Australia and the Colombo Plan: 1949–1957* (Barton, ACT, 2004).

O'Connor, Brendon, 'Anti-Americanism in Australia', in Vol. 3: *Comparative Perspectives of B. O'Connor, Anti-Americanism: History, Causes and Themes*, 4 vols (Westport, CT, 2007).

Osgood, Kenneth A., 'Hearts and Minds: The Unconventional Cold War', *Journal of Cold War Studies*, vol. 4:2 (2002), pp. 85–107.

Osgood, Kenneth A. and Brian C. Etheridge, eds, *United States and Public Diplomacy: New Directions in Cultural and International History* (Leiden and Boston, 2010).

Patterson, James, *Grand Expectations: The U.S. 1945–74* (New York, 1997).

Payne, Trish, *War and Words: The Australian Press and the Vietnam War* (Melbourne, 2007).

Pells, Richard, *Not Like Us: How Europeans Have Loved, Hated, and Transformed American Culture Since World War II* (New York, 1997).

Pemberton, Greg, *All the Way: Australia's Road to Vietnam* (Sydney, 1987).

Pemberton, Greg, 'Australia, the United States, and the Indochina Crisis of 1954', *Diplomatic History*, vol. 13:1 (January 1989), pp. 45–66.

Rabel, Roberto, *New Zealand and the Vietnam War: Politics and Diplomacy* (Auckland, 2005).

Read, Peter, *Charles Perkins: A Biography* (Ringwood, Vic., 2001).

Rosenthal, Newman, *Sir Charles Lowe: A Biographical Memoir* (Melbourne, 1968).

Rowse, Tim, *Nugget Coombs: A Reforming Life* (Cambridge, 2002).

Rupp, Jan C., 'The Fulbright Program or the Surplus Value of Officially Organized Academic Exchange', *Journal of Studies in International Education*, vol. 3:1 (Spring 1999), pp. 57–81.

St.J. Barclay, Glen, *Friends in High Places: Australian-American Diplomatic Relations since 1945* (Melbourne, 1985).

Saunders, Frances Stonor, *The Cultural Cold War: The CIA and the World of Arts and Letters* (New York, 2000).

Scott-Smith, Giles, 'The Fulbright Program in the Netherlands: An Example of Science Diplomacy', in Jeroen van Dongen, ed., *Cold War Science and the Transatlantic Circulation of Knowledge* (Leiden, 2015), pp. 128–54.

Scott-Smith, Giles, *Networks of Empire: The US State Department's Foreign Leader Program in the Netherlands, France, and Britain 1950–1970* (Brussels, 2008).

Scott-Smith, Giles, *The Politics of Apolitical Culture: The Congress for Cultural Freedom, the CIA and Post-War American Hegemony* (London and New York, 2002).

Scott-Smith, Giles and Hans Krabbendam, *The Cultural Cold War in Western Europe, 1945–1960* (London, 2003).

Sexton, Michael, *War for the Asking: How Australia Invited Itself to Vietnam* (Sydney, 1981).

Sharp, Andrew and Dale Flesher, 'Mary Elizabeth Murphy's Contributions to the Development of International Accounting', *The CPA Journal*, vol. 81:3 (March 2011).

Starke, J.G., *The ANZUS Treaty Alliance* (Melbourne and New York, 1965).

Sussman, Leonard, *The Culture of Freedom: The Small World of Fulbright Scholars* (Lanham, 1992).

Tavan, Gwenda, *The Long Slow Death of White Australia* (Melbourne, 2005).

Theobald, Marjorie and Donna Dwyer, 'An Episode in Feminist Politics: the Married Women (Lecturers and Teachers) Act, 1932–47', *Labour History*, vol. 76 (May 1999), pp. 59–77.

Thornton, Margaret, ed., *Through a Glass Darkly: The Social Sciences Look at the Neoliberal University* (Canberra, 2014).

Tobia, Simona, 'Introduction: Europe Americanized? Popular Reception of Western Cold War Propaganda in Europe', *Cold War History*, vol. 11:1 (2011), pp. 1–7.

Tyrrell, Ian R., 'Anti-Americanism Historicized' (review), *Reviews in American History*, vol. 41:3 (September 2013), pp. 445–50.

Walker, Robert, ed., *American Studies Abroad* (Westport, CT, 1975).

Walton, Whitney, *Internationalism, National Identities, and Study Abroad: France and the United States, 1890–1970* (Stanford, 2010).

Wilks, Judith and Katie Wilson, 'A Profile of the Aboriginal and Torres Strait Islander Higher Education Student Population', *Australian Universities' Review*, vol. 57:2 (2015), pp. 17–30.

Williams, William Appleman, Thomas McCormick, Lloyd Gardner and Walter LaFeber, eds, *America in Vietnam: A Documentary History* (New York, 1985).

Woodard, Garry and Joan Beaumont, 'Paul Hasluck as Minister for External Affairs: Towards a Reappraisal', *Australian Journal of International Affairs*, vol. 52:1 (1998), pp. 63–75.

Woods, Randall Bennett, *Fulbright: A Biography* (Cambridge, 1995).

Woods, Randall Bennett, 'Fulbright Internationalism', *Annals of the American Academy of Political and Social Sciences*, vol. 491 (May 1987), pp. 22–35.

Ziegler, Philip, *Legacy: Cecil Rhodes, the Rhodes Trust and Rhodes Scholarships* (New Haven, 2008).

Index

Note: page numbers in *italic* refer to illustrations